Faith in Britain

Faith in Britain

DAVID ALTON

"If not now, when?
If not us, who?"

Hodder & Stoughton
LONDON SYDNEY AUCKLAND TORONTO

To Lizzie, Marianne and Padraig

The poem on page 74, *I Will Live and Survive*, is reprinted by permission of Bloodaxe Books Ltd from *No, I'm Not Afraid* by Irina Ratushinskaya, translated by David McDuff (Bloodaxe Books 1986).

British Library Cataloguing in Publication Data
Alton, David *1951–*
Faith in Britain.
1. Great Britain. Political parties. Christian viewpoints
I. Title
261.70941

ISBN 0-340-54488-0

First published in Great Britain 1991

Published by Hodder and Stoughton,
a division of Hodder and Stoughton Ltd,
Mill Road, Dunton Green, Sevenoaks, Kent TN13 2YA
Editorial Office: 47 Bedford Square, London WC1B 3DP

Typeset by Hewer Text Composition Services, Edinburgh
Printed in Great Britain by Clays Ltd, St. Ives plc

Contents

Foreword

by John Cushnahan MEP

David Alton and I first met and became friends in the early 1980s when we shared a joint platform at the Liberal Assembly in Eastbourne. The subject was the continuing trauma of Northern Ireland – I was then Chief Whip of the non-sectarian Alliance Party of Northern Ireland. David subsequently became Liberal Chief Whip and I became leader of the Alliance Party. Together, as kindred spirits, we brought our two parties into a political alliance. Our views on social and economic matters were in tune: both parties were strongly committed to reconciliation as the basis for resolving the Northern Ireland conflict and we both shared a passionate pro-European outlook.

By 1989 I had left full-time politics in Northern Ireland and became a Fine Gael MP for the Euro-Constituency of Munster in the Irish Republic. Fine Gael is a member of the Christian Democratic grouping within the European Parliament and, since joining them, I have been very encouraged to see the increasing importance and influence of Christian Democratic policies based on the ideals of personalism, pluralism and reconciliation. Indeed, Christian Democrats have been the inspirational and driving force behind the formation of the European Community and have played a similar role in the growth of freedom in the fledgling democracies of Eastern Europe.

This book by David Alton draws upon the significant historical contribution of Christian Democracy to creating the 'European home'. It puts Christian Democratic ideas into the context of British politics.

Hitherto, the Anglo-Saxon and European models of Christian Democracy have been based on vastly different values. One example of this is the traditional class-based politics of Britain which finds little parallel in Europe. Furthermore, European liberalism is a very different concept from British liberalism, as illustrated by the stance of Labour and Conservative MEPs in Brussels and Strasbourg who are markedly different in emphasis to their national parties at home. European politics is changing things, and always for the better.

I believe that our future lies in Europe and that the biggest influence for most of us will come from Christian Democracy. Therefore, it is timely that a broadly-based Movement for Christian Democracy has been founded in Britain. It fills a political gap – as does this important book.

Strasbourg 1991

Introduction

It is becoming increasingly clear that the trend towards secularism and the dominance of materialistic considerations will lead our country towards a crisis of values. The logic of moral relativism – it doesn't matter what you do or believe as long as you're sincere – has removed objective morality and the primacy of ethical behaviour from public life. Doing what you want, regardless of the consequences, is now the unchallengeable dogma of this new age. Argued so unremittingly by the Government in the area of economics, this dogma reflects the public mood and in turn legitimises it. A biblical proverb says, 'Where there is no vision, the people perish.' We see this decay in our divorce rate (the highest in Europe), our neglect of the poor, the debt crisis (personal and international), our treatment of the unborn and the exploitation of the environment.

Who can doubt that we are an increasingly materialistic society? The worth of every social policy and public service is known by its price in pounds, shillings and pence. Worse, the test of personal choices in life has become the answer to the question, 'What is there in this for me?' The State has sanctified greed and turned it from a vice into a virtue. This has led to greedy and selfish attitudes among those able to benefit from the free market, and the overlooking of the needs of the weaker members of society. Regressive taxation, not based on ability to pay, is one example of unfairness; attempts to deregulate Sunday trading is an example of the market's needs coming before personal and community ones.

In the face of this sea change of attitudes, how are

Christians living in a democratic and pluralist society to respond? Some look back with nostalgia to the Middle Ages, when the Church exercised a powerful influence. The Golden Age is a myth: the Church became too easily corrupted and compromised by its involvement in secular power. It also fell to the danger of forgetting its primary calling to preach the Gospel.

Our first task is to restore the right balance of emphasis in the Church on spiritual and temporal questions. To avoid forfeiting their right to comment on issues of public policy, Churches, as institutions, must be renewed as bodies with moral authority. This demands the creation of a new Christian consensus, based on biblical values and Holy Spirit-led priorities. The Decade of Evangelism in the 1990s may help serve this purpose. The arrival of a new Archbishop at Canterbury will also give new opportunities. There must be renewal of the whole Body of Christ in its social and spiritual vision. At the same time, Christians as individuals must challenge the outcome of post-Enlightenment thinking, which has created a secular consensus around the lie that State and legislation must be value-neutral. The best way to do this is get involved.

The disastrous experiment of Marxist Communism was the logical outcome of the desire for government without reference to the sovereign Creator. Its bankruptcy stemmed from its denial that humanity is made in the Maker's image. Yet as a supremely materialist philosophy some of its assumptions are shared by the dominant creed in the West: possessive individualism. This has reduced society to a mere collection of free-roaming selves, whose main purpose in life is to consume. It has emphasised the right to unlimited individual freedom and choice, provided that it does not cause harm to others. It has turned the State into a guarantor of 'rights' in previously unheard of areas, but fosters violent indignation whenever duties are spoken of in equally forceful terms. Paradoxically this creed also seeks to limit those issues about which government can express judgments of right and wrong.

This book aims to contribute to the debate on how a

new model of politics might look. It sets out to do so with a Christian view of the person and society. This new politics will emphasise the community as well as the individual; responsibilities as well as rights. It won't be a model created from nothing. As this book argues, there is a rich Christian tradition within British politics on which we can draw. Though this tradition is temporarily submerged, the aim of the new Movement for Christian Democracy is to be a vehicle which will help bring about its re-emergence.

The tradition in Britain of Christian involvement in politics will also inevitably form part of a richer weave of Christian influence in the fabric of European politics. The post Second World War reconstruction of Europe was led by great Christian politicians. The peoples set free in the revolutions of East Central Europe of 1989 are now pressing for an alternative form of society which rejects the extremes of socialism and the extremes of market capitalism. The importance of their demands will continue to challenge the basis of Western political culture. With the impact of the European Single Act and the forthcoming economic and political union, there will also be another new start for Europe. There is a democratic vacuum in Europe created by a European Commission with all-embracing responsibilities and powers, but with little democratic accountability. This situation will change. In the new Europe that is being created before us, the challenge now is for Christians to rise and play their part in how the continent will be shaped.

Our approach must be fully democratic. Some people worry when they hear of Christians getting involved in politics. They ask, 'Why should you thrust your values down our throats?' Or as one American rabbi put it, 'When I hear talk of a Christian society, I see barbed wire.' Yet, this is to dismiss the outstanding Christian legacy and contribution to the evolution of just laws across our continent. Since Christians must abide by the biblical injunction to submit themselves to the governing authorities we must accept that others who may not share our faith must be convinced of the rightness of our views. The Christian community must also abide by the results of the democratic process.

What is the Christian basis of democracy? There are many different approaches and arguments. They may be based on questions of justice, personal autonomy or on the symbolic equality which humanity shares before God. A biblical approach to democracy will also want to add reference to the political implications of Pentecost. The empowerment given by the Holy Spirit gave all, from slaves upwards, the right and boldness to speak out. In politics this right is best symbolised through giving everyone the right to vote and participate in the democratic process. Christians therefore identify with a political system which preserves the basic dignity of human beings through creating conditions under which they may fully develop, spiritually and materially, through co-operation with others. Related to this is the conviction that social and political power should be distributed to different groups and bodies at every level of society so that neither the State (nor for that matter the Church) monopolises it. Within the British political context, but drawing on the European practice of Christian democracy, this approach may be summarised thus. It constitutes a defence of traditional values against secular philosophies. It seeks to provide the order and values conservatism pledges to protect, the freedom liberalism espouses, and the social justice and equality promised by social democracy. It simply believes all three can be accomplished only if the Christian emphasis on the spiritual dimension and fundamental worth of each human being is the starting point.

Christians can argue for these values in different ways. Our shared goal is to maintain a Christian prophetic witness. This will involve speaking out and using our votes, but also lobbying politicians, joining pressure group campaigns and being involved at the level of grassroots action. It also involves being informed about our heritage and being able to argue our cause with gentle conviction.

This book – like the new Movement for Christian Democracy – is a contribution to the debate. I am grateful to Hodder and Stoughton that their invitation to write the book came at such a timely moment, this probably being a General Election year.

It also comes in a year when Evangelical Christians have been celebrating and relearning the implications of the victories of their predecessors, Wilberforce and Shaftesbury, who radically reformed unjust social structures; and it comes in the centenary year of the publication of the great Catholic call to social and political engagement, the papal encyclical *Rerum Novarum*.

Faith in Britain examines the Christian contribution to Britain's politics. It contrasts this with the different experience of Western and Eastern Europe. It then examines the condition of Britain's social ecology and why a small group of people – drawn across the political and denominational divide – felt it necessary to establish the Movement for Christian Democracy.

The final six chapters are devoted to the six foundation principles of the movement: social justice, respect for life, reconciliation, empowerment, active compassion and good stewardship. It argues that we should evaluate our success or failure in addressing these themes in terms of relationships and the impact on the human personality, families and communities.

Whilst taking full responsibility for what has been written, I would like to thank those who have been good enough to read the proofs, especially Dr Robert Song, Chairman of the MCD's Drafting Committee, Martyn Eden, David Campanale, Dr Michael Schluter of the Jubilee Centre, and Professor Jack Scarisbrick.

I would also like to express my appreciation to my staff in Liverpool and at Westminster for their technical assistance in the midst of numerous other political and constituency pressures; in particular, thanks to Chris Graffius, Peter McGrath, Barbara Lewis and Oonagh Scott.

Finally, I would like to thank my wife, Lizzie, for her encouragement and help throughout.

Liverpool, January 1991

Chapter 1

The Christian Democratic Tradition in Britain

Every Western European political system has been moulded by Judaeo-Christian values. When these values have been combined with democratic ideals, nations have been well governed.

Britain's contemporary democratic institutions are the product of this powerful cocktail. Our rights and freedoms, duties and responsibilities, have not easily been won and only gradually defined. Since Thomas Becket was murdered by Henry II's men in Canterbury Cathedral the role played in this process by the formal Church and by individual believers has been of the highest significance.

In our own times, in pre-war Germany and in the tyrannies of Eastern Europe, there have been graphic illustrations of what happens when Christians and the formal Church fail to engage actively in political life – by withdrawing into privatised religion – and what happens when they stand boldly against evil.

The Church as a formal institution can become badly compromised when it fails to take a stand or when it identifies too closely with a State or with a partisan cause.

Uppermost in the minds of Christians wondering whether they should get their own hands dirty in politics should be the Easter story. When one man with civic and political power washed his hands of his responsibility and said it had nothing to do with him, it led to the Crucifixion of Jesus Christ.

Our own country's history demonstrates that in a parliamentary democracy there is no great desire to see political priests or ministers standing for public office or being caught up in the legislative process. Nor is there a great demand for an American-style Moral Majority, which fails to admit either its own sinfulness or to see morality as about anything other than sex. Christians must also guard against the evil of sectarianism.

However, what many yearn for is a prophetic Church and for Christian values to be at the heart of our politics. Perhaps that is why so many thousands have responded to the 1990 call by such House Church leaders as Gerald Coates to petition the Government for change. That desire is also reflected in the growth and outlook of Evangelical Alliance, whose director, Clive Calver, says, 'Vote in line with your beliefs, don't just slip into mere political allegiance.'[1]

The Church will influence our nation and our politics when it speaks out clearly and forcibly; when it is not bullied by the Right into believing that morality extends merely to matters of sex, by the Left who deny its right to give a lead on bio-ethical questions but wants to hear it speak about poverty; or by the Centre who patronisingly see it as an anachronism. The Church must not allow the Gospel to be diluted or divided as it suits a particular cause – the 'prosperity gospel' any more than the 'social gospel' – nor by procrastinating when giving a lead might cause offence. No doubt the money-lenders in the Temple felt offended when Christ angrily turned them out.

Prophetic Voices and Christian Tap Roots

I think it is of the greatest significance that, as our modern British political parties were evolving, Christian voices were uncompromisingly speaking out about the key issues of the day. Each of our parties has its tap roots in a tradition taking shape while Britain was enjoying a religious revival, sparked off first in the fields and open places as Wesley and his friends found the institutionalised Established Church closed to the individual renewal of heart and soul which they preached.

As this revival got under way and the first of our nineteenth-century measures of emancipation were being enacted, British institutions, attitudes and conditions were on a wholly different track from the rest of Europe's – with implications for the twentieth century.

As in Europe, humanism and secularism emerged in Britain but we withstood the rise of anti-clericalism which swept the Continent. The radical writer, John Wade, was typical of those who tried to identify the Church with reaction. Writing after the rejection of the second Reform Bill in October 1831 he was bitter and scathing:

> The clergy, from superior education, from their wealth and sacred profession, possess greater influence than any other order of men, and all the influence they possess is subservient to government . . . whenever a loyal address is to be obtained, a popular petition opposed, or hard measure carried against the poor, it is almost certain that some reverend rector, very reverend dean, or a venerable archdeacon, will make himself conspicuous.[2]

But Wade's incitements fell largely on deaf ears. This was also the time of Wilberforce and Shaftesbury, and of growing Christian renewal amongst the masses. The 'old Dissent', represented by Presbyterians, Congregationalists and Baptists, increased its combined membership by about seventy-seven per cent to 734,000 between 1800 and 1830. Recently established Methodism increased its numbers by more than three times, to about 300,000 over the same period, though riven by factionalism after John Wesley's death. Catholics doubled their numbers between 1800 to 1830 and the base of the Church changed from a small number of recusants, born amongst the gentry, to the thriving new populations of the industrial towns of Lancashire – Manchester, Preston, Wigan and Liverpool.

The absence of anti-clericalism in Great Britain was largely due to the settlement of the issues which to a great extent fuelled it in other countries three centuries earlier, during the English Reformation. Paradoxically, while the increased subservience of the Church to the State prevented the institutionalised Church from being the catalyst which led to religious renewal, its impotence also protected it.

To be effective, believers got out from under the shelter of the Church's gothic porches and became a formative influence in the new political parties. When Church membership grew the political aims connected with it flourished; when it was in decline the aims withered.

Although today's politicians will often genuflect in the direction of Christians by telling them that Christ was a great teacher and that they are influenced by Christ's teachings, the victories gained by men such as Wilberforce over anti-clericalists such as Hazlitt have been largely reversed and secularism is as strong today in influencing the political parties as Christianity was a century ago. Tony Benn sums up this attitude by saying, 'I regard myself as a serious student of the teachings of Jesus – no more, no less'.[3] Neil Kinnock was even more revealing, when he said in 1989: 'My relationship with God is virtually non-existent, at least as far as I am concerned. What I embrace and uphold are social and moral commitments of what we understand by Christianity, shared in common with a lot of other religions.'[4] But Christian involvement in politics has not always settled for this lowest common denominator.

The Conservative Party

An article in the Church of England newspaper just after the 1987 Election, recalled the Conservative Party's Christian origins:

> It used to be a jibe that the Church of England was the Tory Party at prayer. More positively, we might note that once upon a time the Tory Party used to pray. Lord Shaftesbury, the leading Christian social reformer of the last century (and founder of the Church Pastoral Society), was just such a Tory.

So, of course, was the Tory MP William Wilberforce.

Wilberforce and Shaftesbury

In his account of Wilberforce's forty-year-long struggle to end the evil of the slave trade, Garth Lean, in his book *God's Politician*,[5] reminds us that, with Henry Thornton, Wilberforce established what these days we would call a base-community. At the village of Clapham, four miles south of Westminster, the Queen Anne house, Battersea Rise, became the centre of the prayer life which Wilberforce uncompromisingly believed had to be central to parliamentary efforts to outlaw slavery. Many years after Wilberforce died the fellowship was given the misleading name, the Clapham Sect. They were never an insular sect and their appeal was universal.

One of the leading critics of William Wilberforce was the radical, William Hazlitt, who criticised him for being preoccupied with evils abroad, saying, 'He preaches untutored Christianity to untutored savages: and tolerates its worst abuses in civilised states.' Those who defended Wilberforce said this was like criticising Christopher Columbus for discovering America but for not going on to discover Australia and New Zealand as well.

John Wesley – who in 1780 had published his *Thoughts on Slavery* – described slavery as 'the execrable sum of all villainy'. Government and the population at large turned their backs on the atrocities and degradation connived at with the full authority of Parliament and British law.

The secularists and humanists of the day – still lionised by today's Left – were bitter in their attacks on Wilberforce. The reformer William Cobbett said Wilberforce worked for the 'fat, lazy negroes', while, 'doing nothing' for white wage slaves of England, and that he had 'never done one single act in favour of the labourers of this country'.

Though his best-remembered achievement lies in the Bill to abolish the slave trade, the trafficking in human lives was not Wilberforce's sole concern. He and his friends – whom he gathered from across the political divide – took the first steps towards humanising the prisons and the penal code, and they pioneered popular education at a time when even a radical such as Cobbett thought it 'despicable cant and nonsense'. Wilberforce also championed Catholic emancipation and that of the dissenting sects and helped found the Church Missionary Society and the British and Foreign Bible Society. Wilberforce and his friends intervened on behalf of the victims of the Napoleonic Wars, spoke up for Greeks seeking independence, for British responsibility in India, for North Americans and groups as diverse as the Haitians and Hottentots. Wilberforce raised his voice against the Game Laws, criticised the Government for the cruelties of transportation to the penal colonies in Australia's Botany Bay, and he opposed the brutal use of flogging in the British Army, as indeed did Cobbett.

It was Wilberforce's friend and colleague, the MP Thomas Gisborne[6] who first raised the issue of the plight of children working in factories. The two men then turned their attention to the condition of climbing boys employed by chimney sweeps, the conditions in coal mines, and the shortening of working hours for children. It was to take many more years of campaigning, particularly by Lord Shaftesbury, before the conscience of the country was finally aroused to these social horrors. The enactment of such reforming measures was thanks to the engagement of Evangelical Christians, who did not shy away from unpopular causes and who were ready to challenge the status quo.

Wilberforce had been elected to Parliament in October 1780, at the age of twenty-one, for the constituency of Hull. He secured 1126 votes. For the following forty years he sat as a Tory Member of the House of Commons and, literally while he was on his death bed, he heard that his life's great work, the abolition of slavery, had reached a successful conclusion. 'Thank God,' he said, 'that I should have lived to witness a day when England is willing to give twenty millions sterling for the Abolition of Slavery.' Parliament had paid off the slave owners.

Today's director of the Evangelical Alliance, Clive Calver, recently reflected on the example of Wilberforce:

> We need a gospel that differs from the philanthropy of the nineteenth century. We should challenge and seek to

> change the decision-making organisations in our secular society. Wilberforce swam against the tide – he was told that the British economy would collapse with the abolition of slavery. But he kept going in order to change his world and show that human institutions are not above the heartbeat and demands of Christ's love.[7]

Shaftesbury was the second great nineteenth-century Tory to put his Christian desire for reform before political expediency. His biographer, John Pollock, notes that the work of the two great reformers overlapped, for on August 28th, 1833, one day after the Abolition of Slavery Act received its Royal Assent, Shaftesbury's Factory Act became law. On the 29th, Wilberforce was dead.

The baton of reform, in what seemed like a relay race across the nineteenth century, was passed to Shaftesbury. Representing first the 'rotten borough' of Woodstock, he spent from 1826 to 1851 in the House of Commons, then succeeded to his father's title and took his place in the Lords.

Among his achievements were reforms which transformed the degrading conditions in asylums such as Bethlehem Hospital – Bedlam, as it was known – the Factory Act, the Mines Act, and the establishment of the Ragged Schools Union. The poor man's earl – like Wilberforce before him – set the agenda for social reform and thereby affected the attitudes of both Christian laity and his Party. His example prompted countless other Evangelical Christians to engage in political action.

The One-Nation Tradition of Conservatism

Classical Conservatism was pragmatic and suspicious of ideology. The 'one-nationism'[8] of Disraeli clearly had its origins in the interventionism of Shaftesbury and Wilberforce. The one-nation Conservatives held that leadership was best exercised by an élite and that a broad consensus would emerge so long as policies were seen to be fair. Hence, it is not surprising that it was succeeding Conservative governments who gave the middle classes and later the working classes the vote, and that they enacted a whole raft of social legislation. Underlying this concern to preserve the fabric of the nation was the classical Conservative understanding of tradition, the past and continuity. Out of this came a love of our institutions, a care for tried and tested values, and a sense of both patriotism and duty.[9] As Christian influence within the Conservative Party has diminished, the 'one-nation' tradition has also been eclipsed.

Throughout the twentieth century the Conservative Party has continued to fall into two camps, with the 'one-nation' tradition best represented in our own times by Harold Macmillan and Edward Heath. Churchill expressed a fairly typical view of mainstream Conservative attitudes towards the Christian religion when, in March 1943, he said:

> Religion has been the rock in the life and character of the British people upon which they have built their hopes and cast their cares. This fundamental element must never be taken from our schools, and I rejoice to learn of the enormous progress that is being made among all religious bodies in freeing themselves from sectarian jealousies and feuds, while preserving fervently the tenets of their own faith.[10]

Writing in a more personal vein in *A Sparrow's Flight*,[11] the former Lord Chancellor, Lord Hailsham, says that Christianity is the abiding religious background to his personal, family and public life. He describes the paradox of Christ crucified:

> I seek God and behold a bedraggled human figure impaled for public ridicule upon a gibbet . . . Remaining Christian, I am constantly reassured in my wandering, in my doubting, and as constantly led back by my trusting. I do not know. I do not pretend to know. But I trust and therefore I believe.

The Anglicanism of Hailsham and Heath, and before

them Macmillan and Churchill, have been submerged by the ascendency of the New Right in the Conservative Party. However, the battle is by no means over. Chris Patten, the Chairman of the Conservative Party, is a Christian, and in an interview with *Marxism Today*[12] he signalled his determination to see 'one nationism' emerge in the new clothes of Christian Democracy:

> I find myself very much at home talking to German Christian Democrats. They've constructed a political philosophy which works and delivers not only in terms of the prosperity which it helps to produce but also in terms of – to use a rather Christian Democrat word – the solidarity which it establishes.

New Right Conservatism has its roots in the thinking of Locke and Mill and in the Utilitarianism of the nineteenth century.[13] Mrs Thatcher used to say that there is no such thing as society, simply individuals. The individual's freedom is paramount. New Right thinkers emphasise freedom of choice and self interest. A leading supporter of Mrs Thatcher was Lord Harris. In his 'The Morality of the Market' which appears in *The New Right and Christian Values*,[14] he says the market is the central instrument for determining our needs, attitudes and requirements: 'The market is neutral; it will supply what consumers want, from prayer books to communion wine to pornography and hard liquor.'

Peter Broadbent, a Christian active in the London Labour Party, in an article which appeared in *Third Way*, in March 1989, entitled 'The Soul of the Parties', attacks the New Right for playing down the values of justice and interdependence. He says they become virtually incidental to the ordering of society:

> If freedom is freedom to operate within the market place unfettered by the interference of politics and state, then there can be no question of injustice in the operation of that neutral market . . . I may recognise my responsibility

to my neighbours, but it is an individual responsibility and I must not be coerced into caring for my neighbours by, for example, being forced to subsidise them through taxation or other forms of redistribution.

It was thinking like this which led Mrs Thatcher to reinterpret the parable of the Good Samaritan by claiming that the real moral of the story was that the Samaritan would not have been in a position to help if he hadn't had some money in his pocket in the first place. I suppose this was a reaction against those who think the moral of the story of the Good Samaritan is that because of cuts in public expenditure there was a shortage of social workers on call that day. Neither view seems to coincide with the emphasis Jesus places on the need for each person to show charitable love to others. Lord Harris even claims it is self-interest rather than love which motivates people to do good.

Another of Mrs Thatcher's key policy advisors was Professor Brian Griffiths, himself a Christian. His theological defence of the New Right seems to be based on six principles:

* God reveals His character in justice, and most obviously in the moral law.
* Individuals, made in the image of God, are created for freedom.
* The Fall is cataclysmic, and there is no redemption through politics, and no possibility of a utopia.
* We live in two Kingdoms, and the Kingdom of God is synonymous with the Church. It does not give us a basis for social ethics.
* The Kingdom of God is no more or less than an example of the life of the Church.
* Creation order is the basis of state order, and is expressed most cogently in the law of God.

Although I appreciate the attempts which Griffiths has made to create a Christian context for the operation of the present Government's policies, it is open to criticism for narrowing the relationship between faith and politics. The points of entry in the Griffiths critique are God as law-giver and creator. This is an Old Testament God, not the Christian one.

While the Conservative Party has become increasingly secular and the thinking of the New Right has tried to side-line religion into a purely private affair, British Evangelicals and Catholics have been travelling in a different direction.

The Evangelical Alliance has been discovering a diversity of approaches, whilst simultaneously crusading on a whole range of social and ethical questions. In so doing it has avoided the American evangelical caricature – whose politics are largely 'New Right' – and has been true to its roots. The Alliance, under Clive Calver, has seen substantial growth, with the 419 churches affiliated in 1980 increasing to 1429 by 1989.

In rediscovering their highly influential political role, Evangelicals have come into conflict with the political parties. When EA and CARE (Christian Action, Research and Education), led by Charles Colchester and the Reverend Lyndon Bowring, mounted campaigns against the legalisation of experimentation on human embryos, their principal opponents in the Conservative Party were New Right MPs such as Teresa Gorman and Andrew Mackay.

They found themselves pitted against the free choice arguments of New Right MPs who advocate abortion on demand. During the debate on the Human Fertilisation and Embryology Bill Teresa Gorman mounted what one national newspaper described as the most extraordinary attack ever made on Christianity in the House of Commons. The MP for Maidstone, Ann Widdecombe, a committed Christian and Conservative, complained after the division was taken on that Bill that other MPs – from the Hard Left and the New Right – were trying to deter Members from supporting pro-life lobby amendments by standing at the door to the division lobby scornfully making the sign of the cross and telling them, 'The Pope says this way'.

The debate on the secularisation of Sunday was no less fierce and hard fought. Classical Conservatives such as Sir

Bernard Braine and Michael Alison, both Anglicans, were to the fore in opposing the Sunday Trading Bill. It would have been unthinkable a generation earlier that a Conservative Government would have introduced such a Bill. Churchill had once described Sunday as the greatest of British institutions, essential as a time for families and communities. These would be secondary considerations for today's New Right who, encouraged by the former Prime Minister – and to a lesser extent by John Major – say that the Market should be totally unrestricted. The largely evangelical Jubilee Centre, undoubtedly the leading Christian 'think-tank' in Britain, successfully opposed the New Right, mobilising USDAW – the Shop Worker's Union – the National Chamber of Trade representing small shop-keepers, some of the big stores, the Churches and a majority of cross-party parliamentary opinion. A succession of Conservative knights from the shires, mostly Anglican churchwardens, spoke in the Commons debate and the Sunday Trading Bill was defeated.

The Jubilee Centre has developed links with the Catholic hierarchy, including Cardinal Hume, as well as its natural evangelical constituency. Within the British Churches it has successfully opened up the debate on issues as different as consumer credit, debt and support for those who care for the elderly.

Like the Evangelical Movement in the early nineteenth century, the Evangelical Alliance itself has been growing as its political and social concerns extend beyond the individual into the community. Its Director, Clive Calver, would partly attribute this to its return to its roots: those of Wilberforce and Shaftesbury. Wilberforce, it must always be remembered, was not simply a 'single-issue' politician. He specifically set out his two priorities as the abolition of slavery and the changing of public attitudes so that people might have a greater concern for their fellow citizens. These were the cornerstones of a consistent and coherent approach to politics.

The development of a contemporary Christian social and political critique has been mirrored in the Catholic Church. In England since the Second Vatican Council it has increasingly emerged from its ghetto. Through the social teachings of bishops such as Liverpool's Derek Worlock, the laity has been encouraged to engage in the issues of the day. It also has a rich legacy of social teaching which lays great stress on the importance of the person and the community. Catholics fundamentally repudiate the notion that freedom of choice is an absolute and that freedom and the individual are to exist in a vacuum which never recognises the need for equality of opportunity and community. Catholic rejection of the individual as free agent, and the espousal of the interdependence of both people and their communities, runs headlong into the claim of the New Right that the Gospel does not give us a basis for social ethics.

Conservatism in Post-Christian Britain

The New Right, who dominate today's Conservative Party, would feel distinctly uneasy with William Wilberforce's assertion that 'Christianity calls her professors to a state of diligent watchfulness and active service'.

The conflict between many Christians and the dominant element of Mrs Thatcher's Government led to substantial differences opening up within the Party on issues such as the family and relief for the least well off. MPs such as Patrick Cormack, an Anglican, and Ken Hargreaves, a Catholic, have been formidable critics of policies which they say conflict with their beliefs. Conflict has also opened up between Westminster MPs and the more 'one-nation' MEPs in Strasbourg – and not merely on how 'European' we should be (although the more to the Right the Member the more anti-European he or she tends to be).

In a little pamphlet, *An Introduction to Modern Conservatism*,[15] three MEPs, Ben Patterson, Lord Bethell and Amadee Turner, QC, describe a Conservative Party which has long ceased to exist. The pamphlet was distributed widely amongst Christian Democrat MEPs, and it was an open secret in Strasbourg that many Conservative MEPs wished to ally themselves with the Christian Democrats.

This led to a furious reaction among Christian Democrats. The Dutch MEP, Arie Oostlander, told me that they regarded the Conservative Party as 'too far to the Right', the then leader of the Conservative Party, Mrs Thatcher, as 'too right wing'. The leader of the Portuguese Christian Democrat group at Strasbourg, Professor Lucas Pires, told me, 'I have been to Latin America many times. After what I have seen there how could I describe myself as a Conservative?' And the Italian Christian Democrats went even further: Rosy Bindi said, 'We must stand apart from those whose speeches are inspired by Christian ideals but whose deeds betray arch Conservatism.' She said that Christian Democrats were inspired by 'a solidarity-orientated vision of values and social justice'. She for one clearly did not believe the claim in the pamphlet circulated by the British MEPs that the Conservative Party 'generally accepts the inspiration and values of Christianity'.[16] But is Labour any better?

The Labour Party

The Labour Party reverses the Conservative hierarchy of values. With the emphasis on equality rather than liberty, the socialist is prone to overlook the importance of each person and lay too much stress on the role of the State. Peter Broadbent, despite his Labour sympathies, admits as much: 'If it is true that the New Right has swallowed "possessive individualism" uncritically, it is also true that the old utopian Christian socialism, which has often come nearer to baptising Moscow than to postulating anything distinctively Christian, simply will not do.'[17]

Tony Benn, in *The Church And The State*[18] says that although 'I was confirmed as an Anglican I have, over the years, become more and more interested in the relevance of the social message of Jesus, the carpenter of Nazareth, about peace, justice and the brotherhood and sisterhood of all humanity, from which so much of the Socialist faith derives'. C. S. Lewis would have dismissed this relegation of Christ to 'great teacher' by reminding his audience that anyone who went around claiming to be God, but wasn't, must have been a charlatan and fraud: hardly a great teacher.

After the formation of the Independent Labour Party in 1893, the battle for the English socialist soul took place. On one side were those socialists who had a deep Christian commitment, and no doubt some who would broadly subscribe to Tony Benn's (patronising and erroneous) view of Christianity without God. On the other side were those socialists with a Marxist ideology who wished to take the Labour Party into a more revolutionary mode. This battle continues into our own times.

Christian Socialism

Labour roots, like those of the trades unions, were primarily in Methodism. The Party identified with the interests of the industrial working class and its heartlands remain the industrial (and de-industrialised) urban areas. Unlike other European socialist parties, Labour's origins were significantly influenced by Christianity rather than Marxism. In this respect it mirrored the Conservative and Liberal Parties.

Reminders of these early Christian influences are still to be found in the print and publishing unions such as SOGAT and the NUJ, which are organised in 'chapels', not branches, and where the Chairman is the 'Father of the Chapel'. Biblical texts can be seen woven into the fabric of many of the old banners carried on union marches or displayed at events such as the Durham Miners' Gala.

Brooke Foss Westcott, Bishop of Durham

Brooke Foss Westcott, Bishop of Durham from 1890 until 1901, was one of the foremost Christian socialist influences of his day. He believed that his task was to persuade Christians themselves that 'behind every social question there lies not only a moral but also a religious question'. He dismissed the discussion which was raging about differing forms of socialism – 'the paternal socialism of Owen, the State socialism of Bismarck, the international socialism of Marx, the Christian socialism of F. D. Maurice, or the evolutionary socialism of the Fabian Essays'[19] – and opted instead for what he called 'the obligations which are seen to follow from the sense of the solidarity of mankind, from the application, that is, of the Incarnation to life.'[20] Application was, of course, the problem. He drew back from discussing the distribution of wealth by asserting that the question is not 'How do we get our incomes?' but 'How do we use them?' He believed that thoughts of personal gain should be subordinated to the thought of public service, and advocated simplicity of living by the rich, adopted by choice and not of necessity. He conceded that some of his objectives were utopian but 'unattainable ideals are the guiding stars of life. I have suggested nothing which has not been realised on a larger scale, under harsher circumstances, and with scantier knowledge than our own, by Franciscans, by Moravians and by Quakers.'

Westcott looked for the victory of larger human sympathies over the narrowness of class. His lack of preoccupation with the Marxist class struggle was reflected in his belief that every true nation had 'wide differences in power, in fortune, in duty' and the aim of the Christian was not to wipe out these differences but to harmonise them by showing that 'they can minister to the vigour of one life'. He did not wish to 'confound class with class, but to bind all classes together in their characteristic distinctiveness by the consciousness of mutual service'.[21] He echoed the teachings of Carlyle and Ruskin that great men have a destiny to lead and the generality to follow. In this respect he had much in common with one-nation Conservatives and Social Liberals. He had no revolutionary objective of destroying capitalism, simply to see it take up the neglected duties of bygone days. He was extremely shocked by Leo XIII's encyclical, *Rerum Novarum*,[22] and regarded as 'revolutionary' the suggestion that property rights should be based upon labour. He was strongly opposed, as were other Christian Socialists, to collectivism.

Nineteenth-century Christian Socialism was essentially moral rather than political. The views held by some of their number have a curious ring today. One of their prominent members, Charles Kingsley who wrote *The Water Babies*, was a racist: in an article in *The Christian Socialist* in 1850 he said blacks were savages who impeded the spread of enlightenment and used the description of the extermination of the Canaanites to justify their elimination; congenital differences, he claimed, marked out those who were fit, and those who were not, for self-government. These early stirrings of National Socialism no doubt prompted John Ludlow, one of the founders of the Christian Socialist Movement,[23] to reflect that 'We dare not forget that the laws of politics have to be applied by the spirit of man.'

Britain's Christian Socialists emphasised voluntary solutions to social ills rather than the collectivist ones which socialism subsequently embraced. They made a notable contribution to the advancement of education, especially adult education, in England; they furthered the social emancipation of women; and they encouraged co-operative economic enterprise. Their abiding influence on the Church and Labour movement was that they allied the Church with some of the most dynamic forces emerging in society and in so doing both activated and shaped Christian opinion with social criticism.

In his *Politics of Paradise*[24] the Labour MP, Frank Field, says that the Christian Socialist tradition was left high and dry by the events of 1914:

> The view that man was increasingly virtuous, and that the Kingdom's establishment was thereby guaranteed, was impaled on the barbed wire in the no-man's-land of World War One. The Christian Socialist tradition of Maurice and his followers has yet to recover fully from that iconoclastic event.

Nevertheless, Labour itself went on to pioneer reforms, such as the establishment of the National Health Service and the Welfare State, which have considerably added to the betterment of life in Britain. Among those who deeply influenced Labour during the inter-war years was William Temple.[25]

William Temple, Archbishop of Canterbury

Christians within the Social Democratic and Democratic Socialist currents of today's Labour Party would both call Archbishop William Temple in their aid. On many issues (excepting education, see Chapter 9), he acted as a prophetic and challenging voice in the nation's affairs.

In 1912, then the thirty-one-year-old Headmaster of Repton, Temple carefully distinguished between the position of the Church and the political parties: 'The Church and the official representatives of the Church must keep themselves free from the entanglements of party politics,' he wrote. 'Their business is something far more fundamental and important; it is the formation of that mind and temper in the whole community which will lead to wholesome legislation by any party and all parties.'[26] He said that the Church had to teach about ends, not means. The ends he prescribed were 'freedom, fellowship and service – these are the three principles of a Christian social order derived from the still more fundamental Christian postulates that Man is a child of God and is destined for a life of eternal fellowship with Him'.[27]

In *Christianity and The Social Order*, Temple argued that social justice based on Christian principle should be enshrined in British social policy. He chaired the team of investigators who in 1938 produced a report into unemployment, *Men Without Work*,[28] and would have shared Tawney's (see p. 22) view that unemployment was an involuntary, structural phenomenon. As early as 1927 he argued for a 'Universal Living Income' (not just a 'living wage'). Many of his views were foundation pieces in the creation of the Welfare State. Perhaps when state welfare became an integral part of post-war national identity the Church's work appeared done. Frank Field argues in *The Politics of Paradise* that at the time Temple was writing 'the Christian message was only too clearly understood, and the failure to embrace it stemmed from the revolutionary change it requires of us, rather than a confusion about what the message was'.

However, a clear Christian critique of social ethics disappeared from political thinking. What there was seemed largely time-warped and without a clear definition until David Sheppard and Derek Worlock and others from the Seventies onwards began to grapple again with social and political ethics. One manifestation of this was the publication, in 1985, of the Church of England Board for Social Responsibility report, *Faith in the City*.[29] This element of Christian thinking has once again been called in aid by Labour and many of its recommendations on the alleviation of poverty have been incorporated into their programme.

Temple's three principles – freedom, fellowship, service – would form the bedrock of thinking and motivation in the work of an MP such as Birkenhead's Frank Field. But in today's Parliamentary Labour Party Field is a rarity, not least because he is a Christian. His courage in speaking out on a whole range of issues, from the role of trades unions in determining the selection of Members of Parliament, to his assertion in Parliament that embryo farms would be created to facilitate the destructive use of human embryos, has made him a target for Labour's Left. He has been subjected to regular attempts to deselect and discipline him for his outspoken views.

Field's consistent option for the poor, which dates from his days as Director of Child Poverty Action Group, should make him one of the Labour Party's foremost voices. Instead, he has been relegated to the position of maverick. His predicament has made many Christians suspicious that Labour is no longer a 'Broad Church' with room for them: so has Labour's imitative espousal of New Right policies such as abortion and embryo experimentation; and by advocating 'new and changing forms of the family'. Indeed, they have gone further, by removing the right of individual Party members to hold 'conscience' positions on these issues. In addition to making this a Party policy question there were even attempts at their 1990 Conference to ban the small Labour for Life group. Like its political counterparts, Labour has moved a long way from its early Christian influences and origins.

Keir Hardie and John Wheatley

The first Labour MP, Keir Hardie, wrote a tract which might need to be revised in these inflationary times, entitled, 'Can a Man Be A Christian On a Pound a Week?' Hardie was raised an atheist but was converted to Christianity in 1897 and later became a lay preacher of the Evangelical Union Church. He was a member of the Good Templars and a temperance lecturer. Although he had met Friedrich Engels, Eleanor Marx and other prominent Marxist Socialists, was well acquainted with Marxist and revisionist socialist literature, and had worked closely with the Fabian intellectuals, Hardie's socialism was neither scientific nor utopian, neither political nor economic. He said that his socialism was the result of 'his own thought and feeling, the plight of the workers, and the state of the world'.

In 1910 he wrote: 'I have said, both in writing and from the platform many times, that the impetus which drove me first of all into the Labour movement, and the inspiration which has carried me on it has been derived more from the teachings of Jesus of Nazareth than all other sources combined.'[30] Hardie tended to see all social and economic questions from a Christian and moral standpoint. He was often a lone and ineffective figure in the House of Commons during pre-First World War days, perceiving his role as prophetic, a voice for the coming capture of power by mass democracy. He used the Commons to speak to the voiceless people outside the House of Commons who lived in the slums and the back streets, rather than to play parliamentary games or give polished 'good' parliamentary performances.

He scandalised Members when he took his seat in 1892 by wearing his cloth cap and tweed suit. With puritanical contempt he spoke in Parliament on one occasion of the lavish menus provided in the House of Commons' restaurants and savaged those Members anxious to suspend the day's sitting because it was Derby day. Hardie's words were backed up by an intimate knowledge of the deprivations of working people. This was born of the hardship of his own youth. His courage in expressing his convictions won him the respect of the poor and deprived.

Although Hardie was one of the key influences in establishing the Independent Labour Party, he retained an affinity with Gladstone and the Liberal Party. It was Hardie who persuaded the Labour Representation Committee of the advantage of negotiating the secret 1906 pact with the Liberals. The two parties agreed not to fight one another in thirty seats, thus preventing the Conservatives from winning these seats. The result was the overwhelming 1906 Liberal landslide – but also the election of twenty-nine Labour Members. When Paddy Ashdown and Neil Kinnock rule out the possibility of their parties standing down in one another's favour on the grounds of 'dangerous precedent', they should bear in mind it has been done before. Not only was the Election won by a landslide but the Government which was formed was arguably the best administration we have ever had.

Hardie was subsequently elected as the Parliamentary Labour Party's first Chairman. Until his death in 1915, the man born in a one-room cottage in Lanarkshire was perhaps the best loved, and – by some – the most hated man in Great Britain.

Scotland's socialist movement was particularly influenced by Christianity. It remains so to this day, with a far higher ratio of committed Christians representing its interests in Parliament than its English and Welsh counterparts: from the reformed Churches men such as John Smith, the shadow Chancellor, and from the fiery Left, the Catholic, Denis Canavan.

Writing early in 1990 in the Catholic newspaper, *The Universe*, Liverpool Walton MP, Eric Heffer, recalled another Scottish Socialist MP, John Wheatley, a Catholic. Son of an Irish labourer, his family came to the West of Scotland seeking employment before the First World War. Father and son both worked in the mines. After his election to Parliament in 1922, Wheatley became involved in what Heffer described as a number of 'parliamentary scenes'. He also became involved in clashes with the hierarchy of the Catholic

Church, who he claimed were insufficiently committed to Leo XIII's social teachings contained in the 1891 encyclical, *Rerum Novarum*. He argued his case in a pamphlet, *The Catholic Working Man*, published in 1909. Like Hardie, Wheatley never accepted the historical materialism theories of Marx and Engels, and in the sectarian Glasgow of the day was an early voice in seeking to create a unity between Catholic and Protestant. He told fellow Catholic workers: 'Your interests and those of your fellow Protestant workers are identical. Your enemies are their enemies. Workers of every race and creed must unite.' In 1924, in the first Labour Government, Wheatley became Housing Minister and was responsible for the 'Wheatley' Housing Act which led to the construction of 250,000 publicly owned homes.

The Emergence of Social Democracy

During the inter-war years the Christian Socialist tradition increasingly became estranged from the social democracy of R.H. Tawney. The differences are perhaps best symbolised today in the differing outlook of men like Frank Field and Eric Heffer.[31]

R.H. Tawney

Tawney, in his *Commonplace Book*,[32] refuted the notion that the stark choice is between individual enterprise and collective action. Although he would be called in aid by later generations of socialists, such as Anthony Crosland, who, like Tawney, emphasised the ability of the government to bring about socialism by economic reforms, Tawney was also claimed as a leading formative thinker by the Social Democratic Party (SDP) in the 1980s. Their Tawney Society did much of the SDP's conceptual thinking.

Tawney put the clash of ideas inside the Labour movement like this:

> It will be said: 'Abolish economic privileges, and there will be enough wealth for all to live, and for all to lead

> a spiritual life' . . . Now economic privileges must be abolished, not, primarily, because they hinder the production of wealth, but because they produce wickedness. But, supposing unearned incomes, rents, et cetera are pooled, will not the world, with its present philosophy, do anything but gobble them up and look with an impatient grunt for more.[33]

Tawney was rejected. For more than fifty years the world did look on as socialism did impatiently grunt for more.

At Oxford Tawney had been greatly influenced by the social idealism of Edward Caird and the socially-orientated religious liberalism of Bishop Charles Gore. He joined the Independent Labour Party in 1909, his socialism deeply affected by his Christianity. When he talked of the erosion of values, or conflicts between spiritual and material values, he had biblical values in mind: 'Give me neither riches nor poverty, but enough for my sustenance' was both a personal rule and precept for society. In 1918 he was one of the draughtsmen of an Anglican report, *Christianity and Industrial Problems*. 1921 brought the publication of *The Acquisitive Society*. This was a stinging indictment of capitalism for its encouragement of economic power without a concomitant sense of social responsibility. It is worthy of reconsideration by a new generation of readers today.

Tawney vehemently attacked capitalism for subordinating human relationships to economic productivity and argued that man cannot be whole or dignified until he lives in a community where his private motives lead him to seek the public good. In 1926, in his *Religion and the Rise of Capitalism*, he dealt with the origins of 'acquisitive individualism' and the elaborate ethical support given to this creed by religious opinion. He argued that by the abuse of the Puritan ethic, which placed a premium on individualism, thrift and hard work, capitalism had clothed itself in unquestioned respectability. Writing with great moral purpose, he deprecated modern economic ethics for their selfishness and praised the medieval view of economics which condemned as sinful the relentless increase of wealth for its own sake.

Tawney believed man had been degraded from a spiritual being into an animal. He also believed modern capitalism to be ungodly because instead of stimulating man's desire for the divine creation, it placed a premium on the limitless exploitation of nature. The civilised world was turned into a jungle where the economic rat race took precedence over social endeavour. Tawney's vision of a Christian 'functional society' as a replacement for the 'acquisitive society', his emphasis on the value of each person before God, and his attacks on the subordination of human relationships to economic objectives finds echoes in the *personalism* and *communitarianism* of European Christian Democracy which remain largely unrepresented in the values of Britain's political parties.

Tawney's view of socialism caused him strongly to disagree with the Webbs about Communism. The battle lines were drawn between the Labour Party's centralisers and decentralisers. Tawney, G. D. H. Cole[34] and the social democrats who followed, tapped the rich vein of thought expounded primarily by William Morris, who had promoted Guild Socialism. They were highly critical of the Webbs and Fabianism whose arguments in favour of state control had won the day at the crucial 'Clause 4' 1929 Labour Conference. Cole said:

> The familiar brands of collective socialism were somehow things one wanted for other people than oneself, in order to eradicate the deprivations and injustices of capitalism, whereas the Guild doctrine offered me a kind of socialism that I could want as well as think right . . . as having personalities to be expressed as well as stomachs to be filled.[35]

Social democrats recognised that the human personality mattered and that Socialist four year plans, impersonalised systems and dehumanising politics destroyed the personality. Cole advocated an early form of 'subsidiarity' or decentralisation. Like Tawney, his thinking mirrored that of Christian Democrats in many European countries and his call for the establishment of the greatest amount of industrial democracy possible and practicable was not so far removed from the calls of the Catholic Church, in its 1931 encyclical, *Quadragesimo Anno* – taken up by Adenauer in Germany in 1945 (see Chapter 2) – for industrial democracy.

The Argument Lost

But Cole, Tawney and the social democrats had lost the arguments. The British Labour Party, unlike many of the other Western European socialist parties, now became increasingly corporatist and centralist and committed to material prosperity, efficiency and technology – all personified in 1960s Wilsonism and now inherited by Neil Kinnock. Only the British Labour Party retained direct trades union affiliation and organic links with trades unions, leading to a sectional domination and class orientation which is still not resolved. While the Western European socialist movement went largely Social Democratic, and the East went Marxist, Britain's Labour Party produced its own model – like the rest of our parties and British institutions generally. Unlike countries such as Sweden, Austria, Germany, Holland and Denmark, where there is little perception of social democratic parties being an appendage of the trade union movement, the Labour Party model has still not entirely accepted that the trades unions and Labour Party have different (and sometimes conflicting) jobs to do.

In 1979, Social Democracy and Democratic Socialism in Britain collided in head-on confrontation. It would take another ten years of internal battles before Labour donned the clothes of the SDP. The continuing civil war between the two factions in cities such as Liverpool demonstrates that it will be a long time yet before the basic problem of two unreconcilable forces living inside one party is resolved. Elsewhere in Europe, in the Federal Republic of Germany, for instance, the conflicting visions of socialist and social democrat came to a head thirty years before. At the Bad Godesberg special conference in 1959, a new 'Basic

Programme' had been hammered out and the old socialist objective of nationalisation of industry abandoned.

Shirley Williams

Of the 'Gang of Four' social democrats who left Labour in 1981 to form their separate party, the SDP, David Owen and Shirley Williams both admitted to Christian convictions. David Owen always regarded this as essentially a private matter however and, perhaps surprisingly, says nothing about the connections between faith and politics in his book, *Face the Future*.[36] Nor does he reveal any interest in Tawney. Owen toyed with the idea of seeking membership of the European People's Party for the SDP. His Whip, John Cartwright, MP, came to the conclusion that such a link with the Christian Democrats was not possible. Perhaps this was because the SDP had accepted the secular aspects of Tawney's politics, but not the spiritual ones.

Although the SDP may have ended in tears in 1990, as a movement for challenging the accepted politics it made an incalculable contribution towards change. Most of its objectives – with the temporary exception of electoral reform – are the policies on which Labour or Conservative are now campaigning. Nowhere is this more so than in the promotion of Dr. Owen's 'tough and tender' social market policies.

Unlike David Owen, Shirley Williams publicly voiced her desire to see Christian values on the political agenda. In *The Church and State*[37] she said that the teaching of Christ is 'as valid and as much in conflict with the established values of secular society as when it was first uttered 2,000 years ago'. Taking up the personalist theme she said that 'the amazing technological and scientific capacity, the vast potential of the human brain is out of symmetry with the moral development of human beings'.

She spoke of the need for a rounded pro-life ethic, condemning capital punishment and the destruction of the unborn; the need to recognise degradation of humanity, whether manifested in pornography or the way we treat our prisoners; the obligation of the rich towards the poor, and the abuse of the 'heritage of nature and of intellect that God has given us'. Seeing the need for the Church and State to remain separate but for the Churches to act with a prophetic role she said: 'I think it is excellent that the Archbishop of Canterbury should now be a controversial figure, because the only way the Churches will be listened to is if, sometimes, they say the things we do not want to hear.'

The Fox and the Hedgehog

During its brief but influential life the SDP had a very vibrant Christian Forum and along with its Alliance partners, the Liberals, attracted the active support of many British Christians – even inheriting the nineteenth-century description of the symbiotic relationship of the Conservative Party and the Church of England, the Alliance itself becoming known as the Church of England at Prayer.

David Owen built on Isaiah Berlin's famous analogy of the relationship between the Fox and the Hedgehog to spell out the differences between the centralist socialists and the decentralist social democrats:

> The fox knows many things, but the hedgehog knows one big thing. The personality of the hedgehog relates everything to a single central vision, one system less or more coherent or articulate, in terms of which they understand, think and feel – a single, universal organizing principle. The foxes pursue many ends, often unrelated and even contradictory, connected, if at all, only in some de facto way, for some psychological or physiological cause. The foxes are the decentralisers who lead lives, perform acts, and entertain ideas that are centrifugal rather than centripetal.[38]

The hedgehog, of course, is also a slower animal than the fox. Unlike the fox it does not arouse the passions of the hunter and turn itself into a quarry. The more dangerous existence of the fox is certainly one which the social democrats have been living.

Social Democracy versus Christian Democracy

With the changing face of Europe and the collapse of Marxism in the East, the old and sterile debates between socialism and social democracy are increasingly redundant. The principal reason for the disappearance of an independent SDP was that David Owen had won. Paradoxically, as he sat in the ruins of his castle, he could see Neil Kinnock raising the standard of social democracy in the new building down the road. Owen's most abiding achievement in politics will surely be assessed as the pressure he exerted on Labour to become a social democratic party like its European neighbours. It just left Eric Heffer to complain that Labour had become the SDP Mark One.

As we continue to face Europe, our institutions, our parties and our politics will increasingly be influenced by European realities. Britain will have to address the reality of a system of politics based, not on Socialism and Conservatism, but on Social Democracy and Christian Democracy. The realignment which eluded the Gang of Four will be wrought by the mould-breakers of Strasbourg and the East.

The Liberal Party

British Liberals often trace their Christian roots back to the seventeenth century and the Puritans. Parliament and the Parliamentary Army during the English Civil War and Revolution were a ferment of political and theological opinion. After much complicated evolution, gradually some puritan values came to be represented by the Whigs and later by the Liberals.

Many early industrialists were Nonconformists. This meant that in the nineteenth century the Liberal Party accommodated industrial interests. It was only after the First World War when Lloyd George and Asquith began a bitter feud, in a precursor of events which troubled the Alliance after the election of 1987, that rivalries led to the abandonment of the party by these interests.

Gladstone Converts

The name of the Liverpool-born William Gladstone became synonymous with nineteenth-century Liberalism. Born of a slave trading family, he entered the Commons as a high Tory (and remained one until the mid 1840s). He voted against the 1833 Abolition of Slavery Bill but underwent a conversion in both his attitude to slavery and his politics.

During the last days of William Wilberforce's life, in July 1833, and just before the abolition measure was passed, Wilberforce's son, Henry, brought Gladstone to see his dying father. Gladstone's own first major speech in the Commons had been just a few weeks earlier in defence of his father's estate manager, whom Lord Howick had described in debate as 'a murderer of slaves'.

Gladstone's entry into his diary described Wilberforce as 'cheerful and serene, a beautiful picture of old age in immortality. Heard him pray with his family. Blessing and honour are upon his head.'[39]

Gladstone attended Wilberforce's funeral at Westminster Abbey ten days later and said: 'It brought me solemn thoughts, particularly about the slaves. This is a burdensome question.'[40]

Gladstone later renounced his support of slavery and admitted that Wilberforce had profoundly influenced him: 'I can see plainly enough the sad defects, the real illiberalism of my opinions on that subject.' Gladstone had learnt that only free people are fully human.

A high Anglican in his churchmanship, Gladstone joined the Liberals when he became convinced that the higher spiritual interests of the Church would suffer from Conservative attempts to bolster the privileged material position of the Church of England. Between 1852 and 1865 he was a prime mover in the ecclesiastical battles of the day, especially against the Divorce Bill of 1857, which permitted divorce on grounds of adultery.

Partnership with Nonconformism

Gladstone gradually came to share the belief of Nonconformists that a form of moral regeneration was needed in England: the second of Wilberforce's original objectives. He extended his Manchester School laissez-faire view of economics towards the Church, believing that if competition was increased between the denominations, with none of them privileged through establishment, they would increase their zeal for evangelising missionary work. Neither would Parliament any longer have to become involved with legislation. Under Gladstone, Campbell-Bannerman, Asquith and Lloyd George the Liberal Party remained defiantly disestablishmentarian in outlook.

Gladstone's support for evangelism, his admiration for popular religious and moral passion, and his assault on Erastianism (particularly Palmerston's Divorce Bill)[41] won him the general support of nonconformity in the early 1860s; and this was in tandem with the popular support which he gained during his tax cutting years as Chancellor of the Exchequer (1859-66) in Lord Palmerston's second administration.

His support of disestablishment made him a popular figure amongst Irish Catholics too. His own theological and spiritual outlook was in some sympathy with theirs, although he remained fervently opposed to ultramontanism and was deeply opposed to the Oxford Movement after Newman's secession to Rome in 1845 and Manning's in 1851.[42] Henry Wilberforce, who had brought the young Gladstone to his father's deathbed had, along with his brother Robert, also become Catholic, although the third brother, Samuel, stayed in the Church of England and became the 'High Church' Bishop of Oxford. Notwithstanding his antagonism to the Oxford Movement, Gladstone believed that Catholics should have full denominational rights in education and ultimately he came to believe that in Ireland they were entitled to control their religious and political destiny.

In his fine book *Democracy and Religion*,[43] J. J. Parry

says that after 1867 there is a broad distinction which can be made between most whig-liberals and the Gladstonians and radicals:

> Both believed that religion – understood as including education and the role of the Church – was the most important component in ensuring that society was well ordered. But the first was more anxious than the second for the wise state to superintend the community's religious life, so that the success of anti-social forces could be checked . . . The other camp distrusted the capacity of those in authority to regulate morality and promote spirituality without repression and formalism.

The rigidity of these divisions must not be over-stressed but they help to explain the antagonism in the party by 1874 when the Liberals lost the General Election, and when Gladstone split the Liberal Party on the Irish Question in 1886 they were the underlying reason for the break between Liberals and Unionists.

When the anti-clerical scientist, T. H. Huxley came to write in 1889 that the English 'care for nothing but religion and politics', he was writing against this background of Gladstonian influence on public life. Gladstone and his followers had an immeasurable distrust of human authority, because of the power of evil and sin in the human condition, and the particular susceptibility to temptation of the richest and the most powerful. They believed that out of the competition of genuinely zealous men would spring a popular morality. They recognised that, as with any human undertaking, the product would be flawed but they believed that such an approach represented the best guarantee that society would be regulated along lines acceptable to God – a God who spoke with equal force to all mankind, rather than primarily to the thinking classes. They therefore saw politicians who sought to dictate a position to God's creatures as being in error. In the words of the proverb which Gladstone recalled in 1876 – *Vox populi vox Dei*. The purpose of the politician was to inspire, not to direct.

The job of the political activist was to maintain the public mind in a state of alertness against the manifestations of evil. The dissemination of knowledge would enable those manifestations to be checked. This was why the connection between faith and politics was essential. In 1874 Gladstone wrote of his faith in Britain and the role of religion: 'As to its politics, this country has much less, I think, to fear than to hope; unless through a corruption of its religion – against which, as Conservative or Liberal, I can perhaps say I have striven all my life long.'[44]

Gladstone's Influence and Legacy

Gladstone's lasting impact as a great spiritual leader of our nation is difficult to quantify. He won the respect and devotion of the great majority of Nonconformists and working men. His performance was inspiring enough to lead Keir Hardie, Arthur Henderson,[45] and George Lansbury,[46] all devout Christians, to revere him. But he also won the affection of Irish Catholic MPs as well as the leading Catholic Liberal, Lord Acton. In 1880 Acton described Gladstone's vision as unique because it blended a sympathy for tradition and institutions with a conviction that employers 'ought not to be the political masters of their employees'. Acton believed that for the poor 'misgovernment means not mortified pride or stinted luxury, but want and pain, and degradation and risk to their own lives and to their children's souls . . . the poor have a claim on the wealth of the rich, so far that they may be relieved from the immoral, demoralising effects of poverty'.[47] Although Gladstone was himself resolutely opposed to economic interventionism the logical progression from Acton's thinking to the social-liberalism of the 1906 Government, and especially Lloyd George's 1909 People's Budget is not hard to decipher.[48]

Gladstone refused to tolerate the anti-clericalism which was shaping continental liberalism. Instead he invigorated British liberalism by turning its attention to great questions and harnessing it to moral crusades: in the Balkans, Turkey and Ireland. His anti-clericalism and internationalism might account for a curious reference in a document published in Turin in 1899 by the Italian Young Christian Democrats. Amongst demands for proportional representation, decentralisation, protection of labour and legalisation of trades unions, is one for 'a transformation of the conscience of the nation . . . a universal renewal of Christian and popular humanism . . . in accordance with the desire of such men of genius as Gladstone, Leo XIII and Guiseppe Toniolo, which will be the glory of the twentieth century'.[49] It is not surprising that nineteenth-century Christian Democrats, formed as a reaction against liberal anti-clericalism, could feel so much empathy with a British statesman who believed a nation's progress had to be in accordance with the directions desired by God.

Until the Eclipse

After the Liberal Party split over the Irish Question it effectively had twenty wilderness years until the landslide victory of 1906. Then, after this victory, Nonconformists looked for satisfaction over education and Welsh disestablishment. However, with Catholics wanting to retain denominational schools maintained by public funds and most Nonconformists wishing to see denominational education abolished, considerable controversy ensued. A great Catholic gathering at the Royal Albert Hall in May 1908 was attended by 60,000 people inside and outside the building and was addressed by the Catholic Liberal MP and writer, Hilaire Belloc. The Liberation Society and the Free Church Council supported the Education Bill but the legislation was emasculated in the House of Lords and ultimately dropped by the Prime Minister, Campbell-Bannerman. The *Baptist Times* said the House of Lords 'stands for the denial of democratic Government in England' and the *Bible Christian Magazine* said the country could scarcely tolerate the House of Lords 'as at present constituted'.

By 1914 such questions seemed of minor importance. Christians, like Liberal and Labour politicians and trade unionists, were passionately at odds over support for the

First World War, and over compulsory conscription in particular. The war tore asunder the whole fabric of British society and destroyed the Edwardian political consensus. As late as 1917 Lloyd George, by then leading the wartime coalition government, called many Dissenting ministers to breakfast at Downing Street. He tried to spatchcock together Nonconformist support by promising to resurrect the Education Bill and to implement Welsh Church disestablishment. It was too late. The bitter split between Asquith and Lloyd George had destroyed the political force which Nonconformism had traditionally looked to as their means of expression. Increasingly in the 1920s, as Labour eclipsed Liberalism, the trades unions also eclipsed Nonconformism as the challenger to the established order.

The Flickering Spirit

The collapse of the Evangelical/Liberal alliance deprived the Liberal Party of any real political power, with two exceptions. They participated in Churchill's wartime Coalition Government. Then, in 1977 through the Lib-Lab pact David Steel propped up Jim Callaghan's failing Labour Government as a joint act of self-preservation. In the General Elections of 1983 and 1987, when in Alliance with the SDP, the Liberals polled twenty-five per cent and twenty per cent of the British electorate's votes, the Party achieved its most significant election results since before the First World War. That ended in mutual recriminations and the collapse of another alliance.

At most elections since the break-up of the Evangelical/Liberal consensus the Liberal Party has returned only a handful of MPs. During its nadir in the 1950s all of its half a dozen Members of Parliament were returned from 'Celtic fringe' seats, which through no coincidence remained bastions of Nonconformism. Even when the 1980s Liberal/SDP Alliance was at its height the areas in which it polled most significantly (the Highlands and Islands, the West Country, the Scottish Borders and the West of Wales) were areas where nonconformism remains strong.

During the 1920s and 1930s, although the Liberals attracted thinking men and women – such as the economist J.M. Keynes and Lord Beveridge (the founding father of the Welfare State and Tawney's brother-in-law) – its political base would have totally disappeared without its traditional Christian support.

In the Parliamentary Party of which I became a Member in 1979 a number of colleagues still had those ties. One of the most active is probably Alan Beith, the Berwick-Upon-Tweed MP, and a Methodist lay preacher. Geraint Howells, MP for Ceredigion and Pembrokeshire North preaches in the Welsh chapels; Richard Wainwright, the former MP for Colne Valley, in the Yorkshire Methodist chapels. Sir Cyril Smith is an active Unitarian, and after he won the Bermondsey by-election in 1983, Simon Hughes added the voice of evangelical Anglicanism. Jim Wallace, the Orkney and Shetland MP, is a member of the Church of Scotland, along with former leader, Sir David Steel.

However, the Christian tap roots of the old Liberal Party have largely been dislodged. In the October 1990 edition of *The Liberal Movement News*, Tower Hamlets councillor, Stuart Rayment, writing about the Party's decision at that year's Annual Conference to support the repeal of the Blasphemy Laws wrote: 'The secular fundamentalists are, of course, in house, so theirs was the day.' At the same Conference delegates voted to abolish Christian school assemblies. Both of these decisions – along with the Paddy Ashdown's Policy Committee's support for a pro-abortion policy – will have distressed many Christians and others.

Obviously perceptions about faith and politics differ but many old-time Liberals would have concurred with Ramsay Muir's description of the historic links. Muir was a Liberal thinker and historian who held the chair in contemporary history at Liverpool University, and who set out his beliefs in the 1920s publication *The New Liberalism*:[50]

> I describe this belief as a 'faith' because ultimately it has a religious character. For many of us, at all events, it rests on the conviction that the Spirit Who has guided man in

> his toilsome struggle out of the mire of animalism is perpetually working upon every mind, goading it by means of those insatiable aspirations after rightness which are the torment and the glory of man . . . These aspirations are the source of all advance.

Sixty years later, in 1987, when with John Gummer and Eric Heffer, Alan Beith compiled the election scene-setter *Faith in Politics – Which Way Should Christians Vote*[51] the then Liberal Deputy Leader said:

> Many of the values characteristic of Liberalism appeal directly to Christian thinking. For example, there is the drawing together of individualism with recognition of the need for collective effort to tackle serious problems . . . Jesus emphasised our responsibilities to others, and any Christian model for the political and social order must surely seek to promote that sense of responsibility of each of us for our fellow human beings.

Beith also pointed to the creation of the Liberal/SDP Alliance and argued that a different approach in politics, based not on mutual recriminations but co-operation, was an example of the New Testament's call to find good in others: 'The very creation of the Alliance depends on that humility and willingness to learn from others which is at the heart of the gospel.' Beith's conciliary approach to politics was rejected by party members when he unsuccessfully stood against Paddy Ashdown in the Liberal Democrat leadership election.

Living in Sin: The Time Didn't Come

Shirley Williams had once described the early relationship between the Liberal and SDP parties as like a couple 'living together'. The Alliance, forged in 1981, was the formal wedding ceremony. Perhaps it is symptomatic of the present unwillingness to work at relationships which run into difficulty that in 1987 the Liberals and SDP took the easy way out. By aborting the Alliance and the whole concept of co-operative, partnership politics David Steel and David Owen put paid to their aspirations of forming a Government. Millions of bewildered former Alliance voters, who voted for a non-confrontational form of politics, were left disillusioned. Party activists profoundly misunderstood their own voters. People had not been voting in their millions for the Liberal Party or the SDP but for the non-adversarial spirit which the Alliance represented. That was what made it so attractive to the many Christians who wholeheartedly backed it.

As soon as it became clear that David Owen would not support the merger of the two parties David Steel should have put his merger proposals on ice. Although the majority of members wanted a merger, more notice should have been taken of the implications of ignoring those who could not share this approach – both the Owenites who were determined to continue with the SDP, and those Liberals, like the former Leeds MP, Michael Meadowcroft, who also felt unable to join the new merged party. Attempts were made to heal the rift. John Cartwright had been SDP Chief Whip while I was Liberal Chief Whip during the pre 1987 General Election period. At a painful meeting at the Social and Liberal Democrats' Conference at Blackpool in 1987 we made a joint appeal for a 'cooling off' period and for reflection before the divorce was concluded. We were shouted down. It is a sad reflection on our system of politics that party activists in all parties are frequently out of step with the electorate's wishes. The Alliance represented a genuine attempt at partnership between parties and it was that conviction which the voters supported in their millions. When asked to identify the strengths and weaknesses of the respective parties, the one area where voters put Liberals and Social Democrats ahead of the others was in their ability to heal the nation's divisions.

The intolerance and bitterness displayed on both sides after the 1987 General Election, and the proclaimed new objective of setting out to eliminate, rather than work with, others, blew apart the one conviction which the electorate identified with Liberal Democrats.

I hope that the Liberal Democrats will learn from this experience and again see the need to make a virtue of a willingness to work with others. They must recognise that – as in the rest of Western Europe – a reformed electoral system will in any event require such a willingness as a precondition of politics.

I joined the old Liberal Party when Jo Grimond was leader. He preached the need for political realignment. On entering Parliament I became convinced that this was an over-riding priority and that our existing system of adversarial politics is deeply destructive. I recently came across something which Wilberforce wrote some 200 years ago describing a House of Commons which has largely remained unchanged. He said that you could recognise our Parliament:

> by that quick resentment, those bitter contentions, those angry retorts, those malicious triumphs, that impatience of inferiority, that wakeful sense of past defeats, and promptness to revenge them, which too often change the character of a Christian deliberative Assembly, into that stage for prize fighters, violating at once the proprieties of public conduct, and the rules of social decorum, and renouncing and chasing away all the charities of the religion of Jesus.

The Liberal Democrats alone argued the case for changing all that. It is to their credit and I hope they will once again realise that a co-operative approach offers the best hope for Britain.

Journey Without Maps

In 1928, in his *The Challenge to Liberalism*, Ramsay Muir said that Liberals need to be like the crusaders. He entered a characteristic note of advice. He warned against the methods of the First Crusade. This was the Crusade of Poor Men, roused to ardour by the preaching of Peter the Hermit and other fanatics. Thousands of poor people joined up and drifted across Europe, ragged and starving. They became a danger to the countryside through which they passed. Towns shut their gates upon them. They were left to starve and never arrived in Jerusalem.

'The real crusading host,' said Muir, 'which not only saw but conquered Jerusalem, had waited to plan its routes and to learn what were the difficulties that had to be overcome. And the only Crusade that has any chance of success is a Crusade with maps.'

In the origins of each of our British parties there is a mixture of the religious and the secular. In each, the balance has tilted from Christianity to humanism. While they now journey without maps, the parties of continental Europe have been travelling routes more clearly signposted.

Chapter 2

The Christian Democratic Tradition in Western Europe

While it is true that the majority of Europe's democratic institutions are bound up with Christian influences and ideas, the Anglo-Saxon tradition of politics has evolved in a markedly different way from that of our continental neighbours. This has led to an ignorance in this country about the Christian Democratic tradition in the rest of Europe. Many commentators, understanding nothing of its roots or outlook, tend to equate it with British Conservatism.

This is to overlook the hostility between Thatcherites and the European Christian Democrats over a whole host of issues, not least the future of Europe and the Social Charter which Mrs Thatcher saw as a first step towards socialism. Not surprisingly, the British Conservative Party's application to join the European People's Party (the Christian Democrats in the European Parliament) was opposed – particularly by the Dutch, Irish and Italians. The Dutch MEP, Arie Oostlander, says they have little in common with the New Right or Conservatism. Even some CDU members in Germany who favoured the Conservative application became more hostile in the light of the British Government's reluctant attitude towards the reunification of Germany.

This has serious implications for Britain's future in Europe. Western European Christian Democrats achieved almost twenty per cent (35 million) votes in the 1989 European Elections. They contested seats throughout the EEC states, Great Britain being the sole exception.

The isolation of British Conservatives may be compounded by future developments: the first free elections in Eastern Europe since the ending of the Cold War resulted in victory in East Germany for the Christian Democrats. As one by one the new Eastern European democracies accede to the Community and its Parliament the Christian Democrat bloc of parties will, along with the Social Democrats, shape the Continent's destiny. While the Left has painfully adjusted to the politics of Western Europe (with the SDP acting as catalyst), the Centre and Right have yet to experience the same inevitable realignment.

Britain has been a notoriously reluctant member of the European Community. Our country has sat on the sidelines, usually criticising, and then only grudgingly accepting the movement towards closer European co-operation. Britain's major parties have been isolationist and still contain many fervent anti-Europeans. Labour, as recently as 1983, campaigned to leave the Community. Despite a more recent enthusiasm they still have a large number of members opposed to closer European ties. The Greens, too, have been surprisingly lukewarm, with only the Liberals (to their credit) consistently pro-Europe since the 1950s. The Conservative Party sits virtually alone in the European Parliament, ineffectual and friendless.

In September 1990, during a visit to the European Parliament, leading Christian Democrats expressed their hope that a positive and constructive British voice would ultimately be heard in Europe. The Portuguese Christian Democrat group leader, Professor Lucas Pires, told me, 'The Conservatives do not agree with us over institutional and social reforms.' He joked that the European Conservative Group 'are against Mrs Thatcher – but not as much as we are!' Some of the continental Christian Democrats have been deeply affected by the experience of their sister parties in poverty-stricken areas of South America.

Barto Pronk, a Dutch MEP, identified support for 'an old-fashioned constitution, an antiquated franchise, and their opposition to a Bill of Rights' as some of the reasons why the CDA (Dutch Christian Democrats) were opposed to the British Conservatives but he added, 'We have much in common with the British people; the same outlook, the same sense of humour – but not the same politics.' He said his party steadfastly supported a pro life ethic . . . a point underlined by their leader, Ruud Lubbers, during a CDA symposium in the Netherlands in October 1990 – opposing abortion, embryo experimentation and euthanasia. Since the successful merger of three Protestant and Catholic parties in 1980 the CDA had more effectively been able to champion Christian values in Dutch society – values which Pronk says are needed throughout Europe.

A crucial issue will remain for Britain: where do we and our parties fit into the new Europe? Central to any vision of Europe will be a clear understanding of Christian Democracy: its origins, its beliefs and its future.

Origins: A Resistance Movement

Thomas Jansen, Secretary to the European People's Party and European Union of Christian Democrats, admits that understanding one another is a two-way street: 'Much of the philosophical thought on which Christian Democracy is based is not particularly well known in English-speaking circles, and the vocabulary sounds strange – just as Edmund Burke sounds strange to Continental ears.'[1]

In Britain the major work on Christian Democracy is *Christian Democracy in Western Europe, 1820-1953*, by Professor Michael Fogarty.[2] Although this is a masterly book it says something about the insularity of Anglo-Saxon politics that the last major appraisal of one of the most significant European political movements was written thirty-five years before the creation of a single European Market and twenty years before Britain finally ratified its membership of the EEC. Little else has been published, and nothing since 1980.

Fogarty first came into contact with Christian Democracy when, as a member of the Labour Party, he attended the Socialist International's Bentveld Conference in 1953, which examined 'Religion and Socialism'. He admits to surprise: 'The extent and unity of Christian Democracy gradually came home to me; a unity extending even beyond the limits of what are conventionally known on the Continent as the Christian Democratic movements.' In 1955 Fogarty was astonished by the lack of interest in the English-speaking world: 'Dutch Protestants,' he pointed out, 'have built up over the last century one of the most successful and in many ways the most instructive political, economic and social movements to be found anywhere in the Christian world. But this achievement has been neglected to an astonishing extent by their co-religionists in the Churches of the Calvinist tradition in the British Isles.'

In an effort to remedy the lack of information available in the English-speaking world the European People's Parties have begun to publish a series of occasional papers from their Brussels offices. One of the most easily digested is 'Christian Democracy: The Different Dimensions of a Modern Movement' by Clay Clemens.

Christian Democracy emerged in the rest of Europe at the beginning of this century. Britain, as we have seen, was still broadly a Christian country in which even the Labour movement was still clearly stamped with the mark of the Free Churches. The divisions in Britain were not between Christians and non-Christians, but between those who took particular positions on economics or politics. Life was different on the Continent where large sections of society had already been lost to Christianity. Atheism was militant and Continental European divisions were between Christians and non-Christians.

Therefore, as the Christian Democratic movements emerged they were not preoccupied with the issues which divided Liberal from Labour and Conservative. They tended to learn from each other and their approach was based on a synthesis. Human relations – what became known as personalism – was their primary concern. The family, base communities, the interdependence of social groups of every complexion and dimension, became their concern. There was no exaggerated concentration on the individual, or the State. Nor was there a preoccupation with technical advancement at the expense of traditional values.

In its first phase Christian Democracy was a resistance movement. Robert Papini in *Tradition und Aktualitat christlich-demokratischen Denkens*,[3] says that: 'Christian Democracy arose in the last century as a movement of defence, but also as a movement of social, cultural, religious and civil renewal that set as its goal the erection of a social and political democracy of Christian inspiration.' It was also a largely Catholic reaction against both unbridled individualism and anti-clericalism. It took differing forms in each European country and was spawned often as a response to particular national circumstances. In the period up until the First World War it was still largely a reactive force. It was fighting for lost causes and its distinctive social ideas were not yet fashioned.

In Belgium, for instance, its roots are to be found in a romantic yearning to return to an idyllic, half imagined, Golden Age of farmers, craftsmen and a traditional way of life worth preserving: 'Christian communities of the old type.' Swiss Catholics rose in 1848 in defence of the ancient rights of the Church; Italian Catholics rallied to the papacy; the Catholic Movement in France was for the King and counter-revolution. In Holland Dutch Protestants were of a similar frame of mind, labelling themselves 'anti-revolutionaries'. In both Holland and Belgium the issue which forced Christians from both sides of the Reformation divide to fight back was the decision to ban Christian teaching in schools. In Prussia, the Centre Party was formed to fend off Bismarck's attacks on church freedoms.

This backward-looking view of Christianity's role in politics was essentially reactive. The distance travelled by 1950 is summed up in the respective positions of Germany's Christian Democrats and Social Democrats in the post Second World War period: with Christian Democrats preaching the need for Germany to subordinate German national aspirations to the needs of European Union; while, like their British counterparts in the Labour Party of the time, German Social Democrats continued to preach nationalism.

Leo XIII and the Turn of a Century

By about 1880 substantial Christian-liberal, if not yet Christian-socialist, bodies of opinion existed within all the Churches. The election of Pope Leo XIII in 1878 was to prove crucial. His twenty-five-year-long reforming papacy at the end of the nineteenth century is the key to understanding how Christian democratic ideas were given form.

His encyclicals are full of denunciations of those who treat the people as the source of power and authority; who fail to distinguish between democracy as a means of conferring the power and authority which rests ultimately with God; and of those who erect a whole philosophy on what they see as the inevitable and absolute character of the class war. Leo XIII also made it clear that so long as the liberal and socialist techniques were seen as techniques and nothing more, they could in appropriate circumstances be perfectly acceptable to Christians. *Libertas Praestantissimum* (1888) approved in the conditions of the modern world the liberal principles of democracy and tolerance. *Rerum Novarum* (1891) accepted the socialist principles of State intervention and class organisation. And *Au Milieu des Solicitudes* (1892) specifically warned Catholic leaders in France not to try to overturn but to work with the liberal Republic.

Leo laid down the ground rules for Christian engagement in political life. In *Immortale Dei* (1885) he said this:

> God, therefore, has appointed the charge of the human race between two powers, the ecclesiastical and the civil, the one being set over divine and the other over human things. Each in its kind is supreme . . . One of the two has for its proximate and chief object the well-being of this mortal life; the other the everlasting joys of heaven. Whatever, therefore, in things human is of a sacred character, whatever belongs either of its own nature or by reason of the end to which it is referred, to the salvation

> of souls, or to the worship of God, is subject to the power and judgment of the Church. Whatever is to be ranged under the civil and political order is rightly subject to the civil authority. Jesus Christ has Himself ordered that what is Caesar's is to be rendered to Caesar, and what is God's to God.

Given this lead, many Catholics felt challenged to elevate Christian compassions for the poor and the weak into an engagement for actual social reform. They also began to urge the Church itself to be less socially conservative and authoritarian. They believed such engagement would provide a bulwark against corrosive materialism while lessening the impact of rapid economic changes upon traditional values and social cohesion.

Fogarty warns against seeing Leo XIII's encyclicals as a flash of revealing light:

> *Rerum Novarum* marked a turning point, it did not create one. Like all papal encyclicals, it represented the summing up of a certain stage of thought and discussion about social problems among Catholics, both clerical and lay. *Rerum Novarum* represented the turn of the screw which brought one part of the picture finally into focus.[4]

Leo XIII believed that Christian Democracy would allow people to 'feel themselves to be men, not mere animals; Christian men and not pagans' (*Graves de Communi*, 1901). He summed this up in a plea for a just social order through the improvement in the conditions of life, especially for the weak and the poor, for those most in need, and for those whose basic human dignity is most at risk. Contemporary Christian Democrat declarations project the same message. The West German Christian Democratic Union pledges: 'We respect every human as a unique and unsubordinated person. Man is created for his free development in life together with others. His freedom depends upon a reality which goes beyond the human world.'[5]

Whether *Rerum Novarum* marked a turning point or created the turning point, there is no doubting the impact which it had on its contemporary readers and the generations who have followed. This is summed up by the French novelist, Georges Bernanos, whose 1936 *Diary of a Country Priest* includes some narrative about the impact of the encyclical on an obscure French parish:

> You read it quietly today, skimming through it, like any Lenten pastoral. But when it came out, my friend, we seemed to feel the earth rock under our feet. Talk about enthusiasm! I was parish priest at Norenfontes then, right in the coalfield. That simple idea that labour is not a commodity subject to the law of supply and demand, that it is wrong to speculate in wages or men's lives as if they were wheat or sugar or coffee – believe me it shook people's consciences.[6]

Catholics after *Rerum Novarum*

From 1919 onwards a number of Catholic-inspired workers' movements and activist groups began to emerge. In Italy, Catholic Action saw its role as religious and moral development while simultaneously preparing the Catholic laity to engage in political and social activities. Civardi, in his *Manuale di Azione Cattolica*,[7] says its prime task had been the 'formation of consciences'.

In France, Holland and Belgium Catholic farmers' organisations were established after the First World War. Young trades unionists groups were also set up. The most significant of these was the Young Christian Workers (YCW), which proved to be a revolutionary influence not only in the organisation of young workers but also in the whole conception of work. The YCW's origins go back to 1912 when Father Cardijn (later to be made Cardinal) was appointed curate at Laeken in Brussels. He began working with a group of young girls from local workshops and factories. He carefully examined their working conditions and encouraged young workers to 'See-Judge-Act'. During the inter-war years the movement steadily grew and became influential among many young people, including the young Jacques Delors.

Germany had been ahead of the field with the establishment of the Kopling Associations in the mid-nineteenth century. Father Kopling, a curate at Elberfield in the Ruhr, brought together young craftsmen for primarily educational purposes. Later the associations expanded their work, admitted factory workers, and supported the rising forces of Christian trade unionism. Their pre-First World War membership peaked at 60,000. In 1929 they boasted 90,000 German members and, with branches in Austria and Switzerland, 117,000 overall.

The Protestant Tradition – Stirrings in the Undergrowth

As Catholic social thinking was assuming this new sense of purpose and clarity, after 1880 there were stirrings in the undergrowth of the reformed Churches. From the world missionary conferences of 1910 on, the Life and Work Movement, the Faith and Order Movement, and the great conferences of the World Council of Churches in 1948 and 1954 were manifestations of this. Each of these laid increasing emphasis on social and political action and challenged the view that religion was merely a matter of private conscience.

Fogarty records that 'the conversion of German Protestants to independent political and social action occurred in three main ways'.[8] First, there was a demand, beginning on a very small scale, to affirm the Christian position against secularism and the ideologies of Communists, socialists, liberals and nationalists. Second, there was the need for 'balance' with the Catholics who were already engaged in political action. And third, came the realisation that now free from State control German Protestants might use their freedom in positive ways.

In 1878 Adolf Stocker founded a Christian social political movement. It had a programme of social reform through State intervention. He then joined forces with the Evangelical workers' movement, whose leader, Pastor Weber of

München-Gladbach, had, from the beginning of the 1880s, been establishing workers' unions. Stocker, who had secured election and then defeat in the Reichstag as a Conservative, contested the 1898 election on a Christian Social platform. In a cliff-hanging and dramatic battle he regained his seat by a majority of twenty-seven votes. From then until 1933 the Christian Social tendency continued to be represented, although it never caught the imagination of the wider Protestant community. Like some of its late nineteenth-century Catholic counterparts it had an intolerant streak which led a number of its followers into the evils of anti-semitism and into National Socialism.

Between the Wars

In the thirty years from 1918 until 1945 there were divergent developments within the reformed Churches. The Nazis suppressed Pastor Weber's workers' movement, which had been the best instrument for independent Protestant action and they absorbed its trade union section. But not all Evangelicals simply capitulated. Influenced by Swiss theologian Karl Barth's writings, some Evangelicals recognised the consequences of political acquiescence rather than activism. Barth's theology insists that it is the Word of God, not the word of man, that is essential for understanding the Christian's place in the world. His destiny depends not on any truth which can be read by natural reasoning out of history, but on the will and grace of God, knowledge which is conveyed by Revelation.

The desire to resist the tyranny at work in their country, and to oppose the idolatry of national socialism led to the birth of the Confessing Church at the Synod of Barmen. That in turn was to lead to the imprisonment and martyrdom of their most noted members. The abiding influence of Pastor Niemoller and Dietrich Bonhoeffer galvanised post-war Protestant Christian opinion. Along with Barth, Niemoller and Bonhoeffer opposed the German Christian Movement, Hitler's compliant Church which tried to make his anti-semitism and military ambitions respectable. The

Confessing Church saw many of their number imprisoned, tortured and, like Bonhoeffer, executed. In Germany after Hitler there could be no further question of Christian neutrality towards the assumptions and practices of parties and governments.

During this same period Catholics in most of the Western European countries made sporadic attempts to create parties out of the various earlier movements. These were often the attempts of Catholics wishing to protect their identity and yet to remain open to the emerging democratic ideals. The Church tended to be afraid of these Christian Democratic movements. Some challenged the practices of the Church itself and were perceived as a threat. After Leo XIII the institutionalised Church drew back from Christian Democracy. Of the two streams of thought the Christian Social thinkers inevitably had the hardest time of it. Confessional conservatism, on the other hand, which had long given precedence to the protection of the Church's political role, had an innate suspicion of social reform and liberal democracy. Anti-parliamentarianism during these inter-war years even led some elements of this conservative wing to work for a form of clerical-fascism. Even during Leo XIII's papacy *Rerum Novarum*'s apparent support for Christian Democracy seemed to be limited by the subsequent publication of *Graves de Communi* (1901) and it was not until Pius XII, in his Christmas address of 1944, that the Church appeared to totally reconcile itself with democracy. Like their Evangelical brethren, Catholics had been chastened by the experiences of 1919-1945.

In 1933, on their coming to power, the Nazis dissolved the two Catholic parties, the Zentrum and the Bayerisher Volkspartei. The concordat between the Vatican and the Third Reich marked the end of independent political Catholicism. The *quid pro quo* was the right of the Catholic Church to maintain its churches and spiritual rights. This ecclesiastical 'peace in our times' was not worth the paper on which it was written and led to many individual Catholics taking up private attitudes of opposition. In a few notable cases – for instance, that of Konrad Adenauer, about whom I will shortly say more – this led to the concentration camp. This struggle and the years of imprisonment are crucial to any understanding of the future contribution which Adenauer and other Catholics would make in the reshaping of post-war Germany and Europe.

In Italy the Fascists used similar methods. The Catholic Party, the Partito Popolare Italiano (PPI), was the victim of the Lateran treaties between the Vatican and Mussolini. Its suppression by the Fascists enhanced its subsequent authority and it played a major role in reconstruction. When, in 1943, the Fascist regime collapsed and armed resistance began, the Christian Democrats played a leading part in it. Their northern Italian forces numbered up to 80,000 men and they incurred 4,800 casualties. Their leader was Alcide de Gasperi, who, like Adenauer, had spent part of the war in a Fascist jail. In the 1948-53 Parliament the Christian Democrats held an absolute majority and have subsequently commanded the largest popular share of the vote at about forty per cent.

In France, the party political position of Catholicism was more limited than in Italy and Germany. The First World War created solidarity between the French political factions and this was the cause of the integration of Catholics into the Third Republic. There was strong Catholic representation in a number of parties in the post-First World War Parliament. A group of thirteen Christian Democrats was formed in 1924 and this became known as the Parti Democrate Populaire. It was highly influenced by Italy's PPI – non-confessional, anti-individualistic – and had an organic view of State and society. In 1928 they won twenty seats but by 1936 had fallen back to ten. As the Second World War approached, a new grouping, Nouvelles Equipes Francaises, was established with the remit of renewing democracy and trying to unite the various Christian tendencies.

In Austria, after the collapse of the Austrian Empire in 1918, the Social Democrats and Christian Socialists took power. The Social Democrats were very quickly deadlocked with the Christian Socialists and after the bitter civil war which followed they were swept aside by the National Socialists. Their innate conservatism, lack of realism and partisan intransigence made them impotent in the face of Nazi Germany, even presuming that they would have wished to fight.

In Switzerland, on the other hand, the Catholic parties in the various cantons federated into one national party in 1912. The first election under proportional representation, in 1919, radically altered the balance of Swiss politics. The Liberal Party, which had held power since 1848, split, the Socialists doubled their seats and the Catholics emerged in the centre. By 1943 this new balance was reflected in the Federal Council. The Christian Social Party saw its strength grow from four deputies in 1919 to fourteen in 1943. The thinking of the Swiss Party was greatly influenced by Kaspar Decurtins, a member of the Fribourg Union, which did much of the preparatory work for the encyclical, *Rerum Novarum*.

In Belgium, the old Catholic Party – born out of the battles over Christian education and Church status – existed until 1940. The rise of the Christian social movements radicalised the party and their thinkers adopted the German Centre Party's tactics summed up by their slogan 'We Must Fight in the Open Field'. By 1945 the Parti Social Chretien had been formed. It abandoned denominationalism and its programme centred on the development of the human personality, on the family and on pluralism.

The same trends occurred in Holland once the schools question was settled in 1920. Reformed and Catholic parties continued to exist but the Catholic Party dropped its denominational basis after the Second World War, while the Dutch Protestant parties tended to remain more denominational during this period.

Out of the Rubble: Reconstruction and Post-Second World War

In the post-war period the German politician, Friedrich Naumann, believed that the way for Christians to proceed was to join the secular parties and influence from within. This, of course, is the Anglo-Saxon model. However, this advice was ignored and in Germany the general trend was to take Christians into political solidarity and to affirm their position in independence.

After the horrific experiences of the previous thirty years great vision was needed in facing the challenges of reconstruction. Here was a chance to heal old national rivalries and deep-seated denominational suspicions.

If the anti-democratic movements of the 1920s and 1930s achieved nothing else, they ensured that many of the narrow interest groups of the same period lay discredited with them in the ruins of Europe. The emerging Christian Democratic movements filled the vacuum and in the Cold War climate of post-war Europe they provided a non-socialist alternative to Communism. Unlike the denominational and sectarian parties of the pre-war era, the new movements and parties were specifically detached from Church control and separate from any specific denomination. The Belgian Party declared in 1945: 'We are Christian because we want to build upon human values that represent the foundations of our Western culture and civilisation. Historically they were brought forth by Christianity; today, however, they are the common inheritance of believers and non-believers.'

Ditching the pre-war strands of Christian socialism and confessional conservatism, the new Christian Democratic movements moved from a narrow base to Christian-inspired pragmatism. Their success at the polls in the period since then has marked them out as the most consistently successful movement in post-war Europe.

Adenauer[9] was a principal influence during this period. He saw the need to reconcile and to unite Protestant and Catholic and his achievement in fulfilling this objective was truly remarkable. He recognised that a 'third way' was needed between unlimited domination of private capitalism or its substitution by some kind of State capitalism. The Ahlen programme put out by the new Christian Democratic Union (CDU) in the British zone therefore opposed both socialism and capitalism. The over-great concentration of economic power was to be countered by limitations on corporations, cartels and share ownership. Nationalisation was demanded for the coal and iron industry. The position of workers was to be strengthened by giving them a share in decisions and a right to information about the situation of the company. This was strongly in line with Pius XI's 1931 encyclical, *Quadragesimo Anno*. On social questions the works council would have the right to be heard. Planning and guiding the economy were accepted in certain circumstances but were not seen as an end in themselves; the well-being of the people was the main aim. The Christian Democratic parties became broad loose alliances or federations, composed of many different groups. They all remained close to the Catholic trades union movement while accepting the disciplines of the market.

Although the West German system of industrial relations clearly benefited from this clear-sighted vision, the major impetus to economic renewal came from the massive investment provided by the American Marshall Plan. This enabled the Federal Republic to achieve a rapid and large-scale reconstruction of its economy. Over-reliance on American funding did, however, wed the Germany system to its sources of finance, and the CDU and its Bavarian sister party, the Christian Social Union (CSU), significantly tempered their criticism of structural capitalism.

A number of the new Christian Democrat parties specifically avoided the word 'party' in their title (eg CDU) in order to highlight the all-embracing non-ideological nature of their politics, compared with the narrow party-based outlook of their socialist and Communist rivals. This was a lesson learnt by the Liberal/SDP Alliance in the British elections of 1983 and 1987, when the word Alliance was specifically used to down-play the party politics and to play up its lack of partisanship. The Social Democrats and latterly the Liberal Democrats also dropped the word 'party' from their popular title.

Adenauer's CDU/CSU scored the first electoral triumphs. They were followed by de Gasperi's Italian Christian Democrats, Robert Schuman's Popular Republican Movement (RPR) in France, and the Belgian Social Christian Party (CVP/PSC). From the late 1940s until the late 1960s Christian Democratic parties were the largest members in multi-party governing coalitions in West Germany, Italy, Luxembourg,

Belgium, and Holland. In Austria and Switzerland they were junior partners in coalition. Only in France did their influence diminish.

The 1970s were fallow years with electoral reverses. In Italy there was scandal following revelations of the Christian Democrat Party's corrupt links with the business world. But reform, rethinking, and renewal led in the 1980s to improved performance and good prospects for the millennium. At the most recent national and European elections Christian Democrats have commanded between one-third and two-fifths of the popular support of the electorate. In 1987 in West Germany they polled forty-four per cent; in 1987 in Italy, thirty-four per cent; and at the most recent elections in Holland, Luxembourg and Belgium a plurality of votes. They have shared power with Left, Right and Centre.

Mr van Rompuy, the Chairman of the Belgian CVP, says that Christian Democrats should see their willingness to act as conciliators and mediators as a real strength; Lubbers talks of their 'healing role'; while Arie Oostlander, the Dutch MEP, says that Christian Democrats' belief in co-operation with others underlined why they could not be 'fitted into the Left-Right-Centre straitjacket of British politics'.

Our Common European Home

Undoubtedly the most significant achievements of Christian Democracy in post-war Europe have been the construction of the European Community, its role in Eastern Europe, and its commitment to a federated Europe.

As each post-war nation strove to rebuild its economy, a handful of statesmen from previously enemy countries united in the conviction that nothing could be rebuilt to last without regard for the dignity of each person and without the unification of Europe. This utopia became reality. First, in 1951, in the Treaty of Paris, with the establishment of the European Coal and Steel Community; and then in 1957, in the Treaty of Rome, through the establishment of the European Economic Community.

These treaties were primarily the work of the German,

Konrad Adenauer, the Frenchman, Robert Schuman, the Italian, Alcide de Gasperi, the Luxembourger, Joseph Bech, and the Belgian, Paul van Zeeland – Christian Democrats all. Their ideals were shared by liberals such as the Dutchman, Dirk Udo Stikker, and the Belgian socialist, Paul-Henri Spaak.

Schuman and Adenauer believed deeply that Christian heritage formed the very basis of Western European civilisation. They saw national antagonism as a major factor in the success of totalitarianism and the outbreak of a cataclysmic conflict. They believed that peace, democracy and pluralism all required reconciliation and ultimate integration. This is why they became adherents not only of reconciliation in the moral sense but of comprehensive integration designed to subsume and eradicate national rivalries. These political leaders provided the mechanism for implementing the 'functionalist' ideas of Jean Monnet, who argued for increasing economic and administrative interdependence as a foundation for political union.

In 1988 Pope John Paul praised 'the living example of sanctity of Robert Schuman'. He is an unlikely patron saint for the much lampooned Brussels Eurocrats, for whom a good lunch with a bottle of claret are part of the trappings of office. Schuman preferred to walk rather than to use his chauffeur and led an austere and simple life, unaffected by the pomp and self-importance of politics.

General Charles de Gaulle, always a vociferous nationalist, dismissed Schuman as a German agent for his pan-European vision: 'He is a Boche, a good Boche, but still a Boche,' President de Gaulle declared.

Schuman himself knew that his vision would not be fulfilled in his lifetime. Clay Clemens, in his appraisal of Christian Democrat achievements[10] cites Schuman as saying: 'Europe cannot be established in one fell swoop . . . it will arise from concrete facts that first create a solidarity of action.' It is not surprising that Helmut Kohl, a successor to this tradition, was instrumental in 1990 in reuniting Germany and paving the way for Schuman's federated Europe.

Christian Democrats have put their commitment into practice through 'solidarity of action'. First, in the 1950s they created a Christian Democrat parliamentary group in the European Parliament. By the 1970s, and the advent of direct elections, a European-wide federation, the European People's Party (EPP) was established. They have also participated in the European Union (EUCD) and, since the 1940s, in the Christian Democrat International – with especially strong groups in Latin and Central America.

They have consolidated their position in the European Parliament. In the 1989 elections the Christian Democrats won 121 out of 518 seats, contesting elections in every part of the Community except Great Britain. With the socialists holding 180 seats, they became the second largest group. In 1984, 31 million Europeans voted for them. By 1989, they had achieved 35 million votes. As Eastern European states join the Community the Christian Democrats' position will become even stronger. Understanding what inspires and motivates them will therefore not be of secondary importance.

The Next Ten Years: The Responsible Society

Egon Klepsch, the Chairman of the European People's Party in the European Parliament, draws on a rich legacy of Christian Democrat involvement when he cites the achievements of the Community's founding father. Today he and the present generation of Christian Democrat leaders – Helmut Kohl, Giulio Andreotti, Ruud Lubbers, Jacques Santer, Wilfried Martens and Konstantinos Mitsotakis – look forward to the fulfilment of Schuman's dream: 'If the Christian Democrats had not had the strength to believe in utopias and to put them into political practice following the destruction caused by World War Two, Europe would not be where it is today. We must all work together and make every effort if European Political Union – the Federal States of Europe – is to become a reality,' Klepsch said in 1990.[11] He resolutely opposes the idea of sealing off the Community, creating a Fortress Europe: 'We have a specific responsibility towards the Third and Fourth worlds, notably through the Rome Conventions which have been decisively influenced by the Christian Democrats.' Nor does he believe that Christian Democrats any longer have to 'prove themselves'. He says, 'The historic developments now taking place in Europe provide ample and impressive confirmation of the correctness of our policies.'

Encumbered by none of the national chauvinism or isolationist baggage which has led to Britain's very negative relationship with the Community, Christian Democrats throughout Europe have been able to think positively and plan for the future. Although they would like to see a constructive role for Britain, Klepsch told the Dutch CDA 1990 Symposium that if the then Prime Minister Mrs Thatcher continued to oppose federalism he 'could live with a Community of less than twelve'.

The Christian Democrats argue strongly for the development of the Community's less prosperous regions, external and internal security arrangements and the strengthening of democratic decision-making processes within the Community. This and their support for the Social Charter (clearly in line with Adenauer's thinking and the teachings of *Rerum Novarum* and *Quadragesimo Anno*) is all anathema to the former British Prime Minister, to say nothing of diehards such as her Trade Secretary, Nicholas Ridley, who shares de Gaulle's view of the Germans. Nor would she have been in agreement with their refusal to support destructive experimentation on human embryos, their opposition to the secularisation of Sunday, or their commitment to raise overseas aid spending to United Nations targets.

In a characteristically visionary speech, the former Belgian Prime Minister and present Member of the European Parliament, Leo Tindemans, told the 1990 Dutch Symposium on The Next Ten Years how he saw the shape of European politics. He said that 'society will be confronted by major problems which science poses. The world fears certain results which science may bring. In the area of communications, for instance television in every home, people fear they will be manipulated by science and technology.'

Tindemans also underlined the growing need for international co-operation and decentralised decision-making:

> Post Gulf, everyone is talking about the role of the UN and Europe. These structures will have a new role.
>
> The Christian Democrat theme of subsidiarity has become a core subject. Every country will have to deal with regional issues and our structures, from home to state, must allow for decisions to be taken at the lowest possible level.

At the same conference, M. Oreja Aguirre, the Spanish chairman of the Institutional Committee of the European Parliament, said that Christian Democrats would have a central role in preparing a federal constitution for European Union, and that this should specifically allow for a unified and common voting system based on proportional representation. Professor Sussmuth, CDU President of the Bundestag, said that German reunification had speeded up the process of European unification. She added that the three basic words of the Christian Democrat vocabulary over the next decade should be 'subsidiarity, personality and solidarity'.

Wim van Velzen, the Dutch CDA Chairman, said that if Christian Democracy were no more than anti-Communist and anti-socialist, the temptation to choose liberal capitalism as a leading principle would be strong. But, he argued, the next ten years will demand a policy which 'offers more than individualism, consumptive behaviour and materialism. The problems we face demand answers based on Christian standards and values.' He defined basic concepts as 'justice, managership, solidarity and decentralised responsibility'. In Europe 'we speak about freedom in responsibility, solidarity, justice and respect for Creation'. He said that the economic order advocated by Christian Democrats is not the liberal-capitalist economy: 'It is a socially and ecologically balanced market economy.' Wilfried Martens, the Belgian Prime Minister, described this approach as 'treasurership' which differs from conservative attitudes because 'the treasurer is more than the financial calculator'.

The CDA's Minister for Justice, Hirsch Ballin, defined the objective of Christian Democracy as 'the creation of a responsible society' while Professor van Dijk of Tilburg University said that 'responsibility refers to values and intentions . . . a responsible society is one where morally and socially orientated citizenship and managership will have to be experienced profoundly and actively by persons, groups and organisations at both local/regional and European and even global levels.'

Clearly the move from a planned economy in Eastern Europe and the excesses of market economics in the West provide an opportunity for Europe to create a socially and ecologically responsible market economy. Christian Democrats seem to understand the need to reinforce the mediating and intermediary institutions which exist in the vacuum between the individual and the State. These institutions have become so weak that they are often incapable of fulfilling their designated responsibilities within a responsible society.

Three Christian Democrats who attended the Dutch Symposium said that the absence of such mediating structures was one of the greatest challenges for the emerging democracies. Mr Antall, the Hungarian Prime Minister, said that for forty years families, voluntary organisations and private ownership had been destroyed or undermined; Mr Charnogursky, the Slovakian Deputy Prime Minister, and Mr Mrsic, the Croatian Minister for Foreign Affairs, both agreed and said that economic reforms were worthless unless accompanied by social, cultural and political reforms.

To understand why Christian Democrats cannot easily be classified as 'Left', 'Right', or 'Centre' in Anglo-Saxon terms, and to understand why they embrace particular positions requires both an understanding of the biblical and the social teaching which have shaped their attitudes. For instance, the Catholic critique of capitalism has been developing far beyond the present Christian Democrat position. From *Mater et Magistra* (1961) and *Pacem in Terris* (1963), on through the documents of the Second Vatican Council[12] – the period of aggiornamento, John XXIII's equivalent of perestroika and glasnost – to *Populorum Progressio* (1967) and John Paul's *Laborem Exercens* (1981), the Catholic Church has been responding to the impulses from the mainly South American base communities and the need to show a preferential commitment to the poor and oppressed. This understanding of the need to share power is perhaps beginning now to affect the thinking of Europe's Christian Democrats, as once *Rerum Novarum* shaped the outlook of an earlier generation. Similarly, the Christian think-tank of the CDA, the Dutch Scientific Institute, with its Protestant Reformed Church outlook has kept its party's thinking informed by Gospel values. The Church's insistence on an option for the poor, on the uniqueness of each person, and the need to share power through subsidiarity, have all left their mark on Christian Democratic thinking.

In March 1990 Klepsch outlined his desire to see politics brought closer to the people and insisted that Christian Democrat policies must be based 'on the principle of subsidiarity'. This commitment to empowerment, together with Christian Democrat support for personalism and communitarianism will be critical in the shaping of the new Europe.

But, most importantly for the future, it is to Eastern Europe that Christian Democrats now look. The first free elections since the Second World War have now been held and it was of signal importance that the first electoral victory, with over forty per cent of the vote, went to the Christian Democrats in East Germany. On October 2nd, 1990, Helmut Kohl saw his party and his country united across Germany's previously divided borders.

Christian Democrats place great importance to the completion of European integration and not merely for internal Community and economic reasons. The European Community provided a special source of hope from which the peoples of the East have derived the strength to overthrow an inhuman and totalitarian system. Klepsch believes: 'They now need help and solidarity from a strong, economically and politically fully operational Community to consolidate their achievements.' He says this solidarity with the newly democratic nations in Eastern and Central Europe is crucial if the divisions of Europe are to be healed.

Chapter 3

The Christian Democratic Tradition in Eastern Europe

The initial emergence of human civilisation was reliant on the defeat of its three greatest enemies: despotism, war and slavery. Each of these conditions was and remains incompatible with any advanced form of civilisation. This side of eternity there will never be a time when humanity is not threatened by the emergence of these old foes.

The three enemies were met by three countercurrents: the Greek ideals of political and intellectual liberty; Roman belief in the sovereignty of a just and rational system of law and administration, combined with the essential unity of the civilised world; and the Judaeo-Christian belief in the equal value of all people before God. The sanctity of the human personality has always been a cornerstone of Christianity. It holds out to its adherents the possibility of personal salvation and a relationship with God.

Christianity became the religion of Europe, and therefore of Western civilisation. For the vast majority Christendom and Western civilisation became virtually conterminous; and during periods of barbarian invasion and destruction, the Church stood as spokesman and guardian, not only of Christian teaching, but of what remained of the traditions of Greece and Rome. There is a natural affinity between a religion which stoutly defends the infinite value of the human personality and a belief in liberty conditioned and entrenched by the rule of law. During the last seventy years of totalitarian domination of Central and Eastern Europe the Church once again became the custodian of those civilising values.

1917 And All That

The Communist revolution of 1917 allegedly established in Russia a dictatorship of the proletariat, and Lenin proclaimed the beginnings of a world revolution. The proletariat never actually had a share in the power wielded by a small clique of fanatics. The revolutionaries set themselves the task of destroying all the elements that might have impeded the execution of their plans.

The instrument which they used to execute their plan was a highly organised and disciplined party. Only members of the party would be eligible for positions of authority; other parties were proscribed. Everyone was to be subservient to the new totalitarian regime.

Those who claimed rights of individual ownership or property – for instance, the landowning peasants – were ruthlessly liquidated. All who expressed criticism or dissent were imprisoned, tortured, used as slave labour, or eliminated often without even the pretence of a sham trial. The secret police initiated a reign of terror which was emulated in each of the Soviet Union's subjugated republics and compliant satellites.

Soviet tyranny scorned democracy, describing it as an instrument of western capitalism. Freedom of speech, freedom to publish, freedom of worship, were all suppressed. The State's distorting mirror of a controlled media fed the people lies and propaganda which painted a deliberately false picture of the rest of the world.

In all its main features the Russian system was the model for the National Socialism of Hitler and Mussolini: the use of a disciplined party controlled by a despot; the banning of all other parties; the use of terror as an instrument of government; the suppression of law; the denial of freedom of speech and publication; the exaltation of brutality and cruelty as proof of manliness; the scapegoating of minorities; the scornful extermination of all human pity and mercy; the skilful use of lying propaganda; the locking out of external ideas and influences; the insistence that young people are trained and marshalled into obedient footsoldiers of the State. These were the crude and harsh realities of the system which Soviet Russia boxed up for export.

After Lenin's death in 1924 Stalin replaced Communism's aim of universal revolution with the priority of Russian industrialisation. Stalin extended the Party apparatus and built a corrupt and inefficient bureaucracy. He remained in conflict with many of the earlier revolutionaries and purged them to secure his own position. In the following years millions were slaughtered.

One hundred years earlier William Wilberforce had written: 'It is a barbarous policy which confronts the troubles of a turbulent land by the extermination of its inhabitants. This is the calm, not of order, but of inaction; it is not tranquillity but the stillness of death.'[1] By the time he had finished, Stalin, it is estimated, had exterminated even more of his own citizens than Hitler killed. An estimated 60 million were dead.

In Moscow in January 1990 I met a Catholic Ukrainian student who told me a period story which I imagine could be replicated by hundreds of thousands of other families. He described how his grandfather had refused to display in his home the statutory portrait of Stalin. Challenged by the local secret police he eventually promised to put it in a prominent place. When the officials returned to check, they discovered that the portrait had been displayed all too publicly: above the toilet. The family were sent to Siberia.

Many people simply complied without protest – as they did in Germany. Others were ingenious in their opposition. Stories abound. During a visit to the Ukraine in October 1989 an old priest told me about a woman who asked for the secret baptism of her baby (as, indeed, Gorbachev's mother arranged for his baptism, and leading dissident, Alexandr Ogorodnikov's grandmother, arranged for his). The priest complied. The woman made the priest promise not to register the baptism and to say nothing to the authorities as her husband was a senior KGB official.

A few weeks later, a man came to see the same priest and asked for his son to be baptised. This time the priest refused. He explained to the father that the boy had already been baptised. It was the same child. This revealing story is a glimpse of a world of distrustful, divided and often frightened families, fearful of confiding in one another lest the slightest slip of a tongue provided incriminating evidence against them.

The Hitler–Stalin Pact

By 1939, with Germany facing war on two fronts, Stalin concluded the infamous Molotov-Ribbentrop Accord. The Soviet Union seized the Western Ukraine from Poland. Stalin also took the Baltic States of Lithuania, Estonia and Latvia, and attacked Finland. Russia under Stalin was as faithless, aggressive and despotic as Nazi Germany herself.

Whilst the war between totalitarianism and democracy resulted in the overthrow of Hitler, its conclusion saw the dismemberment of Europe at the Yalta Conference and the further extension of Stalin's ambitions. In 1924 he had formally abandoned the objective of world revolution and domination. By 1945, with most of Central and Eastern Europe under Soviet control, he had accomplished half of the task.

Appeasement Does Not Pay

If that war taught the Western democracies anything, it was that appeasement does not pay; that if effective steps are taken quickly enough the aggressor can be thwarted; and that if little states remain too preoccupied with their precious 'sovereignty' they remain too individually weak to counter the tyrant.

The way the war was pursued also highlighted the methods of totalitarianism. First the intended victim would be given solemn undertakings that his neutrality would not be violated;

after creating this illusion of false security the pledge would, of course, be broken. Then, agitators would be encouraged within the countries intended for annexation, to whip up instability. Masses of 'peacekeeping' troops would then be sent to provide 'stability'. Finally came the secret police to organise the reign of terror. And for a long while the Western democracies compliantly and tamely accepted it all.

Christian and Apollyon

When they finally appreciated the gravity of the crisis Britain and the remaining democracies stood and fought. Like the struggle between Christian and Apollyon, in Bunyan's *Pilgrim's Progress*, this was a struggle between two totally opposite views of life: Christian, certainly burdened by a sense of his own inadequacy and shortcomings, but facing towards the light; Apollyon, the embodiment of evil, rejoicing in his own wickedness, and wearing down his enemy with trickery, treachery and cunning.

The struggle did not end with the overthrow of Hitler. It wound on for another forty-five years, and is still being played out. Throughout it all the peoples of Eastern Europe never lost their faith, they kept facing the light. Understanding how they came by their hard-won liberties may bring a renewal of faith and an appreciation of the liberties we take for granted in Western Europe.

The Empty Tomb

In his book *Perestroika*, Mikhail Gorbachev praises Lenin for the following quality: 'He had the rare ability to sense the need for radical changes, for a reassessment of values, for a revision of theoretical directives and political slogans.'[2] I suppose much the same could be said of Gorbachev himself. Perhaps that is why he chose the quotation.

Perestroika and glasnost have opened up Eastern and Central Europe in surprising ways. Holiday companies now offer weekends in Moscow. Returning visitors pass around snapshots of themselves pictured against a backdrop of Lenin's tomb.

Lenin's embalmed body seems a suitable symbol for a corrupt state caught in suspended animation, wrapped in a winding sheet of theoretical directives and political slogans. For the Christian the filled tomb also provides an interesting parody of the empty tomb in Jerusalem. The authenticity of Christianity's claims are found in the empty tomb.

For seventy years Lenin's mausoleum became a totem for State centred religion. Latterly, Mikhail Gorbachev's encouragement of New Age religious movements in the Soviet Union provides another example of the substitutes for faith which socialist governments have tried to encourage or impose. Notwithstanding Marx's dictum about religion being the opium of the people, his heirs have had a pretty good stab at inventing their own religion.

All the great tyrants of history – Nero, Stalin, Hitler, Mao Tse-Tung, Pol Pot, Ceausescu – are examples of man making himself into God (which, incidentally, is the core of New Age thinking – see Chapter 10). False ego, power and wealth become a substitute for God.

The suppression of the truth of the Risen Christ became an overwhelming priority of the Soviet State. Systematically, dissenting Christians were rounded up and treated appallingly. The hierarchy of the Russian Orthodox Church was filled with KGB agents and Communist officials, dissenters were sent to forced labour camps or put into psychiatric institutions.

Although the Soviet authorities under Gorbachev appear to renounce some of the most distinctive features of Marxist-Leninism, including the belief that a religious faith necessarily blinds you to a correct understanding of the world, it would be absurd to pretend that there has yet been an irreversible shift. Gorbachev has bowed to the inevitable and taken a number of pragmatic decisions. Russian Christians point out for instance that (at the time of writing) the much-promised new laws guaranteeing religious freedom have yet to be enacted. Given their experiences since 1917 they can be forgiven for harbouring doubts. The brutal assassination of

Father Alexandr Men in September 1990 illustrated how well-founded are their concerns.[3]

Michael Bourdeaux, Varavva and Pronina

Thirty years ago a British Christian, Michael Bourdeaux, began to recognise the enormity of the persecution of the Russian Church. After his ordination in 1964 as an Anglican priest he established Keston College, an institute for the study of religion in Communist countries. Ever since, Keston has relayed the truth to a world which had largely chosen not to know.

In his book, *Risen Indeed, Lessons in Faith from the USSR*,[4] Bourdeaux explains that if it had not been for a bad case of toothache during his National Service he might not have been sent off to learn Russian. In 1960 this enabled him to take advantage of the first British–Russian exchange of students. On his return he subsequently approached twelve publishers before Faber and Faber agreed to print his first book, *Opium of the People*. The general response had been, 'all this talk of persecution can only harm Christians in the Soviet Union, even if it were true.' 'Least said, soonest mended' has given succour to aggressors down the ages.

Today, we adopt precisely the same attitude towards the persecution of Buddhists in Tibet and abase ourselves before the Government of the People's Republic of China. Some 6,000 monasteries have been destroyed, 600,000 Buddhist religious killed or proscribed. Yet one year after the Tiananmen Square Massacre and despite the continued occupation and persecution of Tibet, America renewed China's favourable trading tariffs and Britain's Foreign Office conducts business as usual.

Bourdeaux first started to highlight the truth about Russian persecution in 1964. He received a short duplicated letter on green paper, an English translation of a letter from a Ukrainian Christian. It had come via two intermediaries. One, a schoolteacher in Paris, of Russian origin, had recently been in Moscow and had met some Ukrainian Christians. The letter told of the imminent closure of the

Pochaev Monastery, one of the greatest Christian shrines in the country. It recounted heartbreaking persecutions: monks beaten up by the KGB, humiliating medical examinations, eviction from their monasteries. The letter was signed by two people claiming to be eyewitnesses, Varavva and Pronina.

Later in the year Bourdeaux travelled to Moscow – on one of eleven such visits before the Soviet authorities banned him. While he was there he was told of the impending demolition of the city's Church of St Peter and St Paul. To lay their dynamite, soldiers were reported to have pushed their way through the protesting Christians who had encircled the church. When Bourdeaux reached the site all that remained was a pile of masonry and some twisted metal – remnants of the crosses which had been on the cupolas. Two old women were standing nearby, trying to peer over the fencing which had been erected around the site. Bourdeaux approached them.

When they learnt he was a foreigner they asked him to follow them to where they could speak safely. They asked him why he was interested in St Peter and St Paul's. He told them he was anxious to try to help Christians in Russia, and explained about the document which he had received in London.

They asked who wrote the letter. Two women, he replied. What were their names? Varavva and Pronina. Bourdeaux later recalled that the silence which followed was total. The two women he was talking to were Varavva and Pronina. Six months earlier they had travelled nearly 1,300 kilometers to try to find a foreigner. They had met the French school-teacher. Now, amazingly, they had met Bourdeaux. 'Be our voice, speak out where we cannot,' they begged him. 'From that moment,' he says, 'the direction of my life was set. I had to find some way of serving the persecuted Church full time.'

Over the years which followed, Keston built up a reputation for disseminating extensive and reliable information. It has built up a formidable information chain across Eastern and Central Europe and, along with the BBC World Service, it became a highly valued and respected lifeline. In the 1980s, taking some of his inspiration from Keston and from the 35s – the Women's Campaign for Soviet Jewry – Danny Smith, a Christian journalist and campaigner, began to try to galvanise Evangelical Christians into taking action over particular cases of persecution. He subsequently documented the cases of the Siberian Seven, Valeri Barinov and Raoul Wallenberg.[5] Through this work we met one another and in 1985 established the parliamentary arm of the Jubilee Campaign. Since then over one hundred British MPs, from all parties and denominational backgrounds, have sponsored individual victims of religious persecution.

One of the hidden spin-offs of the campaign was revealed through some unexpected ecumenism when one Ulster Unionist MP was asked to take up the case of a Catholic dissident in Romania. This he dutifully and successfully did, even though some eyebrows were initially raised when he asked local congregations of Presbyterians in Northern Ireland to pray for the man.

By 1983 Michael Bourdeaux became convinced that it was only a matter of time before the Soviet Union disintegrated. He said:

> Stalinism delivered a body blow to Marxism from which it will never recover. Upon the ruins of Soviet ideology something one day will be rebuilt. No one can yet forecast what that will be. Nationalism could in certain areas become explosive enough to force change, but by its very nature it is divisive among the many peoples who inhabit the Soviet Union. Christianity does not overtly contain as much power, yet its inner strength is more cohesive. Furthermore, even though it is sometimes linked with nationalism (for example, the Russian Orthodox Church or the Catholic Church in Lithuania) it has the power at the same time often to transcend such considerations.

He went on to prophesy:

> It is already certain that, whatever else the twenty-first century may bring to the Soviet Union, Christianity will

be a formative influence, perhaps more so than is yet surmised, even by those with inside knowledge . . . It hardly needs stressing that if real Christian unity should make strides in the Soviet Union, this would be something of immense significance for the future, both of that country and of the world.[6]

Alexandr Ogorodnikov

One of the prisoners of conscience whom Keston and the Jubilee Campaign worked for was Alexandr Ogorodnikov. Freed from jail in 1988, he was elected as the first leader and Chairman of the Christian Democratic Union of Russia.

Before a visit in January 1990 to the Soviet Union, to attend the World Global Forum on the Environment, Hodder and Stoughton had asked me to act as postman and to deliver a contract for a book to Ogorodnikov, whom I had not previously met. I had also been asked by Father Dick Rodgers, an Anglican clergyman from Birmingham, to help secure the import of a printing machine. Paid for by British Christians it had already been returned to London once already by Soviet officials.

In 1986 and 1988 Father Rodgers had led public protests on behalf of Ogorodnikov. He was helped by a monk, Brother Aidan. Throughout Lent 1988 he had fasted and lived in a cage the size of Ogorodnikov's cell, erected at the London church of St. Martin-in-the-Fields. At the end of the fast Father Rodgers and Brother Aidan were given the news of Ogorodnikov's release.

In 1990, after our arrival in Moscow with Mark Tedder, a young Baptist, we set off in bitterly cold conditions to try to locate Ogorodnikov.

Over the days which followed the three of us spent hours together at Moscow Airport cajoling officials. We successfully imported the first ever offset-litho printing machine to be obtained by a Russian citizen, and subsequently persuaded the machine to churn out its first pieces of paper. I also had the chance to hear from Alexandr personally about his vision for the Soviet Union. Later in the year he and his son, Dimitri, travelled to Britain to spend three weeks here as my guests. Gerald Coates and his church in Cobham, Surrey, raised the funds to cover travel costs. Alexandr was to return to Britain again in August to attend the Ampleforth Conference for Eastern European Christians, organised by Leo Chamberlain, OSB, and Keston College.

Ogorodnikov spent eight years in Soviet jails and forced labour camps. In 1978, when he was twenty-eight, he was imprisoned as a 'parasite' and 'state enemy'. Although baptised in infancy by his Christian grandmother, he had been brought up as an atheist in a staunchly Communist family.

In 1974 he and a group of friends who had converted to Christianity founded a Christian seminar.[7] Its purpose was to facilitate discussion about faith and to consider its practical implications. This led to tensions with the Orthodox hierarchy and invited the interest of the KGB who quickly suppressed their periodical, *Obshchina* (Community). Ogorodnikov says of the group: 'Each of us had come along a complicated, sometimes agonising path of spiritual searching. From Marxist convictions, through nihilism and through the total rejection of any ideology at all, through an attraction to the "hippy" lifestyle, we have come to the Church.'

This repudiation of state ideology led to imprisonment. In Ogorodnikov's case this included periods of total isolation, during which the authorities tried to break him. He movingly describes how sometimes he would feel physically warmed in the most bitterly cold time – and he took this to be through the intercession of prayer. Amnesty International had produced a poster of Ogorodnikov, pleading with the world: 'Do Not Forget Me'. Not until after his release in 1980 did he learn about the worldwide pressure and prayer on his behalf. During his time in prison he was allowed just one telephone call to his son, and one visit from his wife, whom he was allowed to speak to through a glass partition. He told me how on one occasion his cell was deliberately flooded with sewage by prison officers.

After the authorities refused to give him and a Jewish

prisoner copies of the Bible, Ogorodnikov spent 600 days on hunger strike in protest. He was fed intravenously, which he called 'a most humiliating ordeal'. Although the Jewish and Christian prisoners never did receive their Bibles the protests triggered off political action throughout the West. In the House of Commons the Conservative MP for Hyndburn, Ken Hargreaves, used an adjournment debate to raise his plight and was supported by Basildon's MP, David Amess, and the Liberal MP for Berwick, Alan Beith.

During Ogorodnikov's 1990 British visit I took him to Ken Hargreaves's Lancashire constituency. At a packed and sometimes emotional meeting at Oswaldtwistle Baptist Church, the Russian expressed his thanks to some of the people who had worked and prayed for his release. At a meeting in Liverpool, a woman told him she had put up the Amnesty poster in her kitchen and had written on his behalf to the Soviet Ambassador. She had made a point of praying for him every day and told him it was a miracle that he was now there in her city.

Ogorodnikov's time in prison was not wasted. Not only did he survive his captivity, he emerged a toughened man with infinite inner strength on which to call. His association with Sakharov[8] and other Jewish dissidents, his clandestine sharing of the eucharist with a Lithuanian Catholic priest, his contacts with Ukrainians and other national groups broadened his outlook and shaped his thinking. Prison was also where he learnt his English. By speaking through a sewer pipe he was able to talk with an imprisoned professor from Leningrad. The academic taught Ogorodnikov English, Ogorodnikov taught him theology. The professor became a Christian.

Like Adenauer and de Gasperi in the pre-war German and Italian prisons, Ogorodnikov used his prison years to plan for the future.

Living and Surviving

Tatiana Goricheva in her book *Cry of the Spirit – Christian Testimonies from the Soviet Union* eloquently details how the suffering and privations of Ogorodnikov and others lends new credence to Tertullian's famous declaration that 'the blood of martyrs is the seed of the church'.

Many in Britain have been inspired by the extraordinary example of Irina Ratushinskaya, a young Christian poet sentenced in 1983 to seven years' hard labour, and five years' internal exile. Her crime: writing poetry. In her book *No, I'm Not Afraid*,[9] there is a stark account compiled by Amnesty International of conditions in the Mordovian corrective labour colony where Irina was kept:

> The worst feature is intense cold. The cell has a wooden floor with gaps between its boards, and underneath, a layer of solid cement, said to be 40-50 centimeters thick. The window has bars but often no glass. The prisoners receive food rations only on alternate days. On the 'empty' day, they are just given bread and a hot drink three times. Light bedding is handed out to them at night, and taken away again in the morning, so there is nothing they can use to keep warm.

While detained in this camp, Irina wrote her poem 'I will Live and Survive',[10]

> I will live and survive and be asked:
> How they slammed my head against a trestle,
> How I had to freeze at nights,
> How my hair started to turn grey . . .
> I will smile. And will crack some joke.
> And brush away the encroaching shadow.
> And I will render homage to the dry September.
> That became my second birth . . .
> And I'll be asked: what helped us to live
> When there were neither letters nor any news – only
> walls,
> And the cold of the cell, and the blather of official
> lies,
> And the sickening promises made in exchange for betrayal.

And I will tell of the first beauty
I saw in captivity.
A frost covered window! 'No doors, nor walls,
Nor cell-bars, nor the long endured pain -
Only a blue radiance on a tiny pane of glass,
A cast pattern – none more beautiful could be dreamt!'

Living and surviving has been at great cost and as Irina told *The Independent on Sunday*[11] the future does not promise to be easy either.

A massive spiritual renewal has flowed from the prison experiences, the suffering, witness and prayer of Russian Christians. This renewal has been guided by the *startsy*. Each *starets* – literally 'elder' or holy man – exists outside the formal structure of the church. He will have a circle of spiritual children. Wherever he lives, as a hermit deep in the forest, or in a side street, the people will put him in touch with those who have need of him. If caught, he will provide spiritual guidance to the other prisoners. Ogorodnikov is quite insistent on the importance of his *starets* – and the crucial role which the *startsy* have played in and outside penal times – in giving him guidance and help and in his spiritual development.

The Christian Democratic Union of Russia

Ogorodnikov's political development has been greatly influenced by his Christianity and Orthodoxy. When, with some of his collaborators from the 1974 seminar, he established the Christian Democratic Union of Russia (CDUR) in August 1989 they had just sixteen members. This had risen to 3,000 within a year. Despite the continued obstacles placed in the path of the emerging opposition parties, by July 1990 they had secured the election of one member of the Russian Parliament and four members of the Moscow City Council. At the time of those elections unless candidates were Communists they were still forbidden from identifying their party allegiance on the ballot paper. Therefore, each of these had to be elected as an Independent, and only allowed to describe himself as a Christian Democrat following the election.

This is not the only problem which Ogorodnikov's Christian Democrats face. As recently as August 1990 they were still denied the right to be legally recognised. Without such recognition they have not been allowed to have their own premises. Operating out of small apartments and shared rooms is a major impediment – to say nothing of the pressures on the families sharing their quarters. Similarly, they are denied the right to organise an educational foundation. Ogorodnikov's vision is for a Christian Democratic Institute which will provide educational opportunities for their many supporters hungry to learn about political ideas and how a democracy is organised. Some Westerners have an unrealistically optimistic view about the transition from dead-hand Marxism to a participatory democracy. A foundation akin to Ruskin College is urgently needed. Its independence from the State and from the existing ideology-based educational institutions is a prerequisite for long-term political success.

Old habits die hard, and it is not merely within the educational institutions that the party nomenclatura have dug themselves in. Ogorodnikov told a meeting at Liverpool's St Mary's Church, Edge Hill, that attempts had been made to destabilise his party through infiltration by KGB officials, who had also set up a series of 'pocket' parties. These are parties with no members but with not dissimilar names to the CDUR. The objective is to give the impression of factionalism and disunity and to maximise confusion: 'They no longer beat us up and torture us,' he said, 'but they do everything within their power to thwart us.'

Ogorodnikov described the CDUR's objectives to me: 'Our Party is founded on the idea of Christian Democracy – on a Christian outlook. This is based on the evangelical principle: faith, freedom and the special Orthodox concept that each person is responsible for his own actions. Each person, for instance, is responsible for truth, not only those who are elected. Together we can fulfil this deep process.'

This emphasis on the role of each individual in seeing that truth prevails is not surprising in a society which has lived on a diet of lies and where everyone is under suspicion of being a collaborator.

He says that there is little legacy of early Christian Democracy in Russia, contemporaneous with the early development and growth of the movement in Western Europe. In the short period between the removal of the Tsar and the Marxist-Leninist Revolution there was a brief flowering of such thinking but after 1917 such possibilities ceased to exist.

Since his release in 1988, in an attempt to fill this vacuum, Ogorodnikov has spent much of his time working on samizdat – unofficial, underground – publications: 'There are now 720 different editions of samizdat just in the Russian Republic that we know of. Each week we publish two periodicals, the *Bulletin of the Christian Community*, and the *Christian Democratic Messenger*. We have now published our political programme, and documents from the Christian Democratic heritage from the West. We are about to publish the Christian Democratic programme from West Germany. All of these are published underground. We spend eighty per cent of our time making such publications.'

Ogorodnikov says: 'We are opposed to the totalitarian system in the Soviet Union. Our society must work out stable democratic institutions which people can use to check power and to guarantee irreversible change. This can only be done if we deprive the Communist Party of their monopoly of power. A multi-party system will guarantee every group of people, and every person, the right to express their own outlook. We believe as Christians that we have to give answers to the very painful problems facing our suffering society.'

Ogorodnikov recognises that the Soviet Union is finished as a political entity and he supports the concept of a federation of autonomously governed states, and separation where that is desired by the people: 'We support the Lithuanians, and in the Ukraine self-determination, after a common vote, may well mean separation.'

His vision for Russia is 'a sovereign, free Russia. We want to liberate Russia and look after her interests. We seek a pluralistic democracy, based on law. We think that when Russia becomes free, and we have fulfilled some of our lofty aims, we can then enter the common European home. With our personal faith and traditions we can make our contribution to European civilisation.'

Towards his former jailers and persecutors he shows admirable generosity: 'I have pity for them, no desire for revenge. We preach the idea of reconciliation because it is very dangerous to split our society more and more and more. Our nation has to go through a confession, national repentence, to purify ourselves.'

This spirit of purity and reconciliation is something which Ogorodnikov passionately believes Russian Christian Democrats can bring to the new Europe. Nor is his vision for Russia and for Europe one where the East merely adopts Western materialism and capitalism: 'When we become free and democratic it will be a new dawn. We are a rich country, rich in people and in assets. At the heart of our belief is the certainty that man is made in the image of God. In Europe we must rediscover that belief. I am a little afraid that without faith Europe will have few values. We would like to bring to Europe our heritage and our faith.'

Perhaps Ogorodnikov would agree with Dostoyevsky, who once wrote that the vocation of the Russian people is to prove that man cannot live without Christ. He went on to prophesy that:

> The Russian people will arise and will bring forth the light of Christ from the depths of their soul so as to bring it back to the peoples of Europe who have lost it . . . Europe is distancing itself ever more from Christ and is abandoning itself increasingly to comfort and prosperity. When in this way Europe has come to the brink of the precipice, the Russian people will come with the image of Christ shining forth and with His forgiving love in their hearts. And at the last moment they will save Europe from chaos.[12]

Ivan Hel and The Ukraine

If Ogorodnikov's vision of a federation of Eastern and Central European nations comes to pass, one of the most important of the new States will be the populous Ukraine, inhabited by some 51 million people.

In September 1989 I led a small Jubilee Campaign delegation to the Ukrainian city of Lvov. This coincided with the fiftieth anniversary of the Molotov-Ribbentrop Accord and the forcible assimilation of the Western Ukraine into the Soviet Union. I was accompanied by Kingston Liberal Democrat councillor, David Campanale – an AnaBaptist – and Bill Hampson, Chairman of the Organisation Committee of the Movement for Christian Democracy. He is an Independent Methodist from the Lancashire town of Leigh. In 1986 we had previously travelled together to the Soviet Union visiting a number of key Christian and Jewish dissidents, including Valeri Barinov's family, Inna Begun, and Vladimir and Marsha Slepak. At the conclusion of that visit we held talks with the Kremlin's Religious Affairs Department. The Soviet authorities subsequently issued exit visas for all three of these families.

In 1989, at Lvov, we spent two days with Ivan Hel, the Chairman of the Committee for the Defence of the Ukrainian Catholic Church. We also spent time with an outlawed bishop, Pavlo Vasylyk. I subsequently met Hel and Bishop Vasylyk again in January 1990 in Moscow and again at the Ampleforth Conference in August 1990. By then, having received overwhelming support in the elections of March 4th, 1990, Hel had been elected to the Ukrainian Parliament. He sits as a Christian Democrat.

Hel's appearance reminds you of the bluff exterior of Lech Walesa. So does his indomitable faith and tenacity.

Hel spent fifteen years in jail, first at Mordovia Prison. Like Ogorodnikov he was subsequently held at Perm in the far away Urals, the notorious 'camp of death'. Temperatures frequently plunged below zero. Hel was kept half naked and fed infrequently. He told me that he was 'morally and physically terrorised'. For three years letters from his wife, Maria, and his daughter, were not permitted. He was released in 1987.

Hel's first brush with the KGB was in 1961 while he was a student. He remained active in the movement for the legalisation of the Church and was inevitably arrested in 1972.

Vasylyk was secretly consecrated as a bishop in 1974 – and spent eighteen years in jail. While free, he carried out his ministry by night. During the day he was forced to act as a collector of herbs. From 1946 until 1989 it was illegal to celebrate the liturgies in public. This clandestine church of the Ukrainian catacombs gathered its faithful in the fields, in barns and in forests. Even as recently as January 1990 Bishop Vasylyk had been refused the right to register at his family home, effectively preventing him from taking up other rights. He joked with me, saying that 'For an Englishman your home is your castle, mine has become my prison.' I wrote to Gorbachev on his behalf and in August 1990 he was permitted to travel to Ampleforth; not quite an English castle but in the same class.

Bishop Vasylyk introduced us to a young priest, officially a boiler stoker. Father Makhaylo Havryliv was caught celebrating a public liturgy. His punishment was two and a half months at Chernobyl, clearing radioactive waste. He was issued with no protective clothing.

Great bitterness was expressed about the man responsible for the Chernobyl cover-up, the local Communist boss, Vladimir Shcherbitsky, a staunch neo-Stalinist. Hel told us that Shcherbitsky was detested by the people: 'Stalin destroyed the people physically, Shcherbitsky spiritually.'

Our delegation had a brief glimpse of the less than welcoming methods used by Shcherbitsky's local officials. At about midnight we arrived by train at the border town of Mostiska, having travelled from Przemysl in Poland. Half a dozen Ukrainian officials ordered us to disembark with our luggage. For the next four hours – long after our train had departed with the rest of its passengers – the bureaucrats dissected our luggage and scoured our visas and passports. Subversive and seditious material, such as a biography of Basil Hume, the writings of the English medieval mystic,

Julian of Norwich, and a copy of the *Liverpool Echo*, were all confiscated. Clearly they were not ready for the paper's Scouse Mouse cartoon.

We finally left on an empty train at four a.m. In return for our confiscated belongings the senior official handed me a copy of a pamphlet entitled 'Perestroika' and a copy of *Lenin on the Great Socialist Revolution*. Unfortunately it was written in German. I am sure Lenin didn't have all this trouble on his famous train journey to Petrograd.

We were not upset – and I doubt that many tears were shed in the Ukraine – when we learnt, two days after we left, that Gorbachev had finally dismissed Shcherbitsky.

Flowers in the Ukraine

During the protest demonstrations held that September 1989 weekend some 250,000 people congregated at the centre of Lvov. An illegal Mass was celebrated in the park. There then followed a procession to the Ukrainian Catholic Cathedral of St. George, once the seat of their episcopate and from which Ukrainian Catholics had been banned since 1946, when Stalin had ordered a false synod to dissolve the Ukrainian Catholic Church. All its buildings and assets were seized. Five million believers were told that their Church had simply ceased to exist and had 'self-liquidated'. It was made illegal and its priests outlawed. Some buildings were handed to the State-controlled Orthodox Church and others sealed up. In August 1990 the cathedral was finally handed back. An abiding memory of Lvov remains the closed churches and fresh flowers pinned to the doors.

Outside one of these churches in Lvov there is a broken statue of Christ. The cross had been smashed and Christ's head torn off. Not a day has passed since 1946 without more flowers being left and someone had nailed a crown of thorns to the railings. Every so often Shcherbitsky's men had it removed. Another would always appear in its place.

At the makeshift illicit memorial to the Ukrainian national poet, Taras Sheuchenko, people queued to lay flowers alongside his photograph. Some of the young people wore armbands which carried a phrase coined by the 1930s Ukrainian poet, Khvyloviy, 'Away from Moscow, Towards Europe'.

Out of the Ice Age: The Baltic States

Like the Ukraine, Lithuania, Latvia and Estonia – the three Baltic States – have been the most advanced of the fifteen Russian Republics in demanding autonomy. In 1939 they were forcibly assimilated into the Soviet Union, and in 1991 armed force was once again used to stifle their struggle for self-determination.

Their first moves away from Moscow began in 1988 when the independence movements erupted. Lithuania's President, Vytautas Landsbergis, effectively ended the Soviet Union when on March 11th, 1990, he pre-emptively announced Lithuanian self-government. The Kremlin hit back by encouraging local disruption and pro-Moscow demonstrations. Their Committees for National Salvation might have been better called Committees for the Salvation of Communism.

Christian Democrats have been to the fore of the independence movement in Lithuania and their tactics have much in common with Solidarity in equally Catholic neighbouring Poland.

Latvia and Estonia were particularly subject to post-war Russian immigration which has led to a shift in the balance of population: Russian nationals now comprise a substantial element of the people. Latvia is a mixture of Catholics and Lutherans and Estonia is predominantly Lutheran. In both countries the Protestant Reformed Churches have been encouraging and guiding the independence movements, in a similar role to that played by the Churches in East Germany.

On March 25th, 1990, Estonia's Communist Party voted to split from Moscow and the Estonian Parliament said it would not recognise Moscow's authority on its territory. The inspiration for their courage and determination had its origins in the 1989 revolutions of Eastern and Central Europe.

The Turning Point: Poland

The staggering changes here began with the election of a Polish Pope, John Paul II, in 1978. Secular commentators, trying to discover the catalyst for the changes, frequently make no reference to the powerful cocktail of faith and politics. John Paul's election was the single most important element in the crucial role played by the Churches between 1978 and his summit meeting with Gorbachev in Rome in November 1989. His election kicked open the door to change. Any observer who fails to examine the role of the Churches will not understand the future shape of Europe or the attitude of millions of its people.

Notwithstanding the flexible response of Mikhail Gorbachev to the changes, it is absurd to present him as a twentieth-century Hercules, moving from one task to another – first, cleaning out the Augean Stables, then taking a swipe at a many-headed hydra. Gorbachev was in charge of the KGB. It was inevitable that someone who had spent his life observing how other societies are organised would be amongst the first to realise the corrupt nature of Soviet society in comparison. Brave men and women throughout Eastern and Central Europe have wrested power from his Party's hands. Allowing this to take place was not an altruistic or enlightened measure. Gorbachev simply accepted the inevitable.

In the game of grandmother's footsteps played out across the Soviet colonies, Gorbachev became a bystander, probably as dumbfounded by events as everyone else. Soviet reactions to the collapse of the Berlin Wall, the attempts to form coalitions, to allow limited attempts at power-sharing, and to install reform Communists, all indicate that the Communists did not realise either the depth of their unpopularity or the scale of what would happen. Gorbachev did not have a script which anticipated the collapse of the socialist republics. The Soviet Union lost its colonies more by accident than design. To his credit, Gorbachev ruled out the use of force in the European satellite states (knowing also what it would cost in economic terms and through loss of credibility in the West). In dealing with the Soviet republics the mask of reasonableness has frequently slipped. Many Soviet citizens regard Gorbachev with enmity while the people of Eastern Europe feel no special sense of gratitude. In Eastern Europe they were responsible for their own revolutions and the overthrow of hated tyrannies. So from where did their inspiration spring?

In 1983 Michael Bourdeaux[13] asked the question: 'Is it too much to hope that a Slav Pope may yet have some unforeseen influence?' In January 1990, at the foundation meeting of the British Movement For Christian Democracy, Bourdeaux gave a talk about the changes underway in Eastern Europe. He was in a position to answer his own question: 'It is no exaggeration to say that the momentous events which continue to transform Europe began on the day of John Paul's election in 1978.'

John Paul is a product of the Communist system. He tasted the concentration camps and the Communist repression. His mentor was the great Polish Cardinal, Stefan Wyszynski. From 1948 until 1981 Wyszynski was Archbishop of Warsaw and Primate of Poland. In November 1953 he had been taken into custody by the Communist authorities and was not released until 1956. During the battles which followed with Wladisylaw Gomulka, the Secretary General of the Worker's Party, he demonstrated total resolve. John Paul is a chip off the old block.

Immediately after his 1978 election the new Pope planned a visit to Poland for the following year. Millions of people came out on to the streets. This popular explosion of support was the first manifestation of 'people power' in Eastern Europe. It helped the Polish people to gain a sense of solidarity, to build up their own confidence and to overcome their fear. After that the days of tyranny and oppression were numbered. Poland still had to see the formal creation of Solidarity by Lech Walesa, let alone his election as Polish President. The strikes in the Gdansk shipyards and the imposition of martial law were still to come. The first semi-free elections would not be held until June 1989, when Solidarity was allowed to contest half the seats – and won them all. From the Pope's Polish visit it took ten years to see the appointment of the first non-Communist leader in Eastern Europe in forty years. Prime Minister Tadeusz Mazowiecki, a devout Catholic intellectual, saw himself translated from dissident to premier and negotiating his country's future with his former jailers.

In August 1989, with Conservative MP, Tim Boswell, and Labour MP, Tony Lloyd, I attended a Congress of Young Parliamentarians in Warsaw at the Polish Parliament, the Sejm. We were there on the fiftieth anniversary of the outbreak of the Second World War. Neville Chamberlain had broadcast his declaration of war as a response to the invasion of Poland.

Now, on this anniversary, on giant screens in Warsaw's Old City Square, a special recorded message was being broadcast to the crowds by Pope John Paul. Elsewhere in the city I visited the little church where Father Jerzy Popieuzsko had been a priest. Father Jerzy had been an outspoken critic of the Communist regime. He was brutally murdered by them – a massive miscalculation. His death became a focal point for the people's renewed struggle. I was very struck to see on the noticeboard outside his church a Solidarity poster alongside a poster urging protection for the unborn. The radical Christian view which upholds a respect for life at all stages comes as second nature to many Poles. When Western leader-writers in fashionable newspapers attack the Polish Parliament for upholding the sanctity of human life as 'backward' and 'out of step', they are failing again to understand the faith which motivates a people who cherish authentic human values. When this faith was given a voice into the ear of the free world, the movement for change became unstoppable. Little wonder that the Bulgarian Communists sought the assassination of the Pope.

For the 1990s the obstacles which will face the emerging parties in Poland will be formidable. As Solidarity develops into Social Democratic and Christian Democratic parties they will face the daunting legacy of the corrupt Rakowski Government: one hundred per cent inflation, and $39 billion of foreign debt. In August 1989 the asking price for a pound of chops was £20, a pound of sirloin steak, £40.

The currency was worthless; the economy in a state of collapse; the quality of life abysmal; milk and water have to be boiled before they can be drunk. Pollution is shocking. The nomenclatura system – which reserves important jobs for party nominees – will prove hard to dismantle. Little wonder that Tadeusz Mazowiecki said, on assuming office, that he felt a hundred kilos of rock fall on his head, but 'I am a believer and I also believe Providence cares for us all'.

The Pattern Repeated: Hungary

The same pattern of direct Christian engagement in political change can be traced in virtually every other country in Eastern and Central Europe.

In Hungary, probably the most secular of the states, the bravery of Cardinal Jozsef Mindszenty has continued to be an inspiration. In 1948 he was taken into custody and tortured. In 1949 after a show trial he was sentenced to life imprisonment. During the Hungarian Uprising in 1956 he was released and took refuge in the American Embassy at the fall of the Rising, where he remained until 1971. He told a visitor to tell them in the West: 'Tell your friends not to forget us. Tell them to pray, to pray a lot, and then pray still more. There is a hard struggle ahead for us.'

Other leaders who refused to compromise include Bishop Marton in Transylvania, the Calvinist bishop, Ravasz, and the Lutheran bishop Ordass. However, they were not able to stop and resist the total infiltration of the Church hierarchy. Crypto-Communist priests were allowed to abase the witness of the Churches by justifying the party's ideology with quotes from the Apostle Paul. The State Office of Religious Affairs worked closely with them, and apart from a few uncompromising leaders, untarnished pastors and faithful laymen, many Hungarian Christians look back on the Marxist era as a time of compromises, betrayals and unfaithfulness. Even today, many Communist-imposed bishops are still in position.

But at a grass-roots level, the picture was different. Christians played a key part in the Hungarian Uprising of 1956.

Young Catholics organised resistance to military service, and more recently, other young Christians from the Protestant Reformed tradition were actively involved in the new parties which contested Hungary's first free elections on March 25th, 1990. A small Christian Democratic Party also gained twenty-one seats (5.4 per cent of the votes cast) and one of their number now sits in the Cabinet of the Coalition Government.

One of the leading Christian voices in Hungary is Pastor Geza Nemeth, who works in Budapest. He told the Ampleforth Conference that Communism was only one of the demons which had been stalking the region. Burgeoning nationalism would become a new and dangerous challenge. Pastor Nemeth says that 'after decades of imposed atheist uniformity' it is not surprising that there is a revival of national awareness but he warns that a quite proper rediscovery of values easily turns itself into aggression and intolerance. He says: 'The churches, with their responsibility for peace in Eastern Europe, must underline that Christianity is a common heritage of all Eastern European peoples; the essence of the Christian message is to bind, not to part, and it cannot, under any circumstances be an ideology of antagonism.' The danger for Hungary – and especially Hungarians in Romania's Transylvania – is that rising tensions will lead to vindictive attacks. The whole region could become a Ngorno Karabakh, the Armenian enclave in Azerbaijan which has become a by-word for communal violence and nationalism.

Thus, solidarity with minorities must be an essential part of the West's response to this challenge. Nemeth puts it in Christian terms by referring to the teaching of Jesus to care for 'the little ones'. From his Hungarian vantage point he says the West can help the East by using its spiritual, political and financial capacity to redress the imbalance which the region's minorities suffer. It would therefore support the Turks in Bulgaria, the Protestants and Catholics in the Baltic threatened with Russification, the Protestants in Poland, the Uniates in the Ukraine and Romania, the Hungarian Reformed Church and Catholics in Romania, Czechoslovakia, Sub-Carpathian Ukraine, and so on.

Germany: The Walls Came Tumbling Down

From the 1970s onwards East German Christians from the Reformed Churches became increasingly critical of the State. During 1989 it was they who offered a platform and a sanctuary for dissidents – with the church of Nikolaikirche in Leipzig becoming the focal point for the continuing demonstrations. One banner hung above the altar of an East Berlin church summed up the sad truth of Eastern Europe, where many had propped up a system in which they had been both victim and, through their compliance, aggressor: 'I am Cain and Abel.'

By the time the Berlin Wall had collapsed – on November 9th, 1989, after twenty-eight years of separating the two Germanies – East Germany was also heading for her first and last free elections. The Catholic West Germany Chancellor Helmut Kohl, and his Christian Democrats campaigned strongly for their new sister party in the elections held on March 18th, 1990. The scale of the victory took the commentators by surprise. The Christian Democrats and their allies ran away with nearly fifty per cent of the vote; and the interim government was led by Lothar de Maiziere of the CDU. The Social Democrats limped in with twenty-two per cent. Reunification was finally completed on October 3rd, 1990 – a personal triumph for Kohl and his Foreign Secretary, Free Democrat, Hans Dietrich Genscher.

Vera Wollenberger became a Member of the Volkskammer (the East German Parliament) in the March elections. She is a Christian from the Kirche von Unten. She says that the turning point in the role of the Lutheran Church was in the 1970s. Throughout the 1950s, 60s and 70s the Church steadily lost influence and by the end was playing hardly any role in East German society. The Church scrupulously avoided comment on the political issues of the day. Then in the early 1970s it opposed the introduction of defence studies into every school. The Church's stance brought it moral credit and its first increase in numbers. The independent peace movement – which concerned itself with living at peace with nature and concern for human rights as well as disarmament – was born.

Subsequently, Wollenberger says, the first independent newspapers were produced on church duplicating machines in parish rooms. It was also in the parish rooms that the first independent libraries appeared. The Church's influence became so decisive that three years before it fell, the Honecker government was unable to take any political decisions without first considering how they would be received by the Opposition and the Church.

Archbishop Schinherr, the retired Lutheran Bishop of Berlin-Brandenburg, told the Ampleforth Conference that the Church is now in a position of considerable authority in Germany because 'they were able to some degree to retain their integrity in a system that corrupted its own citizens on a massive scale'. Perhaps that is why, in the Volkskammer elections, twenty-four of those elected had theological qualifications and almost all of them were ordained ministers. Four Government Ministers in the interim government were also ordained ministers and the Prime Minister was, additionally, deputy presiding officer of the Synod of the Federation of Protestant Churches. Many others in the government were in Church service or closely associated with the Church.

The Lutheran role of engagement is not dissimilar to that of Catholics in many other parts of Eastern Europe but in the German Democratic Republic itself the Catholic Church stayed out of politics. During the post 1945 period Heinrich Wienken was Commissary of the Fulda Bishop's Conference and adopted the same attitude towards the Communists as he had adopted earlier towards the Nazis: to secure the existence and survival of the Church, with questions of political order of incidental significance. By the 1960s his successors, men such as Cardinal Bengsch, were boasting openly of having voted against the Vatican Council documents *Lumen Gentium* and *Gaudium et spes*. The call to engage in the problems of society was repudiated by Bengsch because this might have entailed conflict with the State. He also rejected the ecumenical movement. By practising social abstinence and living at a distance in GDR society Catholics marginalised themselves. Even after the encyclicals *Pacem in terris* of John XXIII and *Populorum progressio* of Paul VI, which addressed issues of human survival, the Church in the German Democratic Republic remained insular and remote.

Bishop Georg Sterzinsky, the Bishop of Berlin, admitted the failure to engage or to respond to society's needs in his greeting to the Synod of the Federation of Protestant Churches in East Berlin at the end of February 1990, when he said: 'We had no hope that demonstrations or the expression of people's will could lead to success, and we regret for that reason we held back and played far too small a part in bringing about the new initiatives.' Sterzinsky took the opportunity to thank Protestant Christians and communities for their courageous involvement in the 1989 revolution. Father Hans-Friedrich Fischer, of Leipzig, told the Ampleforth Conference that 'Here at last are plain words which not only confess guilt but also show a readiness for a new policy on the part of the Church. This is a signal which will encourage many committed Catholics to continue their witness.' But it is also a story with significance for us in the West, especially for those who say 'the Church' (meaning Christians) should stay out of politics.

Spring at Last: Czechoslovakia

In 1938 in a broadcast on the eve of the Munich crisis, Neville Chamberlain referred to Czechoslovakia in a famous phrase, as a 'far away country' of whose people 'we know nothing'. He thus justified Britain's continued appeasement of Hitler's Germany, which had invaded Czechoslovakia.

In 1968 Britain was similarly impotent when Alexander Dubcek was displaced by Husak, following the suppression of Dubcek's attempts at reform. Soviet armed intervention ended the Prague Spring. In an attempt to forestall the revolution of 1989 the Communist Government of

Czechoslovakia kicked Husak upstairs, made him President, and replaced him as General Secretary by the man who had purged the Prague Spring. It was to no avail and the writer, Vaclav Havel, led his Civic Forum to victory.

By June 1990 Havel was President and Civic Forum secured a majority of seats in the June 1990 elections (46.6 per cent). In addition, the Union of Christian Democrats secured a further twenty seats (12 per cent) and supported Havel in the formation of the new Government.

Throughout the long years of opposition and in the fashioning of the new democracy the Church played a pivotal role. The Church in Czechoslovakia is not as strong as in Poland. Historically, it has been divided between Catholics (associated with Habsburg counter-reformation and restoration) and Protestants (influenced particularly by Jan Huss and Jan Masaryk),[14] while both Churches were ruthlessly suppressed during the Stalinist period, and again after 1969.

Dr Oto Madr, a Czech theologian present at the Ampleforth Conference, spent time in prison and labour camps for his beliefs. He listed the separate techniques which had been used by the State to try to kill the Church: ideological warfare; defamation; disinformation; gerontisation; isolation; discrimination; surveillance; intimidation; obstruction; atomisation; schismatisation; and secularisation. The Reverend Anton Hlinka, who now works with Pro Libertate Christianorum in Munich, gave further weight to Madr's description from the experience of the Church in Slovakia. Believers were eradicated from certain areas of society, a ban was placed on spiritual renewal movements, the Catholic press was almost entirely dissolved, all monasteries and convents were closed. Christianity was branded as the fifth column of capitalism and imperialism, and physical and psychological methods were used in an attempt to destroy zealous priests and lay people. The effect was to intensify the purity of the Church and increase its determination to survive.

Two of the key figures in the Czech revolution of 1989 were

Vaclav Maly, a banned Catholic priest and Vaclav Benda, a Catholic intellectual, and one of the brains behind the original Charter 77 group of dissidents. Along with Havel and Dubcek, the third great symbol of the Czech movement for democracy was Cardinal Tomasek. At the crucial November 24th Wenceslas Square meeting Tomasek sent the following message: 'The Catholic Church stands entirely on the side of the people in their present struggle. I thank all those who are fighting for the good of us all and I trust completely the Civic Forum which has become a spokesman for the nation.' The following day Tomasek led the celebrations at Prague Cathedral to mark the canonisation of Agnes of Bohemia. The actual canonisation had occurred on November 12th in Rome, five days before the revolution began. An ancient Bohemian legend has it that wonders would occur when Agnes was canonised.

By December 28th the Communist regime had collapsed and on December 29th, with Dubcek in the chair, the Federal Assembly elected Vaclav Havel as the new President. To underline his gratitude for the uncompromising and unflinching response to successive Communist regimes by the ninety-year-old Primate, Cardinal Frantisek Tomasek, Havel made his first official duty as newly-elected President a visit to Prague Cathedral. Havel also paid tribute to the fierce and staunch defence by the Church of liberty in his country and to the importance of Christian tradition and thinking. He said: 'The greatest book is the Bible, and the greatest book in the Bible is St John's Gospel.'

In his first New Year's address as President, Havel said the worst aspect of the wasted years was the 'devastated moral environment. We are all morally sick because we all got used to saying one thing and thinking another . . . All of us have become accustomed to the totalitarian system, accepted it as an unalterable fact and therefore kept it running . . . None of us is merely a victim of it, because all of us helped to create it together.' Cain and Abel again.

On November 28th, 1989, in the midst of these quickly moving events, the Central Committee of the Czechoslovak People's Party – the Christian Democrats – adopted their first post-socialist programme. They solemnly pledged their 'unswerving determination' to imbue their party 'with features and aspects fully reflecting the political and religious convictions of the Christians of our state'.

'Our contribution to the political life we are now entering resides in the great ancestral heritage of Christian values, which are an irreplaceable groundwork for the creation of a new democratic society in this country. Our ideological premises unambiguously accept the Christian grasp of reality, society and man's position in society. In this we proceed from the inviolable and inalienable human and civil rights enshrined in the Universal Declaration of Human Rights.'

Like its Western counterparts, the Czech People's Party is non-denominational and supportive of democratic pluralism. It strongly contends that a society is impoverished when it loses sight of its spiritual values: 'We reject the thesis that religion is simply the citizen's private affair. We regard religion as an integral part of the spiritual culture of society, a component of irreplaceable import and influence in the process of shaping the identity of a nation. Our faith gave the world men and women of the stature of St Wenceslas, St Agnes of Bohemia, John Huss, John Amos Comenius[15] and other men and women of great moral purpose and integrity.'

Czech Christian Democrats also believe that active engagement in political life is an obligation for Christians, not an option: 'It is the duty of Christians to participate in public life. We are convinced that the lasting and genuine good of individuals, nations and states can never be attained through evil, violence and the repression of the rights of other people.'

They see the family as 'the fundamental unit of society, in the spiritual, moral, biological and social sense. In our policies we will seek to give the family a steadily increasing degree of stability and integrity.'

They are also strongly pro life: 'We regard life as a divine gift. It is the duty of the State to protect life legally and physically and to foster the citizen's respect for life. We regard abortion, euthanasia and capital punishment as man's interference with the order of creation.'

And their concern for life extends to the rest of the created environment: 'Our considerations are guided by the principle that peace and a healthy living environment are the natural outcome of man's behaviour consonant with the order established by the Creator.'

The People's Party is one of three parties which comprise Czechoslovakia's Christian Democratic Union. These three components each has a distinctive history.

The stronger of these is probably the Christian Democratic Movement based in Slovenia[16] and which is led by Jan Carnogursky. Carnogursky was a prominent Christian dissident under the old regime and was released from prison to become deputy Prime Minister in the provisional Federal Government. The equivalent Christian Democratic Party in the Czech Republic, led by Vaclav Benda, had a weaker popular base (possibly because of the greater secularism of the Czech lands) and was reluctant at first to join forces. Instead, it operated under the Civic Forum movement until March 24th, 1990. The third party in the union is the Czechoslovakia People's Party which was one of the 'fraternal' parties licensed by the Communists under the old regime. Like its counterparts elsewhere in Eastern Europe, it began to assert itself in the final phase of the Communist collapse and has now been relaunched with new leaders, including Chairman Josef Bartoncik. The other well known figure in the CPP is Richard Sacher, who served as Interior Minister in the provisional government, and became a figure of some controversy.

Balkan Cockpit: Bulgaria and Romania

The role of Christians in bringing the Bulgarian and Romanian Communist dictatorships to an end was also decisive. Before the revolutions in both of these countries the only human rights movements were purely Christian.

In 1984 I visited Romania and in *What Kind of Country?*[17] I wrote:

> We should not be deceived by countries like Romania – who practise a relatively liberal foreign policy – into

> believing that they deal similarly with domestic issues. Romania is probably the most repressive of all the Eastern European countries. President Ceausescu rules with a vice-like grip – with one in four of the population estimated to be in the state's employ as spies.

I went on to describe the methods of Ceausescu's 'Department of Cults' and his programme of demolition of churches: 'It is commonplace for churches to be demolished to make way for 'urban renewal' programmes. Despite the difficulty of access by Christians to the Bible, the government pulped 10,000 editions of the Bible in Hungarian into toilet paper.'

I also highlighted the case of Father Georghe Calciu, a Romanian Orthodox priest who had been a brave voice of dissent. He had been kept in prison for most of twenty-one years; was down to six stone in weight; and his hands had been broken to prevent him from making the sign of the cross. On the day before I left Romania, one of Ceausescu's officials (Dr. Nicko Bujor, former chargé d'affaires in London), gave me the news that Father Calciu would be freed.

With the Conservative MP, David Atkinson, I was subsequently pleased to be able to host a reception for Father Calciu and his wife at the House of Commons. I was even more pleased to see television film of him during Christmas 1989, standing in front of the Romanian Embassy in Washington, claiming it for the revolutionary Government which had overthrown the dictator.

Three Romanian Christians have been particularly to the fore in their country's fight for freedom. The Orthodox priest Georghe Calciu; Doina Cornea, the brave Catholic lay woman; and the Lutheran, Pastor Laszlo Tokes – now Bishop Tokes – bravely withstood the excesses of the evil Ceausescu regime.

It was the kidnapping and arrest of Pastor Tokes at Timisoara which triggered off the events leading to Ceausescu's downfull and his reputation remained unsullied during the difficult post-revolutionary days although the continuing Communist regime has threatened and intimidated him.

A profile of Doina Cornea, which appeared in *The Catholic Herald* on Friday, February 16th, 1990, described her as 'Transylvania's Joan of Arc'. Cornea had been forced to resign as a lecturer at Cluj University in 1983, accused of corrupting the young by introducing them to Western philosophy. She had written innumerable appeals to Ceausescu, pleading with him to put a stop to the destruction of the villages,[18] analysing every aspect of national life, and even asking him to resign. Her condemnations of hypocrisy and exhortations to people to live in accordance with the truth brought her prison, two years of house arrests, beatings and death threats. All her efforts had been inspired by her Christian convictions.

Like Bishop Tokes, Cornea was appointed to the ruling council of Romania's National Salvation Front. On January 26th, 1990, the *Independent* reported that 'the conscience of the revolution' had resigned from the Front in disgust: ' I do not want to participate in the unequal fight for power that is developing between the Front and the merging opposition parties,' she was reported as saying.

Sadly for Romania, and to a lesser extent Bulgaria, the new Governments have found it difficult to disown the methods of earlier years. In Romania and in post-Zhivkov Bulgaria new-face Communists have kept power. Romania's National Salvation Front – also known as the Front for Communist Salvation – has in most respects simply continued where Ceausescu left off. Pictures of their supporters brought in to Bucharest to stem protest meetings had an uncannily familiar feel. In a miniature replica of Tiananmen Square, brawling thugs smashed the faces of teenage girls with iron bars and destroyed the cameras of foreign television crews. Old-face Communism is still thriving.

The sight of a Labour Front Bench Spokesman, Roy Hattersley, and Edwina Currie for the Conservatives, who had travelled to Romania to observe their elections, giving the elections a clean bill, was almost unbelievable. Seventeen million votes were recorded as cast: only 16 million votes were registered. Opposition politicians were persistently intimidated and threatened. Minorities' rights were trampled. Iliescu and Roman were elected in elections which were neither free nor fair.

Escape to the Future: The Conclusion

Again and again it has been the powerful cocktail of faith and politics which has been the catalyst for change. As it now emerges from its state of suspended animation, Eastern and Central Europe will need the same level of commitment from its Churches to building the peace as they have provided in paving the way for revolution. The peoples of Eastern Europe will also need practical help on a more substantial scale than that given so far. A European-based initiative, modelled on the post-war reconstruction of Western Europe's economies mainly through American aid provided via General George Marshall's Aid Plan, will need to be a long-term commitment. Unless we are generous in our commitment we will be right to fear for the stability of Eastern Europe as it emerges from the totalitarian ice age. Self-interest alone should be motive enough to help.

But the giving will not all be one-way. In his *We The People*,[19] Timothy Garton Ash makes the point that Eastern Europeans are not like mendicants arriving at our door bearing only chronicles of wasted time. Underneath their threadbare cloaks there are hidden treasures:

> Examples of great moral courage and intellectual integrity; comradeship, deep friendship, family life, time and space for serious conversation, music, literature, not disturbed by the perpetual noise of our media-driven and obsessively telecommunicative world; Christian witness in its original and purest form; more broadly, qualities of relations between men and women of very different backgrounds, and once bitterly opposed faiths – an ethos of solidarity.

In a West starved of such virtues, treasures indeed.

The fear is that as the euphoria fades Eastern Europe will

simply revert to type. Britons used to an 'orderly' political system have been bemused at the proliferation of political parties – fifty-three in Hungary alone – although only twenty-eight contested the March 1990 elections. There are, incidentally, eleven parties represented in our own House of Commons and how many more – from the Greens to the British Communist Party – contest but do not get elected? I guess that an observer noting the presence of a Monster Raving Looney Party candidate in British parliamentary elections might also fear for the worst about our own Mother of Parliaments.

There is also the fear that nationalism and severe racial tension, which can be set alight by hapless economic circumstances, will lead to massive destabilisation. Living in a country which daily dreads the news from Northern Ireland, we must show some modesty in diagnosing remedies for these ailments.

Do not underestimate anti-semitic organisations such as Russia's Pamyat. The word means 'memory' and this fascist group is dedicated to keeping alive old hatreds. Anti-semitism and pogroms – the massacre of Jews – are nothing new in Russia. Organisations like Pamyat are what a nation gets when it is lied to for seventy years. I was in Moscow when, in January 1990, a meeting of Aprel (reformist writers) at the Soviet Writers Union was broken up. It was the most serious anti-semitic demonstration in Moscow since Gorbachev came to power. But in France and Britain, too, we have seen, throughout 1990, appalling acts of desecration of Jewish cemeteries. Anti-semitism and xenophobia are evils which must be countered wherever they surface.

A wall-poster during the Peking massacre read 'Learn From Romania'. Europeans should now try to learn from each other. History is a great teacher.

Nationalism and Marxism have both brought Europe to the edge of destruction. Both are contradictions of what Europe is, both spiritually and politically. Supranational political, economic and legal institutions based on democracy are the only sure defence against recidivist nationalism and one-party ideology. This is not a super-nation Europe; on the contrary, we must strive to restore Europe's individual regions so that each region's identifying character and importance are strengthened through this diversity. A Europe without frontiers and without barriers will be especially reliant on non-state cultural and religious institutions and forces to bring the Europe of the future to wholeness and life.

In the Christian Europe of the Middle Ages European institutions such as the religious orders were effective because they were European and not nationalistic. Anselm came from Aosta in Italy, was an abbot in Brittany and became Archbishop of Canterbury; Albert the Great originated from Germany, taught in Paris and Cologne as well as serving as Bishop of Regensburg; Thomas Aquinas taught in Naples and Paris while Duns Scotus taught in England, France and Germany. Scholarship, the arts, science, the safeguarding of human rights, conscience, the quality of life and common security, are all areas of life where national considerations need not be uppermost in our minds.

The Brezhnev doctrine led to the strangulation of free expression and common movement in Eastern Europe. It followed a well-worn path: the brutal quashing of freedom in Hungary in 1956 and in Czechoslovakia in 1969, and Poland in 1981. That was the kind of Europe Brezhnev had in mind when he coined the phrase, 'a common European home'.

The Europe of the future must be one where diversity is cherished and where mutual co-operation and interdependence are recognised, where the rights of small nations are upheld and respected. It must also be a place where the inner strength and inner freedom of the human personality is elevated.

In meeting these challenges the same forces that forged the European Community and ended the tyranny of the socialist states of Central and Eastern Europe will mould the future. The question then remains for Britain: 'Where does this leave our politics and our nation?'

Chapter 4

The Movement for Christian Democracy

The received political wisdom is that elections are won or lost on the economic issues. The success of a government's policy is measured against inflation, the strength of the pound, the balance of payments and interest rates. You only have to listen to a succession of daily news broadcasts to know this is the case.

Whilst it would be naive to imply that these things are not important – and the temptation is for those who have material advantages to spend their lives urging restraint on others who are trying to get them – political success should not be measured in terms of material advance alone.

We need a different paradigm. Instead of using crude material indicators we should measure the impact of policies on relationships. There is then a better chance of gauging the true health of contemporary society. This philosophy has much in common with the emphasis which European Christian Democrat thinkers are increasingly placing on the worth of the human personality, the integrity of the community and the taking of decisions as close as possible to those directly affected by them, or at the lowest feasible level of administration.

Measuring Success: Social Ecology

In a society where economics are made to serve humanity,

and not the other way around, a different yardstick for measuring success might consist of the impact which legislation and policies have had on marriage breakdown, suicide, loneliness, drug addiction, homelessness, the abortion rate and debt. The success of policies implemented within the framework of the new paradigm would be in Christian Relationist terms: how and whether families stay together, whether marriages break up less often, whether people are less lonely, and whether old people feel more a part of a community: how our relationships are working at any number of levels.

The new paradigm is constructed as a hexangle and includes six building blocks which consist of the individual, the family, locality, the region, professional services and central government. Four of these blocks – the family, locality, the region and professional services – are mediating structures between the individual and central government. Politics tends to offer either a sole commitment to the individual or to the community, at the exclusion of the other. Narrow individualism and our abandonment of mediating structures based on Judaeo-Christian ideals are why our country is in such a mess.

Imagine then the BBC's political staff compiling a summary of the latest British statistics, not simply regurgitated from the Stock Exchange, the money markets and the World Bank, but assessing the state of Britain's social ecology. They might quickly discover that a filled filofax doesn't necessarily mean a fulfilled life; that, for millions, personal worth and self-respect have reached a low ebb; and that there are deep fissures beneath the surface of our seemingly prosperous society.

Here, then, is the bad news.

The State of the Nation

Marriage breakdown is over 600 per cent higher than in 1961 and involves over 150,000 couples each year. One in three marriages now ends in divorce and we are fast approaching the American norm, where fifty per cent of marriages break up. Three million people will experience a broken marriage during this decade. 150,000 children under sixteen are caught up in divorces every year. One in five British children can now except to experience the divorce of their parents before they are sixteen.

In their document, 'Family Change and Future Policy', the Family Policy Studies Centre predicts that by the year 2000 only one out of every two children will grow up in a 'conventional' family. The number of single parents abandoned and left to shoulder all the responsibility for rearing their child has risen inexorably: one in ten children in 1979, one in four now.

It is estimated that nearly 100,000 children go missing in Britain each year, and although more than half return home safely within twenty-four hours, some simply vanish. In lieu of official statistics (because Government's preoccupation with economic statistics means that no national computerised register of missing children is kept) the best estimate of the scale of the problem comes from the Children's Society. They say that 98,000 children went missing in England and Wales last year. Police records show that more than a third of these young people were in Local Authority care. A hard core of those who run away may be lured into prostitution or drug abuse.

No Place Like Home

In 1989 Shelter estimated that around 150,000 sixteen-to-nineteen-year-olds experience homelessness each year. More than 50,000 of these are in London. The London Housing Survey taken in 1986/87 found that 233,000 seventeen to twenty-five-year-olds were 'living with other households' but said that they needed homes of their own. 830,000 young people currently live in bedsit accommodation which is substandard or unfit for habitation. The Catholic Housing Aid Society estimates that the number of reported homeless families has risen by one hundred per cent over the past decade.

Quality as well as quantity is deplorable: 2.4 million public sector homes need repairs of over £1,000. 909,000 are unfit for human habitation. 463,000 homes lack basic amenities. The National Association of Housing Associations report 'Taking Stock' estimates that in thirty per cent of houses that were inhabited, but regarded as unfit for human habitation, the average income was less than £3,000 per annum.

During ten years as trustee of the charity Crisis (formerly Crisis at Christmas) – which cares for the homeless – I have seen the numbers of people sleeping rough on our streets explode. 30,000 homeless families sleep in hostels each night. Cardboard city now sprawls across large swathes of our capital. Many of the homeless are people with mental illness, supposedly caringly discharged from large institutions to be cared for 'in the community'. In practice, they are callously dumped in the community.

The Next Generation

Just twenty per cent of our children leave school with one or more 'A' level. Six million of the nation's workforce (around twenty-five per cent of the total) are illiterate or innumerate.

A report published in September 1990 showed that of 40,000 children in eight English Local Authorities, the number of seven-year-olds who cannot read has risen by eight per cent: fifteen per cent could not read simple words like cat, mat or sat.

Twenty per cent of all secondary schools in England and Wales (twenty-five per cent of inner city schools) have serious truancy problems; just thirty-five per cent of our sixteen-to-eighteen-year-olds are in full-time education and training. This compares with seventy-seven per cent in Belgium and the Netherlands; forty-seven per cent in Italy and West Germany; and seventy-nine per cent in the USA. The British CBI – and even the High Street banks – have expressed serious reservations about the impact of student loans on the number of young people seeking higher education. And yet the CBI say the demand for graduates will increase by about four per cent per year.

Some children have more pressing problems than education. Britain has 360,000 children with some form of disability: only four per cent of their families are estimated to have received any form of respite care within the previous twelve months.

Child Protection Registers were established in 1974. However, the first year in which information was systematically collected was in 1989. 40,700 children were identified in England as being 'at risk' and placed on Registers. Forty-one per cent were listed because of grave concern that they might be at significant risk of abuse; 4.8 per cent had been subjected to severe emotional ill treatment or rejection; 14.4 per cent had been sexually abused; 23.9 per cent had been physically injured; 12 per cent had been persistently neglected; and a further 3.7 per cent fell into a mixture of these categories.

Our Violent Society

Perhaps we should judge the health of our society against the easy availability of pornographic material. As availability increases, so does evidence of the links between pornography and subsequent violence against women and children.

During the last two years the following cases have been before British courts. A woman and her fourteen-year-old daughter were attacked by a hooded man in their home in a Suffolk village. The mother had her clothes cut off with a knife before she was raped and her daughter was indecently assaulted. At the home of the attacker they found a scrapbook containing sordid and sinister stories with a recurring theme of complete domination and defilement of women and young girls.

There was a case in Lincoln involving a man who sexually abused a four-year-old girl. He was put on probation only for a year because the court was told the girl 'was extraordinarily well versed in sexual knowledge'. She had been shown pornographic videos in her home.

In Putney a rapist who committed a series of attacks involving a woman whom he threatened with a knife, went to jail for eighteen years. Police say he copied his ideas from the bondage magazine, *The Trap*, which he had been reading.

Crimes of violence and sexual offences affecting all categories of the population rose consistently across England and Wales up until 1988. Total recorded crime reached a record high in 1989.

Prison, Drugs, Gambling, Drink

Our prison population has reached a record with an average of 55,000 people 'inside' on any one day. Of these, 23.7 per cent are young offenders, compared with 0.5 per cent in Belgium, 15.3 per cent in the Netherlands; 1.4 per cent in Italy and 12.2 per cent in France. Our number of young people in jail is on average twice as high as our European neighbours. Simultaneously, there has been an escalation in the use of hard drugs, heroin, crack and ecstasy.

According to a Mori Poll published in 1990 – 'Young People's Health and Lifestyles', commissioned by the Health Education Authority – seven per cent of nine-to-fifteen-year-olds admit to having tried drugs. One thousand new drug addicts were added to the Home Office Register last year. Department of Health research suggests that the levels of addiction have risen from around 3000 in the so-called drugs-crazed 1960s to about 100,000 today.

The National Housing and Town Planning Council published data in 1987 about young people and gambling. They surveyed 9,655 young people under the age of sixteen. Fifty-seven per cent admitted to visiting amusement arcades or playing on gambling machines. Of those, 21 per cent started playing machines before they were nine years of age, 8 per cent usually spent more than £3 during one visit to an arcade; 7 per cent had stolen to play gambling machines; 6 per cent had gone truant to play gambling machines. Young people often see nothing wrong with gambling and the 'something for nothing' attitude it encourages often becomes as addictive as alcohol and drugs.

Of 33,459 children questioned in another survey, 'substantial numbers of children started drinking alcohol while they were still at primary school'. Fifty per cent of the eleven-year-old boys questioned and thirty-three per cent of the girls said they had at least one alcoholic drink in the previous week.

Our Lack of Ambition

We lack ambition for our children. They are less likely to achieve the academic or skilled excellence of their European counterparts. They are more likely to end up abused, addicted or in prison. They are less likely even to survive in infancy. Child mortality is higher than in eight other European Community countries.

Where it Begins

Back in 1967 many of those who argued for the provision of legal abortion maintained that it would end child abuse: 'Every Child Will Be A Wanted Child', said the slogans. The violent dismemberment of the child is of course the ultimate form of child abuse. Each working day in our British hospitals and clinics (euphemistically called nursing homes) 600 unborn children are aborted; 184,000 last year alone; 3½ million since 1967.

We have one of the highest abortion rates in Europe, with one abortion for every four births. We also have one of the highest upper time limits beyond which social abortions may not occur (twenty-four weeks, compared with twelve weeks in Belgium, twelve weeks in West Germany and twelve weeks in France). The leading immunologist, Dr. Peter McCullogh, says the unborn child can feel pain from seven weeks' gestation.

Far from enhancing the 'rights' of women, the brutal abortion ethic has led to diminished respect for the woman and her child. Nine out of ten women now say they are afraid to go out at night for fear of attack or rape. The abortion ethic, violent attacks and child abuse are all part of life in a society where violence has become part and parcel of everyday living.

This diminished respect for life has led to savage attitudes towards the human being at every point of its development.

In Britain the tiny embryo may now legally be used for experimental purposes. Chemical warfare against the unborn, in the form of the drug RU486,[1] has been authorised by the Health Secretary. And the baby showing any sign of disability may legally be destroyed up until and even during the moment of birth: infanticide.

In 1990 while the Human Fertilisation and Embryology Bill was being enacted Parliament also saw the first attempt by British MPs to make euthanasia legal.

Relationships Shattered

Meanwhile, as the extended family breaks down and community life is destroyed, one survey estimates that over a million old people do not see a friend, relative or a neighbour as often as once a week. Lack of respect for the human person is reflected in the destruction of families, communities and good neighbourliness, and our relationship with the created world. According to a Mori Poll in 1989 'older people still think that maintaining good relationships with neighbours is important but more than 70% of under 35s say it is irrelevant'.

Community based industries have been in decline as family firms are swallowed up by conglomerates. In 1945 forty per cent of industrial output was controlled by the hundred largest companies in Britain. Today it is well over seventy per cent and they largely feel little sense of accountability or responsibility towards the communities where they are based and where their employees live. Companies such as United Biscuits buy out small profitable firms such as Crawfords of Liverpool and then in the name of 'rationalisation', in a year when profits were more than £80 million, the London-based parent company closes the Liverpool factory. There is less and less accountability of business towards the communities in which they are based.

Deeper in Debt

The big financial institutions irresponsibly fuel the worsening cycle of debt. There has been a seventeen per cent annual increase in consumer credit and two million court summonses were issued in England and Wales in 1988. The total repayable arrears amounted to £2.9 billion.

As advertising continues to stimulate demand for more credit, so it leads to more indebtedness. Fifty-two per cent of those who hit trouble don't resolve their problems. The poorer people are, the more debt they face. Last year more than 23,000 gas supplies and 73,000 electricity supplies were disconnected, and 13,780 homes were repossessed. 70,480 households were in mortgage arrears by six months or more.

In answer to questions I tabled last year in Parliament, the Secretary to the Treasury stated that the levels of personal debt in Britain stood at £7,870 per adult. An answer to another of my questions revealed that Britain's debt stood at £378 billion. These figures include mortgage debts on housing. Consumer debt in 1991 stands at £49.6 billion.

Spend now, pay later, is contagious. A Local Authority such as Liverpool City Council now has over £800 million of debt and increases in interest repayments will leave that City's corporate debt at £1 billion by the turn of the century. A one per cent increase in interest rates adds a staggering half a million pounds to the City's corporate debt.

This is a predicament all too familiar to developing nations. The 'two-thirds' world, indebted to the rest of us, is often forced to make larger annual repayments of interest than it receives in help.

Indebtedness is a powerful and destructive pressure on family life. It can force companies into mergers. It leaves communities and even countries in pawn and powerless, hoping that something will turn up.

Ironically, debts are often incurred to fuel development which masquerades under the banner of progress. Redevelopment schemes in British cities and erosion of countryside and ancient woodlands lead to the same destructive results as chain saws in tropical rain forests.

Signs of the Times

These, then, are the signs of the times. Measured in non-materialistic terms we can see a nation in peril. Our country and its people should be part of a seamless garment, woven together with care and love. Instead, the seamless garment has become a tatter of rags.

A Nation in Peril

Our politics and political parties must share much of the blame for the state of Britain's social ecology. Each of our main parties increasingly reflects individualism, materialism and selfishness in its manifestos and policies. Archbishop Temple said in 1942 that the Church may remind politicians of their obligations: 'The Church may remind the engineer that it is his obligation to provide a really safe bridge . . . the Church may tell the politician what ends the social order should promote; but it must leave the politician the devising of the precise means to those ends.'[2]

Today's engineers have forgotten where they left the construction plans. The have become obsessive about claimed rights and silent about duties and responsibilities. Much of this decline can be traced directly to Judaeo-Christian values within our parties and politics being pushed to the sidelines. The new Chief Rabbi, Jonathan Sachs, put it well recently when he said we need a richer language than the language of rights; one which also acknowledges duties and responsibilities.

We have moved a long way from the days when William Wilberforce was able to write about the interplay between faith and politics. He said:

> It is the peculiar glory, and main purpose of Christianity, to bring all the faculties of our nature into their just subordination and dependence; that so the whole man, complete in all his functions, may be restored to the true ends of his being, and be devoted entire and harmonious, to the service and glory of God.[3]

Surveying a country whose churches were experiencing spiritual renewal and the regenerating influence of Wesley and Newman; and whose politics would be confronted by Gladstone's call to action and by Shaftesbury's and his own demands for social reform, Wilberforce also wrote: 'I boldly avow my firm persuasion, that to the decline of religion our national difficulties must be chiefly ascribed and that my only solid hopes for the well-being of my country depends on the persuasion that she still contains many who love and obey the Gospel of Christ.'[4]

As secularism has rebuilt its fortresses in Britain, we have lost our faith in Britain. Cardinal Basil Hume was right when he said in *The Times* in 1990 after Parliament had voted to allow abortion of the handicapped until birth, that Britain may no longer call itself a Christian country. Whether, as this alternative guide to the health of the nation has shown, we can call ourselves a good or happy country is also debatable. As our parties and the people who vote for them have lost their faith, Britain has undergone a corresponding decline. Perhaps that is why it is now right to seek the renewal of our British Christian and democratic traditions, and to reflect on the challenges and dilemmas which European change will pose for Britain.

Questions and Answers

The contours on Europe's political map are now drawn in a form which is markedly different to the Anglo-Saxon model. Those new contours and the changed shape of British society have implications and questions for British politics.

Question: Does our future lie in Europe?

Answer: It is surely inconceivable to think of Britain cutting loose from the European community. Europe will not solve all our problems but there are three reasons why we must be strong in Europe, and none of them is misty or starry eyed: history, necessity and faith. History gave us Fascism followed by Yalta, division, the Cold War and the Iron curtain. I do not want to see history repeat itself. Necessity bids us recognise where our future markets and economic wellbeing lies. Faith tempers self-interest by inspiring us to see inter-dependence and the building of a wider community as fine objectives in their own right.

Question: Should we be enthusiastic Europeans?

Answer: The half-way house of being 'in' but constantly announcing our intention of opting out is untenable. Britain has a rich tradition of diplomacy, of championing the underdog, of maintaining the freedoms associated with a parliamentary democracy. These are gifts which Europe needs and which we should bring with enthusiasm. In 1955 we missed the European bus by not being present at Messina, in Sicily, when the Treaty of Rome was drafted. The will-we won't-we agonising over whether and when to join the Exchange Rate Mechanism of the European Monetary System was only the latest example of missing the bus while Britain agonised over the threadbare trappings of independence and sovereignty.

Question: What difference will Europe make to our politics in Britain?

Answer: The European Parliament will assume increasing importance, even more so as Eastern European nations accede to the Community. Our parties will either have to adapt themselves to functioning in the atmosphere of a political system which requires co-operation and partnership or they can remain isolated combatants, sidelined and impotent. In the first instance they must create a climate of understanding between themselves and their European counterparts. In the new Europe the major political blocs will be the Social Democrats and the Christian Democrats. The smaller Liberal, Socialist, Conservative and Green groups will need to define those areas of their programmes which they hold in common with the two larger blocks and learn to work with them if they wish to see their ideas implemented (as already happens at domestic parliamentary level in all European democracies other than our own).

Question: How Christian are Europe's Christian Democrats?

Answer: They are 'earthen vessels' with the same capacity to get it wrong as the rest of us. They are not exactly the incarnation of the Communion of Saints. But their programme is clearly based on Christian principles – which is more than can be said for any British party – and their achievements since the Second World War (e.g. their primary role in the establishment of the European Community) have been considerable. Their emphasis on families as the basic communities, on the sanctity of human life, on social justice, subsidiarity, 'personalism' and 'communitarianism' will all find an audience amongst British Christians, and many beyond the Christian community. In the 1989 European Elections in the eleven other member States, where they contested elections, one in five Europeans voted for them. The fault line in British politics will increasingly be drawn between belief and unbelief, utilitarianism and faith, rather than between left and right. British Muslims are increasingly looking for political expression of their beliefs for much the same reasons.

Question: Is there a British sister organisation?
Answer: There is now.

The Epiphany Group

In January 1989 I brought together a small group of people who had two things in common: their faith and an interest in politics. We met at Prinknash Abbey in Gloucestershire and spent three days discussing the condition of our country and its politics. It was not that we believed ourselves to be an especially wise group of men and women, although we did have a variety of gifts, but as the meeting was held over the feast of the Epiphany we accepted the suggestion of Father Paul Thompson, Archbishop Worlock's Press and Communications Officer, to call ourselves the Epiphany Group.

The Group consisted of about twenty people and was drawn from across the denominational and political divide. Some who were present had been actively involved in the promotion of my Private Member's Bill to reduce the time limit beyond which abortions might occur. The speakers who led each session ranged from Professor Jack Scarisbrick, the national Chairman of Life, who talked to us about the Christian tradition of involvement in politics, to Denis Wrigley, a Methodist Liberal who helped found Maranatha, the body which works for reconciliation and healing in Northern Ireland. Participants ranged from Lord Hylton, the crossbencher peer, to Dr Michael Schluter of the Jubilee Centre; from Tim Cooper of the Green Party to Peter Hebblethwaite, Catholic theologian and Social Democrat. There was an especially fiery session where Michael Hastings, of the Evangelical Alliance – who has made some contributions to the Downing Street Policy Unit of Professor Brian Griffiths – and Tom Cullinan, OSB, author of *The Passion of Political Love*[5] slugged out different Christian appreciations of liberty/the individual versus equality/the community. Although there were inevitably areas of disagreement – about priorities, emphasis and approach – we nevertheless believed the meeting had been sufficiently useful to warrant meeting again the following year; we used the intervening twelve months to gather our thoughts. At the end of the weekend we agreed that in addition to our common respect for life, there were four other areas which seemed to unite us: social justice; reconciliation; active compassion; and good stewardship.

During the year which followed the Epiphany Group held a number of dinners at the House of Commons, under the chairmanship of David Hall. We invited parliamentarians and others to lead and participate in discussions on various questions, including the position of Hong Kong, embryo experimentation, and how interventionist Government should be. Among the MPs who attended were Ken Hargreaves, Paul Boateng, Alan Beith and Jim Wallace.

How To Be Communitaires

In one of the most important papers prepared for us Peter Hebblethwaite pin-pointed the clash between Mrs Thatcher and Jacques Delors, the President of the European Commission, as being a mainly theological one: 'Cardinal Edward Manning once remarked that at bottom all questions are theological. This was also the view of Mrs Margaret Thatcher.'[6] Delors was a member of Cardinal Cardjin's Young Christian Workers (see Chapter 2) and has never concealed either his

Christian beliefs or his commitment to Social Democracy. Interestingly, the thing which he says most motivates him is his belief in the community: 'For someone like me, still inspired by the communitarian personalism of Emmanuel Mounier [founder of the monthly, *Esprit*], the community dimension is what I find most lacking in political life.' He says he entered politics to help achieve the right balance between the individual and society. Delors says Christian faith 'impels, inspires and motivates, but it does not confer any kind of superiority on Christians'.

Hebblethwaite accused anti-European Conservatives of being stuck in the rut of individualism 'and ignoring the Evangelical tradition of social reform found in Lords Wilberforce and Shaftesbury'. He says they have 'correctly picked out Delors as [their] chief enemy in Europe and the principal obstacle to [their] plan to roll back international "socialism".' The anti-European wing of the Conservative Party confuses Marxism with the Church's social teachings and because it rejects the theology behind these teachings it thinks Christian Democrats such as Helmut Kohl have 'gone soft' when they promote the Social Charter.

Hebblethwaite's paper contends that far from being in opposition, society and communities are made up of human beings and they need one another. Solidarity was not invented in Poland in 1980; it has deep roots in Christian tradition and it comes from shared experience.

These themes are returned to in other Movement for Christian Democracy publications. In the Movement's monthly bulletin, *Christian Democracy*,[7] the editor, Bill Gribbin, gives an account of Jacques Delors' 'Pope Paul VI Memorial Lecture' given at the Bloomsbury Theatre, London, to the Catholic Fund for Overseas Development (CAFOD). In a paper entitled 'United Europe-Divided World', Delors calls for 'a new Europe in solidarity and partnership with the Third World'. In the next edition of *Christian Democracy*[8] Dr Dick Rodgers argues:

> Without a common cause the nations of Europe risk degenerating into a greedy squabble for the largest slice

> of the economic cake. The needy would go to the wall and the earth's resources would soon be exhausted. How much better to lay aside our claims and work together as colleagues on a job which is crying out to be done!

And, in the same publication, David Campanale, in an article entitled 'A Richer Weave for Nationhood', calls for a new vision of Europe:

> Christian Democrats must set before themselves a vision of what kind of Europe we want. With socialism now down and out for the count as an authoritative world-view, and romantic nationalism threatening to bring forward the threat of hard, right-wing governments, we must start with fundamentals . . . Christian communities know that what binds people together can ultimately only be love, mutual tolerance and respect and appreciation for human differences. Christian Democrats must not be ashamed to argue these values are best inculcated in a society where the Gospel is widely proclaimed, and people are compelled by the force of conviction and the work of the Holy Spirit . . . Socialism and nationalism are false all-embracing world-views, both promising to create a spiritual brotherhood for a better world. The failure of one may be giving rise to another. At this moment, Christians in politics must not stand back, for it also offers to us opportunity to say again:
> the Kingdom of God is at hand.

These articles and publications are glimpses of the exploration of ideas and thinking which has been underway.

We Meet Again: Persons or Individuals?

At the 1990 meeting of the Epiphany Group the number of participants had more than doubled. Martyn Eden, Dean of the London Institute of Contemporary Christianity, and a founder member of the SDP, and Tom Cullinan, OSB, opened the meeting with a seminar on scripture and politics.

Cullinan said that people either tried to discredit scripture or chose the parts which suited them. He said we are 'persons' rather than 'individuals' – each made in the image of God. Right at the heart of the human question is the dilemma of whether we are individuals in competition or persons in community and co-operation. Eden contrasted the 'high' standards which the Church is expected to live by with the 'low' standard expected of society as a whole. He said that scripture should not be used in a proof-texting mechanical way but in arguing for a living inter-action with Scripture. This third way, he said, offered an escape route from the arid conflict of Marxism and capitalism, neither of which grappled with human sinfulness.

Ian Linden of the Catholic Institute For International Relations then led a discussion on 'Justice and Peace – Social Responsibility'. Based on his ten years' experience in Africa, he argued that 'holiness and sin are the two compass points' for how we perceive and respond to what he described as 'the two thirds world'. In that world he said Christians were moving away from 'fortress church' and had recaptured something which we had lost by embarking on their pilgrimage. He trenchantly attacked the New Right for their 'fundamental contempt for community'. I strongly agree with this view. The New Right see any clinging to community as atavistic, looking back to a lost past. They have failed to understand that when you destroy community or family – the basic community – you destroy faith. Linden also said that a reliance on the market economy alone was un-Christian, because of the disunity it creates. He contrasted this disunity with the unity of the Trinity, 'which suggests love and equality'. As Christians we cannot remain morally neutral when we come into contact with either the liberal/capitalist structure or Marxist-Leninism.

In his search for a third way, the Christian economist and sociologist, Dr Alan Storkey, presented a paper entitled 'A Christian Programme for a Political Party' and argued strongly for the creation of a political party which was unashamedly Christian in outlook and approach. He warned that 'Christians can mess up politics as well as the next'; that denominational battles had queered the Churches' view of politics; that Christianity can be used by parties; and that since the seventeenth century Christians have retreated into issue related politics, accepting a sacred-secular split and a subjectivism where they do not allow themselves to think and speak as Christians. He considered the nature of political parties and contended that all parties are groups which share convictions, with free membership and no coercion to join. A Christian-based party would be a community of political faithful with shared principles, priorities, practice and evaluation. All parties which exist in the UK at present are analogous: 'predominantly they are humanist.' He said it was not problematic for Christians to be explicit about their faith, so long as they admitted their fallibility, and that their political obedience is to Christ, their leader.

The Jubilee Centre's ideas on Christian relationism were contained in Dr Michael Schluter's address, 'A Political Agenda based on Judaeo-Christian Values'. Dr Schluter said that Evangelical and Catholic social teaching had been converging but this new concern for politics 'has yet to find expression in an agreed consensus among the churches on the principles which should inform the church's approach to the political order'. He said his talk would focus 'specifically on the case for a political party based on Christian principles, and on the platform which such a party might adopt'. In words which were echoed by a number of speakers he recognised that 'to argue for such a party is not to belittle the role of Christians in other political parties, or to suggest that their stance is un-Christian. Almost any political party in any political era will have positive and negative characteristics from a Christian perspective.' However, he said, 'in an age increasingly overwhelmed with material concerns, there is, we believe, a strong case for examining the ideals of a Christian framework for society, and the implications of such ideals for economic and social policy'. Schluter contended that

> A Christian relationist vision for Britain through a party based on Christian ideals relies heavily on policies to

> construct new and strong extended family and community networks, encouraging a new sense of regional identity and building an independent professional class which stands apart from both the regional and central government systems. The complex set of relationships set up through this network of mediating structures would encourage people to see themselves constantly as part of different but overlapping groupings and would help to prevent the polarisation between individuals acting on their own on the one hand and central government on the other.

Such a vision, he said, 'does lead us to hope for a happier tomorrow, as happiness depends on relationships rather than economic growth'.

Salt and Light

The direction of the Epiphany discussion then switched to Europe and lessons which we might learn from experiences in the East. Michael Bourdeaux, Director of Keston College, and Cllr. David Campanale, who had just returned from Romania, outlined their views about how events were likely to unfold. Along with Bill Hampson I reported on our own recent experiences in the Ukraine (see Chapter 3). Mike and Katey Morris concluded the evening with a talk on 'Staying Spiritually Fresh Under Pressure'.

During the concluding session an attempt was made to apply what Martyn Eden had described as an understanding of scripture to politics. Eden saw a logical inevitability in what we were doing. His argument was that for much of the twentieth century, Evangelical Christians in Britain had tended to steer clear of politics:

> It involved too many compromises and they preferred to keep their hands clean. In any case, they believed that their principal calling was to proclaim the Gospel and win souls for Christ. Social and political involvement was

> a distraction from this which seemed so easily to lead believers astray down a 'social gospel' track.

Eden said that the last twenty-five years had seen a rediscovery of the Evangelical tradition, prevalent in the eighteenth and nineteenth centuries, of both proclaiming and living the Gospel, which had inspired the vigorous political campaigning of Wilberforce, Shaftesbury and the Clapham Sect. Present-day attitudes on a host of issues proved that the Evangelical Harry Blamires' warning in 1963, that there was no longer a Christian mind, had come to pass. He said that a turning point came in 1988 at the Evangelical Salt and Light Consultation, which brought together over 300 Evangelical leaders. Increasingly Christians from the Evangelical tradition saw the urgent need for engagement. He said that

> it would be a worthy objective of this group to support today's politicians who aim to operate under the Lordship of Christ, and to encourage a new generation of politicians to follow their example. For without such people Scripture and politics will remain, for the most part, in the separate compartments which secularisation has allocated them.

The Epiphany Group reaffirmed its five principles of social justice, respect for life, reconciliation, active compassion and good stewardship as a basis for our continued work (although the Steering Committee later accepted Dr Schluter's proposal that these should be expanded to six to include the concept of subsidiarity – the idea that decisions should be taken at the lowest possible level – under the title 'empowerment'). It was then decided that the Group might continue to function as an arena for exploring ideas and for bringing people together but a wider more broadly-based movement was needed. Five options were considered for its future role: a pressure group; think-tank; political task force; political party; political movement. It was agreed that the next step should be the fifth of these objectives, the establishment of a movement. Under the chairmanship of Dr Robert Song, of Cranmer College, Durham, three different tasks were isolated.

First, the movement would call the Christian public to include political action within its discipleship. We suggested this might be achieved through (a) concentrating in the first instance on three or four political issues on which there is already some broad consensus within the Christian constituency and which relate to a common theme or vision: such a method we think best calculated to engage people's attention; and (b) contacting different organisations presently involved in the area but not communicating with each other adequately.

Second, we would develop political principles which could serve as a unifying vision for the movement's beliefs and activities.

Third, the movement would take on specific political objectives by pursuing the role of political task force.

Dr Song's Steering Committee was asked to determine a name and to draft a common declaration to be named the Westminster Declaration. Bill Hampson was asked to chair the Organisation Committee and to build up regional groups, to organise the November Rally, and to co-ordinate membership. A third Committee was subsequently established under the chairmanship of Ken Hargreaves, MP, with the remit of seeking the endorsement of the Westminster Declaration by election candidates and by publicising their response.

The Steering Committee appointed at Prinknash consisted of Helen Alford (Cambridge University and the Society for the Protection of the Unborn Child), David Blackmore (local councillor), Francis Davis (parish community worker, Southampton), Martyn Eden (Evangelical Alliance), Christopher Graffius (Interim Secretary-General), Anna Grear (CARE Organiser for SW England), Bill Gribbin (writer, teacher and editor, *Christian Democracy*), Bill Hampson (Jubilee Campaign for prisoners of faith), Ken Hargreaves (Conservative MP for Hyndburn), Michael Hastings (Evangelical Alliance), Jane Mellor (CARE Research Officer), Mike Morris (Director, Foreign Affairs, Evangelical Alliance), Dr Robert Song

(Chairman Drafting Committee, Tutor in Ethics, Durham), Dr Michael Schluter (Director, Jubilee Centre, who acts as consultant to the movement), Dr Alan Storkey (Lecturer, Oakhill College), Chris Townsend (who works with a London law firm) and myself.

The Movement for Christian Democracy

Various names were suggested for the title of the Movement. To emphasise our Christian roots and affinities with the emerging groups of Eastern Europe we chose a title which was self-explanatory and placed us in the European current. Several drafts of the Westminster Declaration were produced and considered by Dr Song's committee. The third draft of the text was then distributed to every person who applied for membership and they were invited to suggest amendments and modifications. Over an eight-month gestation period the document was honed and improved and was ultimately approved by over 1500 delegates at the first major rally of the Movement, held at the Methodist Central Hall, Westminster, on Saturday November 17th, 1990. This was addressed by Members of the European Parliament – Thomas Jansen, the Secretary General of the European People's Party – and key members of the Movement. The day opened in prayer, led by the Reverend Lyndon Bowring of CARE. Since the launch membership applications have continued to arrive at my office, and at Ken Hargreaves' office, on an average of a dozen a day. Several thousand people have now joined.

Thirteen national and regional groups have been established in Scotland, Wales and Northern Ireland, and in the English regions. Appropriately, the first of these inaugural meetings was held in Belfast in September 1990, at the Belfast home of John and Mary Larkin, and Christians interested in politics, from both sides of the divide, have joined. Professor Larkin addressed the Westminster rally on the subject of reconciliation.

Chris Graffius, the Movement's Interim Secretary General, was able to report to the autumn meeting of the Steering

Committee that membership had just passed the 1000 mark and that more than 600 young people had attended the first Youth Day held in July 1990.

The Youth Day brought together students from University Christian Unions and Catholic Chaplaincies and was organised by former Durham student, Andy Dunnett, who had played a key role setting up the 1990 Epiphany meeting. The day included visits to the Commons and a series of seminars and sessions held at Westminster Chapel. These included sessions on 'Women and Public Life' (led by Jane Mellor, Elaine Storkey and Josephine Robinson), 'Social Justice and Economic Success' (led by Michael Hastings, Professor Nicholas Lash, and Dr Schluter) and 'Faith and Politics, Acquiescence or Activism' (led by Clive Calver, Denis Wrigley and Janice Price). The Reverend R.T. Kendall, who had kindly made available the Chapel and its facilities, talked about 'Scripture and Politics'.

In addition to these activities the Movement has published a bulletin, *Christian Democracy*, and has been actively developing international contacts with Christian Democrat International and the European People's Party. Representatives attended the forum on the future of Christian Democracy organised by Dutch Christian Democrats, held in Holland in October 1990; a seminar held in Paris; and the annual international conference of Christian Democrats held in Dublin in November 1990. With the French Christian Democrat parliamentarian, Monsieur Jean-Marie Daillet, Senator Huberta Hanquet, Christian Democrat Chairman of the Foreign Affairs Select Committee of the Belgian Parliament, and Alexandr Ogorodnikov, Chairman of the Christian Democratic Union of the Soviet Union, we launched Democrats Sans Frontières at a meeting in Moscow. M. Daillet, the Vice-Chairman of Christian Democrat International also met Chris Graffius and Bill Gribbin during a London visit. Christian Democrat MEPs, John Cushnahan and Pat Cooney arranged meetings with People's Party members in Strasbourg and Chris Graffius and myself travelled to Brussels to meet Thomas Jansen, and the International Secretary, M. Anton Louis.

By 1991 the Epiphany Group was ready to spend a full weekend considering the history and shape of Christian Democracy – and in reviewing the scale of our task.

In a memorable phrase, Professor Michael Fogarty said that 'movements are founded over the bones of dead pioneers'. In tracing a history of Christian Democracy he challenged us 'to think the unthinkable' and to recognise that the gestation period for creating political change might well be considerable.

In his paper, Professor Fogarty told the Epiphany Group that Christian Democrats had come to stand for personalism; the community; the liberal freedoms of democracy, pluralism and civil liberties; federalism; enabling authority; solidarity around the common good; and change combined with security and continuity. Christian Democrats had also upheld three kinds of justice: 'commutative justice' (fair exchange in a properly regulated market); 'distributive justice' (the supplementing of market forces); and 'social justice' (a framework of social management).

Michael Fogarty's advice in 1991 to the Movement for Christian Democracy was fourfold. Do not be afraid to start small. Build up credible research and ideas, developing the existing vision through practical action. Hit the customers every way, not only through politics but through all forms of social action. Recognise that the core audience for the Movement are believing Christians, so do not neglect the link with the Churches.

Tom Cullinan told the meeting that it was a combination of the political and prophetic which was needed. And the Catholic writer, Jonathan Boswell, who had recently published *Community and The Economy: The Theory of Public Co-operation* provided the Movement with a practical and prophetic approach to handling economics by outlining how the present Market Economy could be replaced by a Community Economy.

The 1991 Prinknash Meeting went on to take some practical decisions about establishing a series of policy panels to monitor Government departments and to develop ideas. Francis Davis and Helen Alford were given the go-ahead to form the Young Christian Democrats, and the finishing touches were put to the preparations for the next four regional launches subsequently held in Manchester, Bristol, Winchester and London, and meetings scheduled for Liverpool, Nottingham, Milton Keynes and Durham.

Peter Hebblethwaite reminded the Group of the Russian Orthodox Epiphany legend of the fourth wise man. He was the one who was waylaid as he travelled to Bethlehem. He was taken prisoner and became a slave, never arriving in time for the nativity. He had to wait through the wilderness years but finally arrived in Jerusalem just over thirty years later and, as the legend has it, was there to witness the Crucifixion and the Resurrection.

The Westminster Declaration

The Westminster Declaration, which was endorsed at the November rally, unashamedly sees the dependence of humanity on its Creator and the interdependence of people and ideas. It has become the foundation document of the Movement.

THE MOVEMENT FOR CHRISTIAN DEMOCRACY THE WESTMINSTER DECLARATION

Our Common Christian Faith

We believe that God is creator of all things and the source of all good. God has made us to worship him, and to live in love, justice and peace with one another and creation. However our lives are marked by sin, which distorts our relationship with God, with each other, and with the natural world. Yet God does not abandon us in our failure, but in his love has met us in Jesus Christ. Through his life, death and resurrection, as Scripture reveals, Jesus Christ has opened the way to reconciliation with God, triumphed over the power of death, and inaugurated a new order of justice and truth. We believe that the Holy Spirit is present and seeks to guide us, to lead us to right living, and to bear witness to the truth.

A Christian Contribution to Politics

We believe that Jesus Christ calls us to follow him in every area of our lives, including the realm of politics. We recognise that the kingdom of God extends beyond this world-order and cannot be simply identified with any political cause; but we also affirm that it demands the pursuit of just government and the promotion of a well-ordered society.

We reject the idea that religion is merely the individual's private affair. Rather we regard religion as fundamental to society and of irreplaceable import and influence in the process of shaping the character of a nation. Hence we bear a responsibility both to challenge and to affirm the social and political order in accordance with our understanding of orthodox Christian principles.

Understanding our Times

We believe that under God the well-being of society should be judged more by the quality of human relationships than by material attainments, more by the richness of human lives than by an abundance of possessions, and more by the realisation of truly human values than by the accomplishments of technology.

We acknowledge and give thanks to God for the many privileges that we enjoy today; the relative stability of our political institutions; the recognition of many civil rights and liberties; comparative economic prosperity; the many advances in industry, science and technology; and the continuing availability of social, educational and health services.

However, we also recognise that our nation has failed in many ways to live as God requires. Our society is marred by poverty, homelessness, family breakdown, neglect of the elderly, child abuse, destruction of the unborn, exploitation of women, racism, violence, crime, drug and alcohol abuse, excessive personal debt, complacency about global suffering and injustice between nations, and careless ravaging of the natural world. Ours is a nation where too often selfishness is rewarded and responsibilities are evaded, and where the fear, loneliness and unhappiness of some are met by the ignorance and indifference of others.

We wholeheartedly affirm the value of industry and commerce and the importance of a productive economy for a nation's wellbeing. Nevertheless we find it inadequate to measure the health of society simply in terms of the growth of the gross national product, or to attribute its greatest problems merely to such causes as poor economic performances or problems with the welfare state, long-term industrial decline or 'the British disease'. The fact that many of our technical and economic solutions serve only to exacerbate the problems confirms that deeper diagnosis is necessary.

Such an analysis would uncover the mistaken beliefs to which we have succumbed and the false idols before which we have bowed. We have placed our faith in the possibilities of self-sufficient science and technology. We have invested our hopes in the quest for endless economic growth. And, to give meaning to our lives, we have turned to the promise of individual freedom, happiness and prosperity, or have found our identity in collective groups such as state, nation or class. Beneath it all, we have deceived ourselves into thinking that we can solve our problems without reference to God and his good purposes for us. It is time for us to break with these false notions and to recognise our need for an individual and corporate change of heart and mind.

The Meaning of Christian Democracy

The Christian Democratic tradition of thought, in our understanding of it, takes its bearing from Christian convictions about the person, society, and political authority. According to these the fundamental worth of each human being is ultimately rooted in God. True human fulfilment is understood as responsible freedom in relation with others, and is found in the development of persons in society.

A society should embody an ethos which is neither selfishly individualistic in sanctioning the pursuit of private satisfactions to the detriment of duties towards others, nor tyrannous in supporting the demands of the state or other collective bodies at the expense of the rightful claims of the individual. Instead it should engender a spirit which respects the freedom and integrity of social and cultural institutions such as the religious organisation, the family, the school, the trade union and the business enterprise, and which thereby serves to equip citizens to pursue the common good together.

The fundamental role of political authority is to ensure justice in the public realm and to create conditions conducive to the common good. The exercise of power by the state must always be equitable and limited, and should be directed to promoting just relations between individuals, associations, communities and other groups, whilst also respecting their proper independence. Although bearers of political authority have the responsibility of encouraging the good and rectifying injustice, it is beyond the competence of government to remedy every social ill, and indeed it is the duty of government not to undertake tasks that lesser organisations or individuals could properly fulfil.

Democratic participation enlarges the horizons of people, empowers them as citizens and limits the power of governments. The expression of opinion through representative elections, political parties, public debate and loyal opposition, together with respect for political office and open and accountable government, are intrinsic to responsible democracy. No party or grouping may claim special legal privileges: while Christian Democratic thinking rejects secularism as a public ideology, it does not seek any governing rule for the institutional church. It also requires the state to acknowledge the rights of religious and cultural minorities and to treat them equitably in public policy.

With regard to the economy, democratic responsibility implies that the economy should not be controlled either by the state, or by business and finance, but should build up the contribution and mutual responsibilities of everyone. Economic activity should serve people rather than dominate them. The full personal, social and ecological implications of national and international market activity needs to be recognised, rather than merely private or accounting calculations, and inequitable and unfair patterns of distribution need redressing. Our emphasis is therefore on the state's concern with economic justice and right structures rather than economic performance alone.

Reworking the Foundations

We do not imagine that in Christian Democracy we possess simple solutions to the problems of our country. Nevertheless we firmly believe that Christianity can make an important contribution to the wellbeing of society, and that participation in the Movement for Christian Democracy is an appropriate way of affirming this.

For this reason we commit ourselves to the following six guiding principles which highlight some basic themes of Christian Democracy:

SOCIAL JUSTICE

Justice is ultimately founded in the character of God and its content is given by divine law. Under this law all men and women are due equal respect and have responsibilities to one another and the wider society. Social justice demands an equal regard for all and consequently a special concern for the needs of the poor, the suffering and the powerless. It requires that exploitation and deprivation be fought, and that appropriate resources and opportunities be available, so that the basic requirements of all are met and each is enabled to take part in the life of society.

RESPECT FOR LIFE

Human beings are created in the image of God. The right to life is the most basic of all human rights, and the intrinsic value of human life at every stage from conception to natural death should be acknowledged and respected. We therefore especially affirm the fundamental dignity of those who are unborn, infirm, mentally or physically disabled, elderly, or unable to speak for themselves. Such respect for human persons also requires a commitment to maintaining a decent quality of life for all, and to meeting the needs of those who for whatever reason do not have the essentials of life. Moreover it implies a disavowal of all armaments whose use is incompatible with the pursuit of a just peace.

RECONCILIATION

The kingdom of God is heralded by a community in which we all are to be reconciled in Jesus Christ. This should be reflected beyond the church in the breaking down of oppression and divisive barriers related to differences of religion, gender, race, class, nation, ideology and political power. These problems have their roots in human sin, expressed through flawed social structures and personal pride and selfishness, which we Christians too often demonstrate as well.

It is a task not only for individuals and social and economic groups but also for those engaged in politics, at local, national and international levels, to work towards reconciliation and healing. We recognise that such goals may never be wholly achieved in this world. Nevertheless humility, repentance, patience and forgiveness are political as well as personal values, and are essential in the process of replacing conflict by common understanding.

ACTIVE COMPASSION

The God of justice is the God of love, and human beings are called to active loving service of others. Instead of an indifference to the distress of others based on passivity, self-concern or ignorance, such compassionate love inspires an attitude not only of detached justice but also of open-hearted generosity.

We all bear the responsibility, individually and corporately, for such service to one another. The government should motivate individuals, families, charities and other associations to active fundamental needs of the poor before satisfying the preference of the rich.

WISE STEWARDSHIP

Human beings are called to be stewards of the creation, and all economic activity involves our responsibility before God for the world entrusted to us. Economic resources are given by God to serve people's needs, to help in developing their capacities, particularly for justice, co-operation, and mutual care, and to be used creatively and with responsible concern for others (including future generations) and for the environment.

Markets are not a law to themselves, but are shaped by people's decisions. They should therefore be instructed in such a way that economic transactions are fair and are undertaken in good faith and with the needs of the community in mind. Concentrations of wealth and power erode responsibility and may cause market distortion. We seek an economy where banks, businesses, trade unions, professional groups and government departments work together with greater mutual understanding and public accountability.

The primary task of government in relation to the economy is to oversee the establishment of just structures in all areas of economic activity; such justice includes distributing wealth and property so as to equip all to participate fully in the economy and using resources in a manner that respects the intrinsic dignity of the natural world.

EMPOWERMENT

All authority is from God and must be exercised responsibly in accordance with the divine ordinances for society. It is given to enable service of the common good, and self-seeking use of it distorts its intended purpose. Different kinds of authority are found in different areas of society, such as the family, the neighbourhood, education, work, business, the media, voluntary organisations, local and central government, and beyond, but in each case authority should have its own proper limits and be directed towards serving and benefiting those under it.

The accumulation of power may often be necessary for the satisfactory performance of certain tasks, but it may also foster patterns of control and domination. Consequently it is wrong to assign to larger organisations what can be adequately done by smaller and more local associations. In particular, those in whom much power is concentrated, such as individual owners of wealth, professional interest groups, trade unions, multinational corporations, national governments, and leaders of political blocs, while they often exercise power with great responsibility, may yet need to be called to account in view of their potential for working against the common good.

Some Goals for the Movement for Christian Democracy

We have outlined the central ideas of Christian Democracy and these six principles in the belief that they offer a better vision for Britain than those prevalent at this time. The task of bringing them to bear on the problems of a complex society will require both vision and patient attention to detail, careful research and wide-ranging discussion. However, at the outset, we put forward the following as a selection of goals for the Movement for Christian Democracy, acknowledging that they need further refinement:

Relationships: with God and with one another

—to encourage an awareness of our accountability to God in all aspects of public and private life, and the evaluation of decisions in terms of how they affect our individual and collective relationships with God;

—to discover ways of enjoying and celebrating our community and membership of one another, locally, at work, in play, in civic and national arenas, and beyond;

The person

—to awaken in persons of all backgrounds and beliefs a greater sense of responsibility for their families and neighbours;

—to promote personal financial security through practical measures which will extend and strengthen the emergence of a culture of stewardship;

The family

—to encourage an appreciation of the central importance of the family, particularly the extended family, for the general welfare;

—to support the concept and practice of family property ownership so as to enable families to develop roots and a greater sense of permanence and security in their communities;

The education system

—to press for improvements in the quality, resourcing and morale of the state system of education;

—to urge the appropriate authorities to make resources available, so that parents may effectively exercise their right to have children educated in conformity with their own religious and philosophical convictions;

The workplace

—to seek measures (including the appropriate provision of training) which would aid genuine participation of employees in decisions made by their companies, in addition to participation in ownership;

—to urge the decentralising of the ownership and management of large-scale corporate, economic and financial enterprises, in order that people may have more direct control over the economic decisions which affect their lives;

Community and region

—to encourage and seek adequate resources for methods of welfare provision which involve family and neighbourhood participation and offer personal care, attention and love as well as financial provision;

—to look for the focusing of state assistance on neglected persons who are in danger of being pushed to the margins of society, such as those who are homeless or mentally or physically disabled, and to promote practical compassion for those who have become unable to help themselves;

National life

—to promote a new perspective on public policy issues so that policy proposals are assessed, not primarily in terms of their economic or political ramifications, but in terms of their impact on the quality and integrity of human relationships in our society, particularly in our homes and local communities;

—to recommend the decentralising of political and administrative decisions, so that they are transferred from central government to local authorities, and from local authorities to neighbourhood councils;

The wider world and the natural world

—to play a full role in the development of Britain as part of Europe in the pursuit of co-operation for the continent;

—to address the issues behind the continuing impoverishment of poorer nations through debt and present international trading practices, and to push for increases in the financial and other support provided by this nation to low-income nations;

—to press for the responsible harnessing of natural resources and the stewardship of them for the use of future generations; also to work for the preservation of the environment, and where it has been ravaged in the past, to promote initiatives to restore it to vitality.

Conclusion

In founding the Movement for Christian Democracy we hope to further Christian understanding of social and political matters, to initiate appropriate forms of action, to stimulate informed discussion, and to influence policy-making. We endeavour above all to be authentically Christian in our approach rather than merely different from other political programmes. As Christians we acknowledge that we are fallible in our grasp of the truth. We also recognise that some Christians will seek other ways of political discipleship. However, we call on all those who share our vision of society to join forces with us across the political and denominational divide, and to promote and act upon the principles and goals outlined in this Declaration.

Endorsed by the Rally of the Movement
Westminster Central Hall
November 17th, 1990

Movement Or Party?

Since the publication of the Declaration many people have written to me expressing enthusiasm for its straight-forwardness and lack of ambiguity. Many have also expressed the hope that it will form the basis of a manifesto for a new political party. On that question the jury must remain out. The immediate task is to return the existing parties to their roots. We are a movement, seeking to influence all parties.

There is no doubt that during the 1970s the New Right and the Socialist Left set the agendas for their parties, but as the 1980s proceeded the Social Democrats and the Greens played an increasingly important part in influencing everyone.

Perhaps, if the Movement for Christian Democracy can become as effective as the Social Democrats and Greens, it will be able to influence either one or all of the British parties. I must admit that after twenty-two years as a member of a party, and after eighteen years as an elected representative – twelve of them in Parliament – I am not hopeful.

I can therefore understand why members of the Movement wished to leave all its options open. If it fails in its primary objective those who wished to do so could proceed with the development of a party and an agenda unashamedly based on Judaeo-Christian values . . . As in the rest of Europe, its appeal would go way beyond the church-going or even a nominally believing community.

The Movement was right not to close off this option for another very good practical political reason. The political parties are more likely to take notice if they think the Movement might sit up and bite. A cosy circle organising genteel tea parties or London dinners will never be listened to.

After the events of 1990 in Eastern Europe secular commentators would be unwise to write off the possibility of European Christian Democrats causing a minor earthquake. Stalin scornfully mocked the churches, asking how many divisions they had. By 1990 we knew the answer. Before the jury feels any need to deliver a verdict, much more intellectual energy must be committed and maps acquired. Declarations are one thing. But how might the six principles be worked out in practice?

Chapter 5

Social Justice

The Charter for Human Responsibility

I was very pleased that the Drafting Committee of the Movement for Christian Democracy listed each of the six foundation principles – social justice, respect for life, reconciliation, active compassion, empowerment and good stewardship – under the working title 'A Charter for Human Responsibility'.

First, it was a recognition that these concerns were not mutually exclusive. I confess to bewilderment when people who say they are for peace have no respect for life; when people tell me they care for the unborn but are indifferent to the vulnerable young woman faced with a whole host of practical challenges; when concern for every other species excludes concern for our own; when human rights are worth defending in Central America but not Eastern Europe, or vice versa; when partnership and co-operation are remedies for others but good old confrontation will do for you; when poverty and social justice are issues solely for Socialists and wealth creation and prosperity matters solely for Conservatives; when the easy distribution of 'hard porn' or the broadcasting of programmes revelling in violence are for the moralists but the same morality excludes a concern for the hungry, powerless and degraded of the under-developed world. All of these things hang together and Christians should be uninhibited in saying so.

Second, the idea of a Charter for Human Responsibility

is refreshing too. We are far too reticent about reminding people of their responsibilities to each other: the next-door neighbour who plays heavy metal throughout the night, as well as the profitable company that closes its local factory without regard for the future of the people who work there; the litter lout or the rubbish tipper, as well as the big river polluter or emitter of acid rain; the lack of responsibility in each case leads to the breakdown of personal relations between offender and aggrieved, and the consequences of such a breakdown are amplified in international relations. In other words from the President or Prime Minister to the churchyard mouse, let's hear less about 'my rights' and more about our duties and our responsibilities.

I have always supported the principle of incorporating the European Convention of Human Rights in a Bill of Rights but I am less and less certain that such legislation would be worth a carrot unless we also enact a Charter for Human Responsibility – and neither of them would be much use unless underlying selfish attitudes are also challenged. 'My right' is usually at someone else's expense. Society should stand up for social justice, not because of claimed rights but because it is irresponsible and unloving to do otherwise.

Lazarus and Dives

People who say they stand up for the poor fall into two camps: those who campaign for an increase in standards of living, basic income, and housing conditions; and those who see poverty as a spiritual condition: yuppies have money but do they lead happy or contented lives? It's very easy to ignore one at the expense of the other. Yuppies, after all, are human too and frequently live and work in the same inner cities as many of the materially poor. Often the two camps become two armies of occupation. Instead of offering each other mutual support systems, and recognising each other's needs, they become new class groupings and treat each other as the enemy. Encouraging an ethic which places a premium on personal responsibility and generosity will help the least well-off. It will also address the spiritual poverty of people fed a diet of self-interest.

Many of the New Right have argued that we should simply leave things to happen of their own accord. The 'trickle-down effect' assumes that as a matter of course the poor will receive some of the wealth. But what happens in practice?

The story of Lazurus and Dives illustrates the problem for both the rich man and the poor man. Despite much pleading by Lazarus, the rich man refuses to part with a single crumb off his sumptuous table. Nothing trickles down. After enduring great bodily distress Lazarus dies. Jesus tells His audience that Lazarus was taken to His father's house.

For the unreformed rich man eternity was Hades and hell-fire and Jesus says, 'That is not all: between us and you a great gulf has been fixed, to stop anyone, if he wanted to, crossing from our side to yours, and to stop any crossing from your side to ours.'[1]

If we rely on the 'trickle-down' effect Lazarus may wait for ever for Dives to respond. Poverty doesn't heal itself. Surely it is the duty of governments to remind Dives of his responsibility towards Lazarus? Our failure to excite the generous and altruistic streaks in man's nature, and our reliance on 'trickle-down', encouraged Dives into his error.

As if to emphasise that you can't pick and choose those parts of Christ's radical vision which suit you, this pointed illustration of what happens when we ignore the poor is preceded by admonitions on the indissolubility of marriage and followed by a rebuke to those who lead others astray. Jesus weaves together a seamless fabric which challenges us at an institutional and very personal level. Of course, some people say Lazarus no longer exists.

Charity Begins At Home . . .

In August 1990 the Institute of Fiscal Studies, an independent body, found that the poorest Britons saw no real rise in their income during the first eight years of Mrs Thatcher's Government. Large numbers were actually worse off. The number of people living on less than half the average income more than doubled, from 4.9 million, in 1979, to 10.5 million in 1987 – one in five of the population.

Frank Field, MP, Chairman of the Commons Social Services Select Committee, commented that the figures were 'worse than we imagined they could be'. He said that the report showed a massive widening of income distribution and demonstrated that there was no evidence to support the Government's theory that a growing economy leads to a 'trickling down from the rich man's table'.

'What they show', he said, 'is that income has been taken from the very poorest and pushed to those at the top end.'

It is impossible to justify an economic policy which during the course of most of the last decade ensured a rise of 23.1 per cent in the incomes of the average Briton. The poorest ten per cent, after allowing for housing costs, saw their income increase by only 0.1 per cent. Amongst the poorest twenty per cent of the population, adults without children, whether couples or single, saw their incomes drop by six per cent. The figures reveal both a massive increase in inequality generally within society and that the gap is getting wider. The harsh end of poverty, like youth homelessness, is becoming increasingly visible and is perhaps a weather vane pointing to the deteriorating position of the less visible.

It has become fashionable to blame the victims themselves. Yes, there are people who abuse social security but some of the country's leading captains of industry are currently serving jail sentences for rigging the stock market. That doesn't make every industrialist a greedy, dishonest crook any more than it makes every poor person a scrounger or a parasite.

Archbishop Winning of Glasgow responded to the Institute of Fiscal Studies findings by underlining this point:

> The cumulative effects of social security legislation and the imposition of the poll tax and a general tendency to denigrate the poor as being responsible for their own plight is surely one of the greatest horror stories in modern Britain. It should not be swept under the carpet.[2]

When we come to evaluate the scale of domestic poverty we should not simply rely on statistics, emotive arguments or political rhetoric. For twenty years I have held weekly advice and help centres in inner-city Liverpool. Over that time I have grown cynical about the claims and counter-claims of self-appointed spokesmen for the poor. The biggest growth industry has been in sociological survey teams. They try out their own pet theories, set up a project, and often depart within the year. People I have represented have developed a fairly healthy scepticism for those who make an occupation out of poverty.

In addition to the social scientists, some politicians make political capital out of poverty while doing nothing to help the individuals affected. It would be hard to live in Liverpool and not be angered by those members of the Labour-Left who used the language of social justice while they simultaneously concocted land deals, entrenched vested interest, preached class struggle and confrontation, and brought a city to its knees. The *Sunday Times* Insight team's investigative exposé and the BBC Panorama investigation into the intimidatory methods used by members of Liverpool's Labour Party were a devastating indictment of a party reputedly committed to the alleviation of poverty. Liverpool in the 1980s also became a text book case of what can happen when a community of half a million people are abandoned by central Government and how festering conditions can create the climate for the unscrupulous and the extreme to thrive: a museum of horrifying example.

Without the regular intervention of the city's church leaders, Archbishop Derek Worlock, Bishop David Sheppard, and Moderator John Newton, I doubt whether Liverpool would now be enjoying the post-Militant improvement in its reputation and relative economic position.

As a direct result of the manipulative and exploitative methods used by Militant and others it actually became harder to raise the profile of the least well off. The extreme positions which were struck alienated public opinion and made it easier for an unsympathetic Government to leave Liverpool to stew in its own juice: it served them right. Just as the individual living in poverty is blamed for his condition, so an entire city can be blamed and then ignored. This blaming the victim has little to do with social justice – about as little as the fanatical exhortations to rise up and smash the Government – any Government – and to destroy every vestige of our present society. All it leads to is people getting hurt.

So, if the self-appointed class warriors and social scientists cannot be trusted, who can be relied on to tell the truth about the poor? The Church. Independent institutes. Campaigning organisations who work directly with the poorest people and who have a long-standing and proven track record.

The Figures

With governments constantly tampering with the way statistics are collected and altering the criteria, it is pretty hopeless to rely on their figures. One of the most reliable independent organisations is the Child Poverty Action Group. Before entering Parliament, Frank Field was their director. In 1989 the Group highlighted twenty examples of the underside of life in Britain:

1. Over 15 million people in the mid 80s were defined as living in poverty or on its margins; with over 2 million children living in families with poverty.
2. Between 1979 and 1985, the real incomes of the richest 10 per cent went up three times more than the poorest 10 per cent.
3. In 1986, 96 per cent of homes with incomes of over £550 a week owned a car; only 24 per cent of homes with incomes of £60 to £80 had one.
4. The richest 1 per cent of the population own 20 per cent of the wealth; the wealthiest 5 per cent own 40 per cent of the wealth – the poorest 50 per cent own just 7 per cent.
5. While tax allowances have increased, the value of child benefit has fallen since 1979: the value of tax allowances has gone up by 22 per cent for married men and 19 per cent for single people but the value of child benefit has gone down by 12 per cent.

6. Babies of fathers in unskilled jobs run twice the risk of still birth and death under one year old than babies of professional fathers.
7. Women earn only two-thirds of men's pay – average hourly pay for women manual workers was £3 to £11 in 1988; £4 to £46 for men.
8. The lowest paid workers are Asian women: the latest available figure (1982) gave them an income of £73 a week compared with £77 to £80 for white women; £109 to £120 for Afro-Caribbean men and £129 for white men.
9. Married mothers returning to work after bringing up two children find that either through lost earnings or reduced salary they have forfeited £135,000 over their working life.
10. Unclaimed benefits of poorer people unaware of their entitlements run to an estimated £1 billion per year.
11. In an average year, over 70,000 homes have their electricity cut off; over 20,000 lose their gas supplies; 7000 have their water turned off; and 14,000 homes are repossessed.
12. Income Support for a couple with two children under eleven is only 37 per cent of average earnings – a fall since 1978, when supplementary benefit was worth over half of earnings.
13. The tax burden falls more heavily on the poor than on the rich, who have gained from tax cuts. Of the £20 billion of tax cuts in the past decade a quarter have gone to the richest 1 per cent; only 17 per cent to the poorest 5 per cent.
14. In one budget alone (Nigel Lawson's Budget of 1988) the richest 1 per cent received fifteen times more in tax cuts than the poorest 12 per cent of taxpayers.
15. The gap between poor and better off widened further as a result of the poll tax: families with £100 to £150 weekly income pay four times more out of their income in this tax than households on £500 plus per week.
16. More people in work are now low paid (about 9 million) – i.e. on less than two-thirds average earnings.
17. Pay for top executives doubled during the 1980s; over 1400 company directors have salaries of at least £100,000 a year (£2,000 a week).

18. Although two families in every three now own their own home, homelessness is also on the increase, doubling in the last decade.
19. 30,000 homeless families sleep in hostels each night, while 70,480 households in 1989 were in mortgage arrears by six months or more.
20. Unemployment in mid 1991 now affects over 2,000,000 people and has been rising at the rate of up to 80,000 per month. 6.5 per cent of the workforce are in receipt of benefit.

The danger of simply regurgitating these lists of economic statistics is that you could easily fall back on to the failed economic analyses of what is wrong with Britain and what needs to be done. Nor is it a case of trying to produce a levelised, supposedly equal, society. We all know where that takes us. What is surely needed is a vision of a fairer Britain and one which is more conscious of the underside. That is the value of these statistics. Behind every 'repossession' or cut supply is a family or a single person in a mess. Poor people will not be helped by breast-beating or by encouraging resentment. Privilege and wealth should be seen as tools by those who are fortunate enough to have them. They should be encouraged to use them wisely in creating a fairer society.

Some Solutions

What sort of policies should therefore be pursued?

In his *Transforming Economics*[3] the Christian economist, Alan Storkey, called for both a new coalition of politicians and policies: 'the old orthodoxies in economic policy are crumbling . . . this is matched politically' and he called for 'a new paradigm based on relationism rather than materialism: Our economic life is fundamentally relational.'[4] I would argue that market economics should be replaced by a Community Economy.

There are key principles by which Christians can steer their response to economic issues. Storkey puts it like this:

> The first is a recognition of the centrality of our relationship with God in economic life. God's blessings, care providence, creation, requirements and mandates are the context for our economic life. We are stewards of God's creation and dependent on its goodness. This means that economic life cannot be considered in a separate compartment (there is no economic man), but is part of our response to our creator.

An approach which upholds social justice must be based on responsible economics. We must reclaim our responsibility for addressing poverty and unemployment. The polarities of market place economics and those which place the State at their heart are both wrong. The community is a better starting point.

Such an approach would therefore mean welcoming the Social Charter, investing more in work and training, encouraging the wider implementation of profit sharing and involvement of employees in their companies, and a renunciation of the old lie that the only purpose of economics is to produce more. The emphasis should surely switch from maximisation – often a synonym for injustice and selfishness – to sharing; and from naked materialism to qualitative enrichment of each person's life.

Our perception of money must also change. In Chapter 9 I will be looking at the issue of debt in more detail, but it is worth saying here also that it is not money which is at the heart of all evil, but our love of it. In other words, we should see money in much the same way as we see water, air, or the countryside: as something which is there to enhance the quality of everyone's lives, not just a few. Encouragement of Credit Unions, restructuring of the housing market and mortgages, and restrictions on the use of interest, would all help tame the excesses which unlimited exploitation of money can produce. I have no desire to see a return to welfarism and agree with Frank Field's conclusion in *Inequality in Britain*[5] that 'Today the traditional welfare state not only fails to combat poverty but all too often operates as a ceiling, making it impossible for the poor to escape from their poverty.'

With our emphasis changed to a personalist and community approach we would no longer be preoccupied at Budget time with obsessions about by how much we might expect standard rates of income tax to be cut. We might instead wish to reflect specific concerns – for instance, the need to give more incentives to the low income groups and those in the 'black' economy to come into the tax system – by cutting the standard rate of the lowest wage earners. A system of tax credits to replace a whole host of benefits might also help reduce dependence, enhance personal status, and more effectively target help to those who most need it. It would certainly be easier to adopt the current populist Labour Party approach of promising uncosted across-the-board concessions, such as free TV licences for all pensioners, but it would stretch belief. It is simply not credible to argue for a fairer Britain and then introduce a proposal that would give every hereditary peer over the age of sixty-five a free TV licence, as well as those who really do need help – it will be a decision made at the expense of the genuinely poor.

If we take a rifle shot rather than scattergun approach to politics we might well wish to simultaneously cut and raise certain taxes. For instance, we might wish to weight taxes to ensure that parents who remain at home with their children are no worse off than the parents who return to work. Maybe taxes should also be substantially cut – or, better still, given as matching money on a pound-for-pound basis – for those who are prepared to covenant some of their income to charitable purposes. Chancellor Lamont's 1991 decision to impose VAT on charities is precisely what we should not be doing. Cutting taxes should be seen as a creative weapon in the quest for fairness instead of an obsessive piece of ideology. Equally, there would also have to be times when for many people an increase in standard rate would be required. This should not simply be a catch-all contribution towards general Government expenditure but a creative contribution for specific purposes, say enhanced health or educational services or environmental improvements.

As long ago as 1934 Archbishop Temple[6] urged the then Chancellor, Neville Chamberlain, to use the opportunity of cuts in taxation to help the most needy: '. . . if the Chancellor of the Exchequer finds himself in a position to reduce taxation, the restoration of the cuts in the allowances for the unemployed should have precedence over any other concessions, including remission of income tax.' The Government complained that the Archbishop had exceeded his remit by sticking his nose into matters of politics: *plus ça change*.

. . . But It Doesn't End There . . . The Two-Thirds World

In March 1989 a packed House of Commons considered Chancellor Nigel Lawson's last Budget. A little later in the week, on a quiet Friday morning, we debated overseas development. About twenty MPs were present.

Three days earlier Mr Lawson had told the Commons that along with cuts in taxation he had budgeted for repayment of £14 billion of Britain's national debt – 3 per cent of our Gross Domestic Product (GDP). He was able to announce that Government debt was lower than at any time since the First World War, and that our net debt interest costs would be lower by £1.5 billion during 1989-90 because of reduced payment on loan charges. Good. But our total aid programme for the same period was £1.4 billion. No doubt many of the debtor nations, facing larger contributions in repayments than they were receiving in aid, would also like to have been in a position of reducing their usurous debt burdens.

Some Figures

In *What Kind of Country*,[7] I set out the arguments for increasing our aid programme (see Chapter 22, 'One World One Day' and Chapter 23, 'Rich Man, Poor Man'). The statistics speak for themselves. In 1980 the World Bank estimated that 800 million people were living in a state of starvation and despair. The United Nations says there are thirty-four countries where over eighty per cent of the population are illiterate; UNICEF says that in one year alone more than

12 million children under the age of five died of starvation. Many millions more died of disease, violence or neglect. In 1980, Robert McNamara, then President of the World Bank, said that 'Up to a million of the world's population live lives of poverty which are so limited by malnutrition, illiteracy, disease, infant mortality and low life expectancy as to be beneath any rational definition of human decency.' The scale of this unspeakable misery and grinding poverty was brought home to the developed world in the prophetic Brandt Report, published in 1980.

Eight years later, Chris Patten, as Overseas Aid Minister, said that 'an effective aid programme is one that stops babies dying'. Yes, but an effective aid programme is also one that does not shackle countries with unrepayable debts. It is one that recognises and addresses the pressures to ravage and exploit forests, land and prized environment. It is one which targets aid at projects which will alleviate poverty direct – rural water supplies, provision of improved seed, simple facilities for crop storage, development of fisheries and village wood lots, primary health care, territorially based livestock grazing projects, minor irrigation using intermediate technology, and so on.

The accelerated growth of international debt provides a graphic illustration of the parable of the unforgiving debtor. Many of the debts were amassed in the 1960s and 1970s when conventional wisdom held that countries could not go bankrupt. Commercial banks in the developed world gave out money with the alacrity of a three-armed man. The sequel is well known – countries did go bankrupt; they defaulted on debts; the banks rescheduled the debts and interest rates soared. The Third World countries have subsequently been forced to generate exports by selling raw materials and plundering their assets to repay debt and service interest.

By 1990 Third World debt was estimated at more than $1,000 billion. The net negative transfer of resources from poorer countries to richer countries (i.e. debt servicing, less aid) rose from $38.100 million in 1987 to $43,000 million in 1988 (World Bank figures). In trying to reduce this colossal sum the International Monetary Fund tends to place burdens disproportionately on the poor. Financial austerity leads to cuts in already minimal health and welfare services and in food subsidies. That leads to hunger, and to babies dying. President Julius Nyerere summed up the choices which he faced: 'They asked me to make a choice between paying the debts of Tanzania and feeding the people of Tanzania. For me, that is no moral choice; it is not even a practical choice.'

Mexico has pursued so severe a programme of structural adjustment for seven years that real wages have fallen by forty per cent, and yet it still owes $100 billion of its debt of $105 billion. Nigeria has suffered severely in seven years of structural adjustment, so that poorer people can only afford one meal a day. Yet, they now owe more than the $30 billion debt they set out to clear with their structural plan in 1983.

Some Solutions

Martin Dent, of the Department of Politics at the University of Keele, and some of his colleagues, have devised a plan entitled Jubilee 2000 which seeks to liberate under-developed countries from the burden of unpayable debt by the end of the decade. Dent points out that at the present rate of progress the total debt of one thousand billion dollars will not be cleared until the year 3000. The Midland Bank have set a good example, in a small way, by converting $800,000 of its Sudan debt into local currency and dedicating it for a UNICEF water sanitation programme in the drought-stricken Kordofan region. Dent's radical plan for remission of debt might really begin to bite into the $440 billion South American debt and the $120 billion debt on Sub-Saharan Africa.

While debt has increased there has been a corresponding cut in Britain's help for the developing nations. Although Chris Patten managed to obtain the first small real increase in overseas aid expenditure in a decade (to £1.5 billion in 1989-90), and was undoubtedly a highly committed and effective Minister, I am sure he would agree that overseas development policy has never been a central question of British politics. The Overseas Aid Minister does not have a Cabinet seat, or even an autonomous Government department. In terms of relative importance the facts speak for themselves: between 1977 and 1987 Britain's aid programme fell by 36 per cent. Even in starving Africa – where, to use the Patten litmus test, babies have been dying in their thousands – there was a decrease in Britain's aid from £386 million in 1979 to £284 million in 1987. In 1979 we contributed 0.5 per cent of our GDP in overseas aid. By 1990 this stood at 0.3 per cent. In 1979 we were sixth in the league table of Western aid givers, today we are fourteenth. In 1983 the Government promised that we would move towards the 0.7 per cent target figure which the United Nations asked us to reach as long ago as 1970 'when economic circumstances permit'. Despite Mrs Thatcher's boast in February 1989 that 'We now have a higher standard of living than we have ever known. We have a great budget surplus',[8] economic circumstances still did not permit the creation of an aid programme that stopped babies dying. This approach is in stark contrast to that of countries such as Germany and Italy.

Another parallel may be drawn. In 1990 John Major, as Chancellor, found ten times as much to pay off domestic debt and eighteen times as much for armaments as he found for aid. Five hours' worth of world military expenditure is equivalent to UNICEF's total annual budget. Over the past decade military expenditure has risen more rapidly in most European countries than that devoted to the civilian economy. Just as disturbingly, developing countries have devoted larger sums to military expenditure: an average of 6 per cent of GDP in 1965, 16 per cent by 1980. This has been fuelled by the arms trade. From 1965 to 1970 the annual growth rate of the conventional arms trade was 10 per cent; in the five subsequent years it was 15 per cent and from 1975 to 1980 it rose to 25 per cent. According to C.M. Klare,[9] the Soviet Union, France, Great Britain and the USA are responsible for the great majority of arms supplies. Money spent on armaments is money lost for other needs. The war with Iraq and the destabilisation of the Middle East was after years of arms sales to countries in the region. In the five years before the Gulf War I tabled parliamentary questions and motions demanding an end to the sale of arms to countries in the region. Despite chemical attacks on the Kurds the Government would not even accept my request to end favourable trade terms with Iraq, saying there was no need to treat it differently to any other country.

How would a government which cared about social justice address these issues?

In a speech in the House of Commons on March 17th, 1989, I set out six principles which bear repetition. First, to reach the 0.7 per cent overseas aid contribution target we will need to increase our aid budget in real terms by 20 per cent each year. Second, we must greatly increase the programme of long term aid. Third, we need a substantial reserve sum to provide prompt and generous aid in emergencies. Fourth, there should be a detailed plan for adequate food aid in times of famine. Fifth, there must be greater remission of the official and commercial debts of the poorest countries; and, sixth, we need a comprehensive plan for improvement in terms and conditions of trade for the poorest countries.

I think I would now add two further points.

Chris Patten rightly called for 'a pretty fundamental review of the working relationship between Government and charities'. In seconding that I would also strongly argue for substantial tax breaks and incentives for those who give to charities such as Christian Aid, CAFOD, and Tear Fund. In addition, a government that took seriously both overseas aid and its relationship to environmental protection would put the Minister in charge into the Cabinet and give him an autonomous department. In other words, political clout. Furthermore, in the future we should pool our efforts with our European counterparts.

Europe and the Developing Nations

An effective aid programme is also one which doesn't duplicate what others are doing. I remember being appalled as I drove through Nepal, probably now the world's poorest country, to see huge billboards advising the traveller that he was lucky enough to be driving on the next piece of road thanks to the Government of Great Britain/Germany/France, etc. What the Nepali people – average annual income £120 – make of this flag-waving I dread to think. But, at another level, it also illustrates the individualistic nature of our bilateral aid programme. Britain currently gives aid to 123 different countries, but many of these programmes are very small and do not get to the roots of poverty and injustice. We could save on administrative costs, and make our aid more effective if the European Development Fund (EDF) was used to co-ordinate all European aid programmes. An internationally respected politician such as Willy Brandt, Hans Dietrich Genscher, David Owen or Edward Heath should be asked to oversee it, and be answerable to the European Parliament.

In 1990 the European People's Party published its document, 'World Economy and Development – A Christian Democratic Contribution'.[10] The party's Secretary General, Thomas Jansen, has a different vision of Europe and its relationship with the rest of the world to the myopic and xenophobic vision of British politicians who regard the world beyond Dover with suspicion and fear. In the Introduction he said:

> World Government remains a desideratum though one hardly dares mention it, not wishing to appear utopian. In the understanding of the Christian Democrats the establishment of the European Community was one contribution amongst others towards the creation of a more just world order. Its onward evolution to political union only becomes wholly meaningful when it is regarded as one step to world federation . . . A social world economy is the counterpart of the social market economy, that was initially designed by Christian Democracy in Europe . . . It is based on the idea that the interplay of market forces is subject not only to its own inherent laws of the market, but also to a social obligation, which is to ensure a social balance, social partnership and social justice.

The Christian Democrats list four key concepts which help

them arrive at their policy for the underdeveloped world: justice, broad responsibility, solidarity and good husbandry. They say:

> Of these, justice is the foremost. It is the main motive for political action aimed at creating conditions in which people are able to practise responsibility, solidarity and good husbandry. Public justice means that government carries out executive tasks where it is competent to do so (such as e.g. to guarantee minimum living conditions, environmental standards and defence) . . . The principle of justice requires that we should attach particular weight to the voice of the poor, the powerless and the oppressed . . . In the field of development co-operation Christians have no reason to remain silent. The Gospel tells us to love our distant neighbour as ourselves.[11]

In their conclusions the Christian Democrats call on all industrialised countries to meet the United Nations 0.7 per cent target figure for overseas aid contributions and conclude that bilateral aid programmes are usually more geared to the interests of the donors than the recipients. They argue that diversification must be the hallmark of development co-operation, both in substance and structure. To achieve this will require 'intense co-ordination of the various activities which are being devised at this moment at the European level.'[12]

Even more fundamentally they say we will combat poverty through structural shifts of power: institutionalised changes which ensure that money and trade are geared to serving the needs of developing countries, rather than crippling them. They warn the West not to project its own standards, customs and institutions on the under-developed countries. They argue that the place of women in the developing countries is central:

> Women in the Third World must be enabled to speak for themselves . . . It is further our opinion that development for man only is no development at all, but a monstrosity

> leading to disaster. The role of women as pillars of development must be given much more prominence.[13]

They see the need for dialogue and honesty in assessing priorities. Wherever possible developing countries must be able, and where necessary enabled, to shape their own development. Where we intervene in the domestic aspects of development it must be done from a sense of responsibility and not paternalism.

As with domestic poverty it has not been a lack of analyses, visions, intentions and rules which have militated against a fundamental shift in political direction, but rather the absence of a mentality orientated towards social justice and development issues in the governments of both the industrialised and the developing countries, in business, international organisations and ourselves.

Not surprisingly, Christian Democrats place the human being at the heart of their philosophy and their approach towards social justice and development. Reflecting themes taken up in Paul VI's encyclical 'The Great Social Problem',[14] they say

> We are each made in the image of God and our right to life, to protection from ill treatment and oppression and to spiritual freedom is inalienable. These rights, which are laid down in the Universal Declaration of Human Rights, must never be violated. Development and growing respect for human rights must be indissolubly linked.[15]

Political success in under-developed countries must not be measured merely in terms of GDP or aid given. The true humanism to which we are called requires us to find ourselves again by embracing the higher values of love and friendship. This enrichment will permit authentic development, a development which is for each and all. It will allow us simultaneously to address social injustice and the lack of material necessities of the starving but also the moral deficiencies of those who are mutilated by selfishness. Less human conditions are abuses of power, abuses of ownership, exploitation of workers, infringements of human rights, unjust and exploitative transactions. We become more human as we progress from misery towards the possession of basic necessities, as we are victorious over social scourges and injustices, and as we facilitate the growth of knowledge and the acquisition of culture.

Aid programmes have been too geared to the needs of the donor rather than the recipients. In some cases they have been downright corrupt. Those who devise them have also regularly failed to listen to the needs of the people and have created systems of dependency. Take a country such as Honduras. It now has more airports in proportion to the size of its population than any other country; yet it cannot find enough milk to give its children. Nothing could be more revealing of the corrupt values of governments and the international order. Honduran people have to grow crops to sell abroad rather than as food to eat; their pitiful earnings can only be spent on over-priced imported goods. Drugs and pesticides which have been banned as unsafe in the West are dumped on Hondurans – as a result the peasants are poisoned and the children are born deformed. This thumbnail sketch of the effects of a policy which is rotten to the core could be painted on a wider canvas in many other parts of the globe.

Christians have increasingly recognised the need to address these questions. The widely-respected evangelical, John Stott[16] says:

> We cannot maintain a good life of extravagance and a good conscience simultaneously. One or other has to be sacrificed. Either we keep our conscience and reduce our affluence, or we keep our affluence and smother our conscience. We have to choose between God and mammon.

Paul VI's encyclical[17] made it clear that such an approach is not an optional extra for believers:

> Countless millions are starving, countless families are destitute, countless men are steeped in ignorance, countless

> people need schools, hospitals and homes worthy of the name. In such circumstances we cannot tolerate public and private expenditures of a wasteful nature: we cannot but condemn lavish displays of wealth by nations or individuals: we cannot approve of a debilitating arms race. It is our solemn duty to speak out against them. If only world leaders would listen to us before it is too late!

The Catholic Bishops of England and Wales put it like this: 'Action on behalf of justice, and participation in the transformation of the world fully appear to us as a constitutive dimension of the preaching of the gospel, or, in other words, of the Church's mission for the redemption of the human race, and its liberation from every oppressive situation.'[18]

As developed nations we can never be sufficiently on guard against the temptation to enrich ourselves at the expense of others. We are not making a gift of what is ours to poor people, but giving back what is theirs. We have appropriated many things provided for the common use of all mankind. The earth belongs to everyone, not just to us.

It does not accord with our innate genius to live by simply gathering more to ourselves in the relentless pursuit of a prosperity gospel and market place economics. But for Christians there is another reason yet for seeking a more truly human and socially just approach. If Lazarus is symbolic of all who live in poverty and Dives is representative of all of us who are privileged to live in wealthy societies, then Christ might well have had us in mind when he starkly asked, 'What will it profit a man, if he gains the whole world and forfeits his life?'[19]

Chapter 6

Respect for Life

From the very first pages on, the Bible teaches that the whole of creation is for every human being, and that it is our responsibility to develop it. Each of us is made in the image of our Maker and all other claimed rights are subordinate to the right of each person to live. We are not expendible raw material but unique people prized by our Maker. The destruction of created life can never be a matter of 'choice' and any logical concern for social justice would see a respect for the most powerless of human beings as an over-riding concern.

To argue that it is our individual right to choose to end another person's life is to place the individual's rights above the rights of the human person. The atheist or secularist should not wonder at Christian insistence on this age-old truth; we do, after all, believe in a God who took the form of humanity in its most vulnerable form. We believe God came as an embryo. His first witness was a foetus, John. The Gospel writer, Luke, a doctor, records how John leapt with joy in his previously infertile mother's womb as he greeted the tiny Jesus – who at that stage was just a 'primitive streak' or 'pre-embryo'.

The utilitarian arguments put forward by those who favour destructive experimentation on human embryos, abortion, limited infanticide on disabled babies, eugenics and euthanasia, all take as their central theme the erroneous belief that they are doing it for the individual's or for the general good. Wilberforce well understood where such thinking led when he proclaimed: 'Resolutely disclaim that dangerous sophistry of doing evil that good may come.'

Our generation has seen a general baptising, in all walks of life, of demanding one's own rights. The language is aggressive and it legitimises the very selfishness about which we moralise when we attack other aspects of the grab-what-you-can society in which we live. This impoverished economic and political language demands rights without duties and responsibilities: we must re-establish balance in the equation. It is not a choice between mother and child: it is a question of love, care and practical help for both of them. What it can never be is simply 'my right' to choose to take another person's life.

This is the supreme human rights issue. The issues at stake are the sovereignty of God and the sanctity of human life. Because the protection of human life is at the heart of the matter, it cannot be dismissed as a topic for 'private morality' or left as merely a subject for Christians and other people of faith. Britain's political parties have all – to a varying extent – adopted anti-life postures. The Movement for Christian Democracy is right to counter this by insisting that a respect for life is a central political question.

Where They Stand: The Church

One of the clearest expositions of the position of British Evangelical Christians on life issues is to be found in John Stott's *Issues Facing Christians Today*.[1] He says:

> All Christian people believe that Almighty God is the only giver, sustainer and taker-away of life. On the one hand 'he himself gives all men life and breath and everything else', and 'in him we live and move and have our being'. On the other, as the psalmist says to God, 'when you take away their breath, they die and return to dust'. Indeed, whenever anybody dies, Christian faith struggles to affirm with Job: 'The Lord gave and the Lord has taken away; may the name of the Lord be praised'. To the Christian, then, both life giving and life taking are divine prerogatives.

Christians from a Catholic tradition would agree with the Nobel Peace Prize Winner, Mother Teresa[2]:

> Only God can decide life and death . . . that is why abortion is such a terrible sin. You are not only killing life but putting self before God; yet people decide who has to live and who has to die. They want to make themselves Almighty God. They want to take the power of God in their hands. They want to say, 'I can do without God. I can decide.' That is the most devilish thing that a human hand can do . . .

When she came to Westminster to urge support for my Bill to end late abortions, Mother Teresa told me that she believed our willingness to destroy unborn life made us an infinitely poorer country than India and is a shocking manifestation of violence: 'To me, the nations with legalised abortions are the poorest nations. The great destroyer of peace today is the crime against the innocent unborn child . . . In destroying the child, we are destroying love, destroying the image of God in the world.'

The Quaker, Gerald Priestland, put it another way: in an abortion 'life is not just prevented or postponed, it is destroyed. As a Christian and a believer that life is a divine gift and that God has a will for each one, I have to agree that his presence does put things in a different light . . . Like war, abortion is a confession of failure.'

Speaking at a 'Care for Life' rally, at the Royal Albert Hall, the Scottish evangelical, Dr Nigel Cameron, said that 'the final act of child abuse' should be 'seen as the dawn of a new barbarism, and challenges our Christian values at a fundamental level'.

And the Christian feminist lawyer, Pauline Connor, argues that:

> abortion cannot solve the problems of violence against women because it is part of the problem of violence against women . . . abortionism has transformed women and children into objects . . . feminism is about attaining justice

> and consequently has nothing to do with killing. Women have not, and we cannot, kill our way to liberation.[3]

Following the Synod of Bishops, held in Rome in 1980, on the theme 'The Role of the Christian Family in the Modern World', John Paul II acceded to the Synod's Request that a Family Charter be prepared. This was published in 1983[4] and Article 4 says:

> Human life must be respected and protected absolutely from the moment of conception. a) Abortion is a direct violation of the fundamental right to life of the human being; b) Respect of the dignity of the human being excludes all experimental manipulation or exploitation of the human embryo; c) All interventions on the genetic heritage of the human person that are not aimed at correcting anomalies constitute a violation of the right to bodily integrity and contradict the good of the family; d) Children, both before and after birth, have the right to special protection and assistance, as do their mothers during pregnancy and for a reasonable period after birth.

Not all Christians hold to such firm convictions. In supporting the passage of the Human Fertilisation and Embryology Bill, the Archbishop of York called for the legalisation of destructive experiments on the embryo. He told the House of Lords: 'The argument is constantly made that such a conceptus might develop into one of us. Indeed, but there is a great difference between reading history backwards and trying to predict it forwards . . . when you are trying to read history forwards you are simply talking of potentialities.'[5] Another Anglican, the Maidstone MP, Ann Widdecombe, poured scorn on this proposition during a meeting which we both addressed in Bradford: 'I should like to be present at an Advent service at York Minster,' she said. 'No doubt the readings will be changed to suit these new circumstances: and the angel said unto Mary, Thou art with potentiality, and the conceptus leaped with joy in her womb.' Many Christians, especially Anglicans, will be looking to the new Archbishop of Canterbury, George Carey, to give a clear and faith-related lead on respect for life issues.

During question time at the end of a meeting at the 1990 Greenbelt Festival for young Christians, an annual Arts festival which attracts around 18,000 young people, a young man said, 'It is easy for white middle-class Evangelicals to speak against abortion. They should take on tougher issues like the poll tax.' I told him he was wrong. Concern about these kind of issues is not mutually exclusive. Furthermore, I have never found that abortion or the defence of life is an 'easy' issue. My experience has been that a quiet life and fulfilment of political ambitions are easier to achieve by giving these questions a wide berth. Anyone who upholds that both divine sovereignty and human dignity are central to 'respect for life' issues, cannot stand aside and say nothing.

Where They Stand: The Politicians

The Archbishop of York's speech to the House of Lords was used by pro-experiment, pro-abortion MPs as a Trojan Horse throughout the passage of the legislation. It is sadly ironic that the pro-experimentation lobby, while accusing its opponents of 'forcing religious views' upon others (in a democracy, where laws are determined by majority votes), relied so heavily on the exegesis of the Archbishop of York to bolster and promote its case. In their book, *Whatever Happened to the Human Race?*,[6] Francis Schaeffer and Everett Koop rightly traced 'the erosion of the sanctity of human life' to 'the loss of the Christian consensus'. There has also been an erosion of the political and medical consensus.

Until the passage of the 1967 Abortion Act doctors upheld the Hippocratic Oath 'I will not give to a woman a pessary to procure abortion'; updated in 1948 at Geneva to say: 'I will maintain the utmost respect for human life from the time of conception' and they believed that if they could not help their patients they would not harm them. The British Medical Association and the Royal Colleges of Gynaecologists, Nurses and Midwives had all held with the general practitioners' view that life was sacred. They were defenders, not destroyers of life.

Politicians had steadfastly opposed the abortion ethic. But in 1967 the Abortion Law Reform Association secured the services of David Steel, who promoted a Private Member's Bill. He assured the House of Commons that the legislation was not designed to provide for abortion on demand. However, more than twenty years later the coach and horses provisions of this legislation have led to an annual abortion rate of over 180,000 and some 3 1/2 million legal abortions in total. Just twenty-nine MPs voted against the Third Reading of that legislation. Prior to 1967, there were no official figures since abortion was illegal, although those campaigning for changes in the law would often talk of 20,000 illegal abortions annually. Immediately after legislation, the figures were about a quarter of what they are now.

In 1967 the issue was a 'conscience' question with no party whip imposed. No party had a policy on abortion. The Steel Act changed that. It legitimised abortion; and with the assumption that because abortion had become legal, *ergo* it was right, each of the parties has become more and more wedded to the abortion ethic. Public opinion, however, is by no means so certain.

When Kenneth Clarke, as Health Secretary, introduced the 1989 Human Fertilisation and Embryology Bill, he told the Commons that there would be free and fair votes and debate. Sir Geoffrey Howe, then Leader of the House of Commons, said that there would be a 'fair balance' on the Committee which was appointed to discuss the Bill. Unlike Private Members Bills – such as my 1988 Bill to limit late abortions – it would not be possible for a minority to 'talk out' this Bill because it would be debated in Government time and a guillotine imposed on the debate. During the passage of the Bill it would be possible to have a vote on late abortions as well as on the principal issue of whether experiments should be allowed on human embryos. What happened in practice was a travesty of these undertakings.

First, the Government did impose a Whip at the Third

Reading of the Bill, which meant that pro-life Ministers such as Chris Patten and John Selwyn Gummer would have been required to resign from the Government if they had refused to vote for the legislation. They also went back on their promise of 'fair balance' on the Committee, which was heavily rigged in favour of the pro-abortion, pro-experimentation lobby. The Committee of eighteen was made up of sixteen from the other side of the argument and just two pro-lifers, Dame Jill Knight and Ann Widdecombe. Undoubtedly Government whips took their lead from Mrs Thatcher, who had expressed herself in favour of destructive experiments on human embryos and opposed any substantial reduction of the upper time limit for abortions. Parliament finally enacted legislation allowing abortions to take place until twenty-four weeks gestation, and in the case of disabled babies right up until and during birth. As babies have been born and lived from twenty-two weeks onwards this is infanticide. It is also discriminatory and based on the weeding-out theories of the eugenicists. It is all too consistent with the view of some of the libertarian New Right who see disabled people as a liability – early detection and destruction saves unnecessary expenditure.

Although Conservative Members like David Amess, Ken Hargreaves, Ann Winterton, Alistair Burt, Alan Amos, Elizabeth Peacock, the redoubtable Sir Bernard Braine and others already mentioned, spoke with passion and conviction against these proposals, the stark truth is that they are outnumbered by those on the other side of the argument.

The situation in the Labour Party is even worse. Speaking for the Opposition, Jo Richardson and Harriet Harman made it clear where the official Opposition stands and what they would do if a Labour government were returned to power. They moved amendments to extend the 1967 Abortion Act to Northern Ireland, to allow abortion on demand up until twelve weeks, and to introduce a public blacklist of any doctor or nurse who refuses to undertake abortions. Support for abortion is no longer a conscience question for individual members of the Party; it is official Party policy.

The Liberal Party had traditionally allowed abortion to be a matter of conscience, although the SDP took up a pro-abortion position. The new Liberal Democrats inherited some of this thinking and Paddy Ashdown's Policy Committee passed a motion committing the Party to abortion up until twenty-eight weeks and the extension of the act to Northern Ireland. After protests from Shirley Williams, Alan Beith, Sir Cyril Smith and others, David Steel suggested to the Liberal Democrats' 1989 Conference that the issue should remain a matter of personal conscience. No vote was taken and although Ashdown privately promised that the Policy Committee decision would be reversed, this had not happened at the time of writing. Along with Neil Kinnock, John Major and Mrs Thatcher, he voted for the Third Reading of the Human Fertilisation and Human Embryology Bill.

The Green Party claims a concern for creation and rightly argues for a holistic approach. However, despite the opposition of Christian members such as Tim Cooper (twice co-chair of the Green Party Council) they have taken pro-abortion positions. Like some Liberal Democrats, the Greens have been greatly influenced by New Age thinking and this pagan view of life emerges in their language and policy positions.

For Right, Left and Centre, this issue raises fundamental questions. It engages with the most highly charged dilemma of liberalism: human rights. But for whom? Is liberalism about human dignity or does it treat people as functional units, to be socially engineered, lacking any essential value?

If the abortion controversy is essentially about the supremacy of liberal values rather than the millions of dead children, what does that say about our ethics and attitudes? What will the liberal do if the State changes its mind and reverses these beliefs? The changes will be denounced as undemocratic and the laws as bad laws. If the people or Parliament produce the 'wrong' majorities they will be ignored or defied. In other words, liberalism in those circumstances will be as willing as the totalitarian ideologies to sacrifice lives and to ignore democratically made law if it furthers its ends. This is a chilling view of law and democracy.

Where They Stand: Europe

Britain has the most open-ended abortion laws in Western Europe. Only four out of five pregnancies now go full term. Last year alone women from over one hundred different countries – from Mongolia to South Africa – came to the UK to avail themselves of laws which allow abortion later than anywhere else in the civilised world. More than £12 million passed hands in the private clinics, mainly based in London, in the lucrative abortion business.

Attitudes in western Europe vary considerably, with Ireland now alone as the only country refusing to sanction the destruction of the unborn. However, the European Parliament contains a high ratio of pro-life MPs and the refusal of the Norwegian and German Parliaments to countenance destructive experiments on human embryos is indicative of the change of attitude which we must hope is gradually emerging.

Unlike the British political parties Christian Democrats in both Western and Eastern Europe have been willing to assert their belief in the inalienable right to life. In their 1989 election manifesto for the European Parliament, the Christian Democrats set out their position.[7] First, unlike the British Parliament, they draw a distinction between research and science used for the benefit of humanity and destructive experiments which use the embryonic human being as their subject:

> Technology should be used in the service of mankind. We are convinced that the meaning of the value of the person is that they should live in peace and responsible freedom, without hunger or need, in a safe natural environment. Science and technology are ethically justified in so far as they serve to provide this.
>
> The continuing development of science and technology is indispensable for the more humane shaping of human life and to secure its survival. Modern technology makes possible effective protection of the environment, economic use of scarce resources, humane work conditions and new types of aid for handicapped people and elderly people.

But not everything which is technically possible or economically advantageous is desirable from a human point of view. For us Christian Democrats, technical progress is an ethical, as well as a political and economic requirement and we must find answers together, in a European framework, to the problems posed. We must decide responsibly on the basis of the contemporary state of knowledge, whether a greater risk lies in the use or in the nonapplication of technical novelties.

The European People's Party favours three ethical ground rules in research and the application of technology:

* Respect for human values and the rights of the person from conception until natural death;
* Responsibility towards Creation; and
* Responsibility towards future generations.

Respect for Creation obliges us to preserve for today and for future generations the beauty and diversity of nature as an essential basis of human existence. We may not destroy the basis of life for future generations; the application of new technology and our relationships with nature must be undertaken with a sense of our responsibility towards future generations.

The value of the human may not be negatively affected by experiments in genetic engineering and the human person may not be reduced to being the object of genetic manipulation.

In another section of their manifesto, which looks at bioethics, the Christian Democrats examine the dilemmas posed by artificial insemination and in-vitro fertilisation. Whilst accepting that such procedures can fulfil the life's wish of a childless couple to have much-wanted children, they say that limits must be set: 'All decisions must be based on the good of the child and have respect for human values. The value of life and the right of marriage and the family must be respected.' They say that 'the Christian concept of marriage and the family' means that IVF must not be 'separated from the mutual love and responsibility of parents'. This, and their insistence that the human embryo must be incorporated in a total concept of the protection of life, is once more in stark contrast to the attitudes and positions taken by British legislators who authorised so-called 'virgin births'.

The Christian Democratic tradition is refreshingly consistent and logical when it puts the rights of the unborn child in the same framework as other human rights and communal duties. The manifesto discussed the issue of abortion in a section which looks at the position of the family:

> The objective of EPP policy is to strengthen the importance of the family as the basic community. For us the family as a community for living and for teaching is the most important source of individual refuge and it is where values are transmitted, and where there should be solidarity and responsibility, with equality between parents and where each has autonomy and there is mutual respect for the aspirations of each . . . The child is obviously the natural extension of the family. The child is the centre of family policy. The effective protection of unborn life is of primary importance for a human Europe. The child has the right, from the moment of conception, to have its life and integrity protected. It has the same right to life as the person after birth.

I was also impressed to see the recognition of the needs of lone parents and the support and encouragement which we must give to parents struggling by themselves to provide a loving home environment for their children. The lack of ambiguity and political 'double speak' in these commitments is startling and refreshing.

Following the Maker's Instructions

The climate for consideration of the 1989 Human Fertilisation and Embryology Bill was created by two things: the Warnock Committee Report and distorted media coverage.

In 1985 Lady Warnock said that only a fool would now say

that life does not begin at conception, and her Committee, which drew up the Warnock report, said: 'Once the process has begun there is no particular part of the development process which is more important than another . . . However, we agreed that this was an area in which some precise decision must be taken in order to allay public anxiety.'[8] They hit on the aptly named 'primitive streak' (the earliest manifestation of humanity) and later (although it was never used in the Report) they invented the term 'pre-embryo' to refer to the human embryo prior to fourteen days. In the House of Lords, the Law Lord, Lord Rawlinson, pointedly asked, 'Fourteen days after what? It must be fourteen days after something or fourteen days into some sort of existence.'

A group of four who served on the Warnock Committee came out against the use of this early-stage human being for experimental purposes. One of these was Professor John Marshall: 'We took the view that from fertilisation this entity was alive and its potential was so great and so important that it was wrong to destroy it . . . we really must insist on this respect for human life.'[9]

Marshall went on to say that if experiments were allowed up until fourteen days, 'they will start pressing for more later on . . . If only we could go on to 20 days we could show you this and that. That's the scientific logic of it.'

With many other scientists Professor Marshall points out that the research which Parliament has authorised is not aimed at finding cures for disability, merely at identification leading to destruction: 'Because the entity has the potential to become a person . . . nothing should be done that prevents it realizing that potential, and things can be done to help it attain that potential.'

Fertilisation is the only event to which each of us can point and say, 'That is when I began and I have been me ever since.' The appearance of the primitive streak is one of thousands of events, not a watershed. It is an incident in a life already begun. Fertilisation determines the colour of our eyes and the colour of our skin, our sex, our uniqueness – not fourteen days.

The conclusions which we draw about the tiny, vulnerable,

powerless human embryo have the highest moral significance. They determine how we regard the status of every individual and how we perceive their human rights and our obligations towards them. Our conclusions will also determine our attitude towards disabled people, the senile, the incurably sick and the terminally ill.

The justification of experiments is that means justify ends, benefits outweigh costs. These unenlightened arguments have a frighteningly logical conclusion. Dr Michael Hall was quoted in *The Guardian* in 1987 on the subject of scientists' long-term intentions: 'It would mean we could manipulate at will the genetic pool, produce super-races, modify ethnic traits, excise socially unacceptable habits – in fact produce people to order.' During the House of Lords debate Lord Reay summed up what MP Rosie Barnes – a strong supporter of experimentation – agreed was 'culling the handicapped'. He said, 'We should also consider society's need to reduce by every means possible the proportion of handicapped children.' Not merely the elimination of handicap, but of handicapped children, by every means possible. This thinking is summed up by the Oxford philosopher, Jonathon Glover, who argues that for utilitarians killing is in no way intrinsically wrong, but is only wrong because of its implications for happiness and misery. This is the thinking of a society which no longer believes in a Maker, and which has lost the Maker's instructions.

Respect Life or Respect Nothing

Care and kill can never be used as synonyms. Quality controls and perfection tests on life are utterly repugnant. They are also defeatist. A society which loses its respect for life respects nothing.

There are radical alternatives to this anti-life ethic. The French geneticist, Professor Jerome Lejeune, the American, Professor Hymie Gordon and Westminster Hospital's Professor Ron Taylor all say that the objective of pursuing research may be reconciled with the highest ethical standards of maintaining a respect for the life of the subject. Professor

Gordon told the 1989 conference of LIFE, held at Coventry, that 'everything we need to learn can be learnt by studying genetic diseases in non-human primates and other animals'. LIFE's Chairman, Professor Jack Scarisbrick added: 'The strength of the case for experimentation clearly does not rest on the cogency of its moral arguments. It rests rather on rash and misleading claims that research on human embryos will lead to the relief of infertility and the overcoming of genetic disease.'

It is, of course, cruel nonsense to manipulate sufferers and their families with tales of cures. Sixty per cent of genetic diseases occur spontaneously, without any family history. Therefore the only way to ensure that no baby is born with a genetic disease would be through every couple planning children to have them by IVF.

IVF itself will fail in ninety per cent of cases. Dr Wagner of the World Health Organisation has published a study which shows that a higher incidence of miscarriage and a fourfold increase in perinatal death rates occurs with children conceived by IVF. The same study shows serious health risks of hypertension, bleeding, strokes and ovarian cancer to the mother. Women undergoing these procedures are rarely aware that they will be drugged to the point where they will superovulate, their embryos will be examined, and those considered superior selected for implantation. Those held to be inferior will be subject to invasive experimentation before being discarded.

Nor are many of those who give tentative support for these procedures always aware that when implantation leads to multiple births it is followed by what is euphemistically called 'selective reduction'. This means that surplus children produced by the process are stabbed to death with potassium chloride through the wall of the womb. What a paradox that these methods are justified as helping to create life when our clinics and hospitals, abattoirs and charnel houses, now destroy 600 unborn children daily, and when countless thousands of childless couples, who will never be able to have children even with IVF, would willingly provide them with loving and safe homes.

I am the first to admit that it would be double standards to argue for a pro-life approach but not to accept the corollary of increased provision for and acceptance of the single parent who bravely goes ahead with the birth of the child or for the parent who accepts that disability should not be a disbarment to life. But is it not also double standards, for instance, to argue for animal welfare, against capital punishment, and for penalties against child abusers when babies are literally dismembered in barbaric abortion procedures. From seven weeks' gestation the unborn child can feel pain and is writhing in agony during an abortion.

No anaesthetic is used on the unborn child during dilation and evacuation. A pliers-like instrument is inserted in the uterus, the baby's skull is crushed, its body broken, and it is removed piece by piece. In NHS hospitals the method known as prostaglandins is used. This involves the premature induction of labour and the baby is poisoned. It does not always work. At Carlisle General Hospital a baby was aborted at twenty-one weeks' gestation. The grounds for abortion were handicap, even though it was not certain that handicap was present. The aborted baby struggled for life for three hours before dying. It was then placed in a black sack and incinerated. Home Office Minister, Douglas Hogg, refused to order an inquest even though the County Coroner for Cumbria, in a letter to me, admitted that it would serve the public interest if such an inquest was held. The baby's birth was never registered nor was its death. As far as the law is concerned it never existed. The nurses on duty gave the baby a rudimentary baptism and because the chaplain voiced his disquiet about what had occurred his contract was not renewed.

I raised this matter in the Commons and my colleague, Ann Widdecombe, again raised the case in two debates which she initiated on June 8th, 1989, and on March 27th, 1990. She doggedly persisted during the April 24th, 1990, debate on the Human Fertilisation and Embryology Bill and pointed out that a reduction in the abortion time limit from twenty-eight weeks to twenty-four weeks would not have saved the Carlisle baby, or, indeed, a single one of the 184,000 babies aborted that year. In fact, the final decision, to extend the abortion time limit of the handicapped until birth actually made the position worse.

With the casting vote of the Deputy Speaker, Sir Paul Dean, the Commons also rejected our proposal that at least the nature of the disability be specified on the abortion authorisation form. Forcing doctors to specify skin disorders, club foot, cleft palate, etc. might at least expose the scandalous litany of reasons why abortions take place – although I have no doubt that many doctors would simply cite a mother's 'mental health' rather than admit the true reasons.

That many of these arguments were never even heard by the public is not surprising. The media grossly distorted the debate and Sir Bernard Braine had to write to the BBC complaining about news items prepared by supposedly objective reporters who, in reality, held and promoted their own highly subjective views. How often was a disabled person, holding pro-life views, asked to appear in reports to balance the views of those who said disability could be 'cured' by experiments? How often were proprietors of private clinics involved in making money, or a reputation, balanced by pro-life medics? How often were strident voices balanced by those of women who had been the victims of abortion? And does it not strike you as odd that virtually every known medical procedure has been shown on television, with the notable exception of abortion?

What the Future Holds

While the Human Fertilisation and Embryology Bill was before the House of Commons for consideration in April 1989 there were two graphic illustrations of where our anti-life mentality has taken us. They point bleakly to the future.

In Liverpool, a court was considering the case of a drunken driver who had mowed down an eight-month pregnant mother on a pedestrian crossing. The baby died. The judge instructed the jury that the unborn child did not count in law. The driver was given a three-month prison sentence and a £1 fine. Neither the Lord Chancellor nor Home Office Ministers, to whom representations were made, were prepared to hold an inquiry into this decision or to criticise the verdict.

Then there was the case of the King's College baby, one of a pair of twins. He had a chromosomal defect that would have left him impotent; in no way life threatening. Using the selective reduction procedure, described above, the baby was killed at twenty-seven weeks' gestation. A letter in *The Lancet* suggested that it might be better if these procedures were renamed 'pregnancy enhancement' as selective reduction – although an accurate medical description of precisely what takes place – had unfortunate connotations.

Cardinal Basil Hume, in a letter to the Duke of Norfolk in February 1989, eloquently described where our lack of respect for life is leading:

> Gene therapy and positive genetic engineering are not the stuff of science fiction but realities of the near future. It is ironic that when Dr Edwards began his work on IVF he found it difficult to obtain serious consideration for his proposals outside a limited circle of medical researchers. Theologians, amongst others, dismissed his programme as hypothetical nonsense. When we see how quickly events have overtaken systematic moral discernment, it is obvious that we must not allow such complacent inaction to occur again. If we do not unambiguously lay the foundations for the future protection of human dignity, integrity and responsibility, we are likely to stumble down the path of pragmatic short-term reactions to profoundly difficult questions. Unless we start laying those foundations now, we are in danger of falling, almost by inadvertence, into permitting deeply immoral solutions, or at best approaches which are incomplete or incoherent.[10]

Kenneth Clarke gave notice to Parliament that for the future the Department of Health intends to encourage the development of both experimental techniques and innovations for abortionism. Among these, he has allowed clinical trials to take place in Liverpool, in my constituency, of the

French abortion drug RU486. Commenting on this refined form of chemical warfare the French journal, *Le Quotidien du Medicine*,[11] has reported that Roussel, the manufacturer, has sent a circular to abortionists in France telling them that one heart attack and another cardiac anomaly have occurred in women after they have undergone an RU486 operation. The company also reported knowledge of more than 3000 further cases of 'less serious' side effects, stating that women must be assessed for risk of cardiac problems before taking the drug and the procedures must be tightened and that 'resuscitation equipment must be available and ready for use whenever the drug is administered'.

In the *Nursing Mirror*,[12] Professor Allen Templeton, head of obstetrics and gynaecology at Aberdeen University stated: 'The main problem [with RU486] was infrequent but severe haemorrhage.' Other problems included nausea, vomiting, diarrhoea, headaches, fever and infections. And *The Pharmaceutical Journal*[13] said that: ' . . . studies of women using RU486 have shown [they have] more guilt and regret than those using surgical methods.' One of the greatest challenges for the future will be how society provides healing and help for those women who have been falsely encouraged or pressurised into having an abortion – often by irresponsible men using their sexuality without a willingness to accept the consequences.

Unless we persevere with our opposition to current laws and attitudes, the future will hold out bleak prospects for handicapped and disabled people. Some of the most vocal advocates of ramps for wheelchairs at public buildings will be in the vanguard of urging the use of amniocentesis tests and chorionic vilus sampling (a method of testing for disability which can be carried out much earlier than amniocentesis) as the best way of dealing with handicap. Debbie Hill, whose disabled son Timothy died aged six months, said: 'In his short time with us, Timothy brought to us a great deal of love. Parents like us have a choice. They can decide whether or not to take the risk of having more children. But to conceive children on a sale-or-return basis is wholly wrong.'

Alison Davis, who runs the handicapped division of the

Society for the Protection of the Unborn Child, and who has spina-bifida, says of the tests: 'They are not prevention. It could not have resulted in me being born without spina-bifida. It would have resulted in me being washed down the laboratory sink at an early age.' The feminist writer, the late Ellen Wilkie, put the arguments in her own characteristic way in *A Pocketful of Dynamite*[14]:

> To abort someone on the grounds of disability is the first step on a very slippery slope. It opens the door to eugenic practices and there are many in our society who are eugenists quite unashamedly. If it is disabled babies today it will be babies with AIDS tomorrow. This is not ludicrous scaremongering . . . Even now it is considered anti-social for a mother to go ahead and have a disabled baby when she knows it is disabled. Such a baby is regarded as a drain on society's resources but many disabled people contribute far more to society than the average able-bodied football hooligan.

Ellen knew. She had muscular dystrophy. In her poem 'Theraputic Termination'[15] she reminds us that ultimately we will all be held to account for the massive destruction of created life:

> Though voiceless
> you will hear us
> though powerless
> we will triumph
>
> outside time
> in another place
> we join the ranks
> for confrontation face to face
>
> we are the ones
> who stand before you
> and demand
> a life before death.

In the future the pressures on parents to have the tests and to then abort will grow. It is not a flight of fancy to suppose that there will come a time when the only people who will give birth to disabled children will be Christians. This will not be because disability had been cured but because disabled people in their earliest form will have been destroyed.

Another challenge, as we confront the eugenic ethic, will be to turn the debate away from mere 'anti-abortionism' to a positive respect for life. Concern for the life of the unborn must be matched by our sensitivity and love for women with unexpected or problem pregnancies.

I am a national patron of the excellent LIFE organisation. It now has a network of a hundred LIFE offices and sixty LIFE houses where vulnerable women – and their babies – may receive practical help and care. Education, resources and practical care will be essential ingredients in an approach which is based on a respect for life, and the movement for Christian Democracy will want to apply pressure on Government to move away from remedies which place such a low value on the premium of life. There are many positive achievements to the credit of the pro-life movement which will continue while the legislative fight goes on. Each year 80,000 women are helped by LIFE, who have a tremendous team of unpaid women busily saving life. In Britain, this manifestation of people power – people determined not to buckle under despite incredible pressure – is a beacon of hope and inspiration. It demonstrates a revolutionary spirit of dissent when it would be so much easier to go with the crowd.

We must re-create the consensus which places a primacy on the right to life and which was broken in the 1960s. Many who should know better have been seduced by the egregious argument that 'Personally I am against abortion, or embryo experiments, but I believe women – or scientists – should have the right to choose'. While this argument has public relations appeal, closer analysis reveals it for what it is. Advocates of this position would never apply such logic to any other serious moral matter, such as racial harassment, child labour, sexual harassment, or racial or religious bigotry.

It would sound pretty bizarre for someone to announce, 'Personally, I am opposed to slavery, but I believe that people should have the right to choose.'

If we employed this approach to all our current social problems – drugs, child abuse, pornography – where would it leave us? We must confront society with the harsh reality that the 'freedom of choice' argument when applied equally to good and evil choices is senseless.

In 1967 the pro-abortion lobby dismissed as scaremongering that the legislation was the 'thin edge of the wedge'; that the legislation would lead to abortion on demand and ultimately to enthanasia. Abortion on demand is a *de facto* reality in Britain. In 1990 the first Bill to make euthanasia legal was introduced before the House of Commons. Although it was defeated this was only the opening salvo. The 1967 Abortion Act was the only conclusive one in a long line of Bills which had been introduced over the years.

Jane Hastings, one of CARE's research team, has provided me with some of the discussion papers already being circulated calling for euthanasia. In the *British Journal of General Practice* of March 1990, M.R. Bellis, a consultant geriatrician at Hackney Hospital in London, says:

> I hope that in future the rights of children to make decisions for their parents who are incapacitated by age or dementia will be so well recognised that 'living wills' will only need to be made by people who wish particular family members, or persons outside the family, to represent them; or if they wish for treatment which they feel their natural proxy might find difficult to support, for example, euthanasia . . . Perhaps it is not even too much to hope that in future the success of the NHS may be able to be measured in terms of a decreasing, rather than the present monotonously cited, increasing life expectancy.

We should not be surprised to hear these arguments being put forward by leading medics. This death-wishing is wholly consistent with our loss of respect for life at the other end of the spectrum.

A basic respect for life is part of a seamless garment. That garment is woven together with a common thread. Here is a concern for life, justice, care and worth. When you consider the degradation of life today – destruction of family life, isolation of the elderly, collapse of communities and of good neighbourliness, contamination and plunder of creation, and indifference to the world's hungry poor – you can see how that seamless garment has become a tatter of rags.

Unequivocally and unambiguously we must affirm the fundamental dignity of the unborn, the infirm, the disabled and the elderly. A respect for life encompasses all those who through poverty, famine or war do not have the essentials of life; it implies a disavowal of the relentless pursuit of violence through armed aggression, assault or attack.

As we have abandoned Judaeo-Christian belief in the sanctity of life, succumbed to the modern heresy of choice, and abased ourselves to the white-coated shamans of science, a respect for life has ceased to be a paramount consideration.

Chapter 7

Reconciliation

On a wet and windy day in September 1990 three identical statues were simultaneously unveiled in the British-Irish cities of Liverpool, Belfast and Glasgow. They were the work of a Liverpool sculptor, Stephen Broadbent, and symbolise, through an embracing couple, the need for reconciliation. Stephen Broadbent had been present at the Epiphany Group Meeting and is a member of the Movement for Christian Democracy.

Working from the abandoned cells of a disused police station in the inner city area of my Liverpool constituency, Stephen conceived the idea of a piece of work which might be sited in places of confrontation in the hope that it would foster a spirit of reconciliation. Together, we travelled to Belfast and over the course of two years Stephen won the support of the local authorities and gained business sponsors.

Two days before the official unveiling I was in Belfast again, and was delighted to see Stephen's work in place at North Belfast's Carlisle Circus. It seemed propitious that at their nearby home John and Mary Larkin had convened the first meeting of the Northern Ireland group of the Movement for Christian Democracy. Bringing together Evangelicals and Catholics – with their respective strengths – in a clear non-sectarian Christian commitment to politics, is a positive and practical move towards reconciliation.

The atheist will often point scornfully to Northern Ireland and say: 'See how these Christians love one another.' Religion has brought the sword instead of peace.

Whilst it is undoubtedly true that Northern Ireland remains a scandal both for Christianity and for a western Europe where coexistence has largely replaced bitter enmities, it is also the case that religion has had less and less to do with the tribalistic hatreds of Northern Ireland. That said, those who believe a secularist non-sectarian formula will provide the answer to the mistrust and hatred of successive generations misunderstand ninety per cent of the people of Northern Ireland. If bitter denominational rivalries are a part of the cause of the conflict, Christians will also have to be involved in providing its resolution. So, too, will nationalist and unionist, loyalist and republican, British and Irish.

Hiding Behind the Flag

Gladstone said that failure to achieve a British-Irish reconciliation was 'the one and only conspicuous failure of our political genius'. After the First World War Churchill commented that despite the upheaval of most of Europe the enmities of Northern Ireland remained firmly in place. Until we are prepared to make the leap of imagination which puts us into the other man's position, and puts us on to the other side of the divide, they will stay in place. Unless we enter into the insecurity, hurt, and history of the other players we will have no chance of understanding the origins or nature of the conflict. The temptation is to run away from this issue – it is easier to care about far-away places – to 'leave it to the Irish', or to hide behind worn-out slogans and clapped-out rhetoric about a 'United Ireland' or 'United Kingdom'. Neither position can lead to reconciliation because either way, one part of the community loses. Either way, someone will feel unable to wrap themselves in the other person's flag.

This is where the British-Irish cities, with their extraordinary mixture of culture, faith, and conflict, can teach one another a thing or two. Although Liverpool's Archbishop Worlock rightly points out that there are still plenty of examples of mindless conflict and division in Liverpool, the city can take great heart from the painful process of reconciliation personified by its three church leaders. Writing in the summer 1990 edition of *Corrymeela Link*, Ray Davey commented on this visit of Archbishop Worlock and Bishop Sheppard to Ballycastle, when they gave the 'Witness For Peace/Corrymeela Lecture'.

Davey says that the lasting memory was the 'very genuine relationship of respect, trust and friendship' between the two men. 'Surely here is a timely reminder for us to grasp again the potential of a personal relationship as a starting point, and a very natural one, in our divided society. It is the only way that trust, understanding and harmony can begin among us.' Davey was struck that for Worlock and Sheppard the Gospel was not something apart from the rest of life but an intimate ingredient in every aspect of life: 'Phrases that came through several times were "the importance of being with people" and "Willingness to be there".'

A Tale of Three Cities

From the bitter experiences of its sectarian past Liverpool's Christians have learnt how to coexist and how to co-operate on a whole range of issues. Glasgow, meanwhile, has turned around an image based on negatives. Belfast's planners and the Northern Ireland Housing Executive have radically improved the North's housing stock in ways which would make tenants in the overspill areas of the other two cities deeply envious. The three British-Irish cities can teach each other a great deal.

Material improvements pale, however, when viewed against the unending lists of casualties and deceased in Northern Ireland. By 1989, the twentieth anniversary of the present 'troubles', 2762 people had been killed, including 415 regular soldiers and 180 members of the Ulster Defence Regiment. There had been 30,000 shootings and more than 8000 explosions. Well over 250,000 lbs of explosives had been used and a further 200,000 lbs recovered. Ten thousand firearms had been siezed with more than one million rounds of ammunition. No one knows how much more remains in circulation.

Barely a day passes without a new story about another murder, bombing or shooting. Military chiefs say there is no military solution, but withdrawal of troops would simply lead to civil war. Political leaders play to their narrow constituencies and posture. At the time of writing the discussion is still about whether talks will take place between the politicians. Invariably, just as dialogue is about to commence, a new condition or prerequisite is discovered which must be met before talks may begin. The people of Northern Ireland deserve better than this.

Twin Houses of Hate

Speaking at Westminster, at the Parliamentary Christian Fellowship, the Catholic Archbishop of Armagh, the Right Reverend Dr Cahal Daly, made a deep and lasting impression on the parliamentarians who crowded into the Speaker's House to hear him. Bishop Daly – as he then was – said that 'secularised religion often retains the loyalties and passion of original belief'. He said that the common Gospel background and shared Christian experience of the people of Northern Ireland had to be reaffirmed. Quoting Bishop Berkeley,[1] he said that to be is to be perceived: that, in Northern Ireland, how something is perceived is more important than the reality.

On one side the increasing insecurity of the Protestant/Unionist community left it open to be easily influenced by extremists. Catholic republicans often held pseudo-nationalist views which were based on quasi-religious emotions and reactions. The nation, the cause, the rising – all were a parody of religion. Whilst this was 'a decidedly minority view it does very serious damage to the Catholic community in Northern Ireland'. Dr Daly told parliamentarians that 'Finding the right relationship between the Church and State needs Christian leadership and a Christian word spoken to it. To work to reconcile the people of our two communities is our bounden duty.'

Dr Daly compared the Protestant Christians of Northern Ireland who are engaged in the quest for reconciliation with the Confessing Church of pre-war Germany. No doubt alluding in this remark to their courage, let it not pass unnoticed that Dr Daly himself has been pilloried and attacked for courageously rebuking and condemning every manifestation of violence by the IRA and other paramilitary groups. He says that 'all physical violence, all verbal violence, is a betrayal. So is equivocation and ambiguity. Christians must be clear and absolute in their condemnation of violence.' It was Martin Luther King who said that 'violence creates bitterness in the survivors and brutality in the destroyers'. Nowhere is that more evident than in Northern Ireland.

In 1988, at Corrymeela, the Antrim-based centre for Christian renewal and reconciliation, Dr Daly had been equally outspoken in his description of the role played by Gerry Adams and Sinn Fein. He recalled that it was exactly twenty years since the civil rights marches: 'Sinn Fein's attempts to present themselves as the heirs of the civil rights movement is an abuse of history', and said that Gerry Adams had 'stolen the mantle of civil rights for their campaign of violence'. Progress in the North of Ireland was being thwarted by the twin obstacles of Sinn Fein violence and Unionist intransigence, he stated: 'both houses of hate are a plague on our society', and said that both sides must abandon any 'solution' that implied a victory for either side.

Finding the Right Relationship

I have no doubt that religion can be taught and organised in such a way as to intensify anxiety and evoke fear in fanatical adherents, rather than bring forth a charitable faith based on love. But this is a travesty and distortion of the Christian faith. In the Garden of Gethsemane Jesus rebuked the over-zealous Peter for physically attacking the soldiers who had come to seize him. Jesus went further and instantly healed the injured man.

During his visit to Ireland Pope John Paul II spelt out the implications of the Gethsemane story to his contemporary listeners as was widely reported in newspapers at the time:

> On my knees I beg you to turn away from the paths of violence and to return to the ways of peace. You may claim to

> seek justice. I, too, believe in justice and seek justice. But violence only delays the day of justice. Violence destroys the work of justice. Further violence in Ireland will only drag down to ruin the land you claim to love and the values you claim to cherish. In the name of God I beg you: return to Christ, who died so that men might live in forgiveness and peace. He is waiting for you, longing for each one of you to come to Him so that He say say to each of you: your sins are forgiven; go in peace.

The relationship which John Paul urged upon his audience is one based on reconciliation. Incitement to violence, the language of hatred, revenge, retaliation and conquest have no place in the vocabulary of the reconciler. Right relationships in Northern Ireland will require a clear repudiation of those who entice young people into the ways of violence and train them in the methods of the terrorist. I have been a regular visitor to Northern Ireland's prisons over many years and I never cease to be angry at the waste of lives: lives lost in the conflict and young lives wasted through years of incarceration.

Although I have met a few prisoners who have renounced violence – some of whom have even become Christians – the vast majority simply fester away feeding one another the old lies about the means justifying the ends. The Church – especially Catholics – must give no succour to leaders who train young people in these violent ways; who falsely proclaim that courage and strength consist in killing, bombing and destroying. It must encourage a full and wholehearted commitment to the service of life: a love of life, a respect for life, and a generous giving of self to the service of life. When it succeeds in doing this the relationships will come right.

Because of shared Gospel values the challenge for Christians from the reformed Protestant tradition is just the same. The Reverend Cecil Kerr, a Church of Ireland Minister, and his wife Myrtle, became, with their three children, founder members of the Rostrevor Christian Renewal Centre. Along with Rostrevor, the Reverend Ray Davey and the Reverend Dr John Morrow's Corrymeela, Father Neil Carlin's St

Columba's House, in Derry, and the integrated Christian School at Laggan, are four of the most hopeful places which I have visited in Northern Ireland. They are also evidence of the growing ministry for reconciliation and healing. In *Just a Moment*,[2] Cecil Kerr says:

> We long for peace in our troubled world. We pray for peace in our broken land. We desire peace in our hearts when all around us there is violence, bitterness and hatred. We can only have real peace when we allow the Prince of Peace to reign and rule in our hearts and lives. I cannot bring peace to others if I am myself a walking battlefield.

In their document *Choose Life*[3] the Inter-Church Group on Faith and Politics makes a declaration of faith and commitment. The Group is sponsored by Corrymeela, the Glencree Centre for Reconciliation and the Irish School of Ecumenics. Within six months of its publication some 34,000 copies of their declaration had been distributed.

They say:

> The whole of creation belongs to God. All human beings are made in God's image. All human life is sacred. Therefore:- we believe that all our land belongs to God: not to Unionists or Nationalists. All of us have to live in it and share it together. We believe that all human life is sacred. All Christians must recognise that murder is evil by whomsoever and for whatsoever reason it is committed. The sin of murder is shared by those who co-operate in it whether before, during or after its execution . . . our differences are no excuse for refusing to seek reconciliation with God and with each other.

The Churches need not wait on events to start getting their relationships right. Catholicism has been over-identified with Gaelic/Nationalist culture. Northern Irish Protestantism has been over-identified with the Unionist ascendency and with the Orange Order. The Church's concern must be with the whole of society.

When the Church fails to seek reconciliation it ceases to be a Sign of God's Kingdom. While locked in division it cannot reflect the Kingdom and without bold manifestations of Christian love no one will take its mission seriously. In places such as Limavady[4] where the Presbyterian Minister, David Armstrong, did reach out across the divide it was not without a price. He was spat at, ostracised and rejected. Churches who claim the Cross of Christ know only too well that the Cross is not a symbol of success, but of pain and rejection. Yet death on the Cross was the precursor for total renewal.

The Church must own up to its share of the blame for what has happened in the North of Ireland. It will have to learn how to pray and worship together. It may find the starting point for co-operation (as in Liverpool) will be most easily discovered in working for commonly agreed values (e.g. social justice, respect for life, and active compassion towards the needy). Certainly, one of the most fruitful meetings which I have ever addressed in Northern Ireland was in November 1987 at the Europa Hotel in Belfast, when 800 Catholic and Protestant people came together to consider safeguards for the unborn child. Politicians, including Rhonda Paisley (Democratic Unionist Party, Protestant), Eddie McGrady, MP, (Social Democratic and Labour Party of Northern Ireland, Catholic) and the Reverend Martin Smyth, MP, (Ulster Unionist, Protestant), joined me on the platform. The meeting was opened in prayer by a Catholic and a Presbyterian clergyman.

The Church will also need to understand the source of violence and understand what sustains it – as well as condemning it – if it wants to be taken seriously in the work of reconciliation. In 1987, at a meeting I organised at the last annual assembly of the Liberal Party, Liam McCloskey told us that Catholics had to understand that they were being taught a version of history which excluded all reference to the atrocities committed against Protestants. This was a remarkable statement: McCloskey had been the last hunger striker at Long Kesh Prison. A former member of the Irish National

Liberation Army (INLA), he was part of the dirty protest and began his strike after the death of hunger-striker Bobby Sands in 1981. McCloskey starved himself for fifty-five days before being taken off the strike after his mother and Fr Neil Carlin had intervened. He later renounced violence, and after he had been moved to Magilligan Prison he risked his own life by exposing an attempt to kill a prison warder. With Neil Carlin he has subsequently been involved in seeking reconciliation and healing. He says that neither side understands the grievances of the other.

The Church – especially Catholics – should also encourage their schools to be more open and objective in the teaching of both history and faith. As a patron of the Belfast Trust (which encourages integrated Christian education[5]) I went to Stormont Castle to see Northern Ireland Education Minister, Brian Mawhinney, to encourage him to support integrated education in a policy which has upset some members of the Catholic hierarchy. Following this meeting in 1987 I spent an hour at Maynooth trying to convince the late Cardinal Tomas O Fiach of the merits of integrated education – without any notable success. I also held talks with Dr Cahal Daly and Bishop Edward Daly. Whilst I understand and share the fears of Catholics that the secularisation of education would deny thousands of parents and children access to Christian schooling, integrated schools need not be part of this process. Indeed, all the more reason actively to participate in Christian-inspired integrated ventures (such as Laggan College), to appoint chaplains, and to bring without fear the Catholic strengths to these schools. Fear is holding back parts of the Church.

The hierarchy of the Church must understand that the Holy Spirit works through Catholics as well as Protestants; that no one has exclusive rights over the Spirit; that confessional articles in the Republic's constitution are perceived as bolstering the position of one Church over another and are an impediment to building Christian trust; and that Christian marriages between Catholic and Protestant are not in any way inferior. Above all, there will need to be some real Christian forgiveness and repentance if we are going to see renewal and get the relationships right.

Getting the Politics Right

In his letter to the Ephesians the Apostle Paul says:

> Christ is the peace between us, and has made the two into one and broken down the barrier which used to keep them apart, actually destroying in his one person the hostility caused by the rules and decrees of the Law. This was to create one single New Man in himself out of the two of them.[6]

Any fantasising about a New Ireland and any political initiative in Northern Ireland which fails to take into account the spiritual and deeply-held beliefs of its people will have only limited impact. Ireland's Christian heritage must be turned to its advantage and reflected in its politics. Just as Adenauer brought together Protestant and Catholic in post-war Germany's Christian Democratic Union and just as Dutch Protestants and Catholics (with an equally bitter past) successfully came together ten years ago in Holland's Christian Democratic Appeal, the same will need to happen in Northern Ireland. Nor is this a distant pipe dream.

In the context of Dublin's Dail, or the Westminster Parliament, it might seem an impossibility that Seamus Mallon or John Hume of the SDLP and Official Unionists, Jim Molyneaux and Martin Smyth, could be members of the same party. But, almost unnoticed, this is precisely what has already happened at the European Parliament.

In September 1990, in Strasbourg, I met Jim Nicholson, the Ulster Unionist MEP for Northern Ireland. Before Nicholson's election in 1989, his predecessor, John Taylor (also a Westminster MP), had briefly taken up membership of the European People's Party (the Christian Democrats). Nicholson applied for membership of the group – where he sits with Irish MEPs from Fine Gael – including the former leader of the Alliance Party in Northern Ireland, John Cushnahan, now MEP for Munster, and Pat Cooney, the formidable and well-respected Leinster lawyer, a former

Irish Justice Minister and past Chairman of the Fine Gael group in the Irish Senate. So, as part of the same political group in Europe, Catholic and Protestant men and women, sharing a common Christian and democratic belief, are already working with one another.

In 1988 in *What Kind of Country?*[7] I expressed the view that

> The future cannot consist of rabble-rousing marches and displays of triumphalism . . . a fundamental political choice now faces Northern Ireland . . . Unionists can now create a relationship with their fellow citizens, a relationship which recognises the legitimacy of the two traditions and the need to share power and responsibility.

The Unionist will continue to look towards Westminster and the Nationalist to Dublin. For the future, both can look towards Europe – something the Northern Consensus Group[8] recognised in their paper, 'Untying the Knot', in February 1990.

Christian Democracy can be both a healing and stimulating influence in the context of British-Irish affairs. Arguably, after the disintegration of the Iron Curtain mending the rifts between Great Britain and Ireland could be its greatest challenge. With its emphasis on the human personality and the importance of community and family life, with its belief in a Creator and the implications which flow from this in the making of law, and with its profound respect for life, Christian Democracy will have enormous appeal throughout Ireland.

Christian Democrats would see any attempt to make an absolute out of political structures or ideology as idolatry. Their allegiance is to Christ. They recognise that the political claims of republicanism or loyalism, socialism, conservatism, or liberalism, must be subordinate to the Kingdom of God. The failure of socialism to take root in Ireland lends support to the proposition that Irish outlook will be especially responsive to Christian Democracy.

In a talk to the Cork University Legal Society, in February

1989, I said that people had been duped into believing that the political choices consisted of the Scylla and Charybdis of redundant socialism and uncaring monetarism. On even the most generous reading of Irish history socialist activism has been at the margins of Irish political life for the last sixty years – and socialist thought has been virtually non-existent. The first Irish socialist, William Thompson, had been born in Cork in 1775. Influenced by Jeremy Bentham and by Robert Owen, Thompson correctly observed that enforced competition can corrupt human relations and bring spiritual suffering. He also said that over-centralisation is both tyrannical and inefficient. Not a bad description of the socialist states of the twentieth century; and of the present-day position of European Christian Democrats, with their emphasis on subsidiarity.

At the time, Thompson's ideas took little root in Ireland. It was not until the late nineteenth century that socialist thought emerged in a more militant guise. The Marxist Fenians erected their own socialist standard. Michael Davitt had sown the seeds following his arrival from Lancashire in the 1870s.[9] James Connolly had imbibed his socialism in the slums of Edinburgh and Jim Larkin was the son of an Irish emigrant from Liverpool.[10] None of these essentially alien ideas took root. In the first elections to the Dail in 1922 of the 128 seats contested, Labour won only seventeen. As in the United States of America since 1917 socialism has been on the margins. Instead, both Fine Gael and Fianna Fail developed an essentially Irish outlook and their policy differences have been more about application than about ideology. In the North, the Social Democratic and Labour Party had its roots in the Nationalist Party and within its ranks are Social Democrats, Liberals and Christian Democrats. Many of its voters would recoil at the notion of supporting the objectives of the socialist group in Europe to which it has become affiliated. It was significant that Mary Robinson did not use the socialist label and played down Labour Party support when she successfully contested the 1990 Irish Presidential election.

Amongst Unionists there exists also a variety of political

views and although MPs such as the late Harold McCusker could, in quieter and politically normal times, have happily found a home in the British Labour Party, Unionists would regard socialism with suspicion. Their link with the British Conservative Party was made when Gladstone's Liberal Party embraced Home Rule in the 1880s. Lord Randolph Churchill played the 'Orange Card'[11] and for reasons of mutual convenience and self-preservation Unionism and Conservatism supported one another until the 1970s. The Anglo-Irish Agreement finally severed any reasons for links based on expediency and Mrs Thatcher's Conservative Government came high on the list of Unionist demonology.

The British Labour Party does not contest elections in Northern Ireland and although there is no formal accord between the SDLP, the Irish Labour Party and the British Labour Party, they all sit in the socialist group of the European Parliament. In the event of a 'hung' or balanced, Parliament after the next UK elections the three SDLP MPs would back a Labour Government (and might even enter it as Ministers in the Northern Ireland Office). The Unionists would trade their support for the suspension of the Anglo-Irish Agreement and although there is a 1970s precedent for Labour striking a deal with the Unionists over additional seats in Northern Ireland, I do not believe that this time there would be any takers. However, it is worth remembering that in the 1880s Parnell's Home Rule Party dominated the British Parliament by virtue of its balancing position within it.

In 1988 I helped to seal the agreement between the British Liberal Party, the Alliance Party of Northern Ireland and the Republic's Progressive Democrats, who all have membership of the Liberal Democratic and Reform Group of the European Parliament (although there are only two MEPs, both from the Republic). Each of the parties is secular in outlook and has made an honest contribution to the political debate. Their political positions will inevitably limit their appeal to a tiny share of the electorate.

Ireland's Fine Gael – previously led by Dr Garret Fitzgerald – already campaigns under the title of Christian

Democrats. Within the European Parliament they sit with the Official Unionist, Jim Nicholson. Two of their MEPs, John Cushnahan and Pat Cooney arranged a series of high level meetings in Strasbourg in September 1989 between the Movement for Christian Democracy and leading European Christian Democrats. Cushnahan's has been one of the clearest and most consistent voices arguing for reconciliation in Northern Ireland, while Cooney's integrity and coherent approach to politics has made him a widely respected figure in Irish and European politics. His approach to 'respect for life' issues, for instance, has led him strongly and staunchly to oppose the IRA paramilitaries. He addressed the Movement's Rally held in London in November 1990.

In 1964, on the eve of his entry into politics, Dr Garret Fitzgerald expressed his vision of Ireland in Europe:

> The sense of nationality enjoyed by Irish people in such a society would be simply pride in their country and their roots in it, and in the society of which they form a part. It would be neither narrow nor exclusive, containing no hatred of any other country, nor passion for revenge or self-assertion. This local loyalty would be accompanied by a sense of belonging to Europe, and by a sense of inter-dependence with the rest of the world.[12]

Mary Robinson said much the same thing after her 1990 election victory. By 1972 in *Towards a New Ireland* Fitzgerald was able more clearly to define that vision by arguing that commitment to faith would shape Ireland's politics: 'The strength of the religious tradition in Ireland, however distorted it may have been by bigotry and intolerance, adds a dimension to Irish society that is lacking in Britain.' He adds that Irish society 'is much more intensely personal in its orientation than society in Britain' and that Ireland will never be a miniature reflection of Britain because politics will 'be tempered by their deeply-rooted system of Christian values'. Looking towards Europe, Fitzgerald says that there is

> among believing Christians a growing sense of Christian

> solidarity against neo-paganism. The sectarian differences of the past have come to seem increasingly irrelevant to Christians in many European countries as these Christians have become an embattled minority, more conscious of what they share in common than what divides them.

Prophetically he adds that in Northern Ireland the passage of time will give rise to a new cleavage 'between Christians and non-Christians, which may eventually come to seem a lot more relevant and important than the traditional Protestant/Catholic confrontation.[13]

Within Ireland the validity of different traditions – Ulster Scots, Anglo-Irish, non-Gaelic urban and Gaelic rural – must all be recognised and given voice in its institutions and forms of Government. Cross-fertilisation of these traditions has been a great deal more common than the occupants of the besieged fortresses would sometimes care to admit. I remember meeting the former Fianna Fail Speaker of the Dail, Jim Tuney, at Corrymeela in 1988. He told me that as a boy, my mother, born in the West of Ireland, had taught him his Irish. I am a Cockney representing a Liverpool constituency. Many similar links show how absurd it is to say our islands have nothing in common.

British-Irish politics, set in Europe, can give way to a pluralism and reconciliation impossible in the straitjacket of a purely British or Irish non-solution. In a talk at the Ulster town of Lisburn in 1989, I argued that Northern Ireland – and Europe generally – needs a system of politics which does not see everything in terms of the victors and the vanquished.

Any enlightened view of human nature must surely address the unresolved tensions which are always seeking reconciliation; each of us is both competitive and co-operative; personal and social; self-seeking and altruistic. Any single view ideology, whether untramelled laissez-faire, or Marxism, which tries to deny half our nature will cramp our individual and our common life. The Christian would also admit that each of us also has the attributes of both Martha and Mary – the spiritual and the practical – and we neglect one to the detriment of the other.

A wise administration would recognise that democratic self-government ultimately depends upon voluntary association, people coming together, as nature intended, to work out a common future. It would also see that a waste land of arid and sterile political slogans and postures, devoid of authentic human values, is worthless.

In his *Dialogue for Peace*[14] Cahal Daly says, 'The problem in Northern Ireland is fundamentally a political one. It is the problem of establishing credible institutions of government able to win the allegiance and merit the trust of both communities.' The security problem mirrors this.

True Security

Security operations, just like the legitimate pursuit of politics, require the confidence of both parts of the community and must respect the rule of law. Where politics is perverted by violence and where the security service is perverted by illegal actions it is confidence undermined and reconciliation jeopardised. The Stalker Affair, the cases of Annie Maguire and the Guildford Four, and the case of the Birmingham Six – all of which I raised in Parliament – illustrate how not to win the trust of an already hostile and alienated community.

In 1985 the Donaldson Commission, of which I was a member, published its report 'What Future for Northern Ireland?' We proposed the creation of a Joint Security Commission, with consultative and deliberative powers. We also called for the phasing out of the clearly sectarian Ulster Defence Regiment and for a greater Catholic commitment to recruitment to the RUC. There is more support than either side would have us believe for such propositions. A Mori/Weekend TV poll, conducted in 1984, showed that combined patrols of British and Irish police and troops on both sides of the border were acceptable to the majority (51 per cent of Protestants and 56 per cent of Catholics; unacceptable to 38 per cent of Protestants and 25 per cent of Catholics).

I would go further and advocate the abolition of the Diplock Courts – where one Judge sits alone without a jury – and whilst I recognise that until there is stability, jury trials are not practical, why could terrorist trials not be handled on both sides of the border by a mixture of Irish and British judges? Or, as with politics, maybe a European option could be explored, using the European Court and a system of examining magistrates. Legislation such as the Emergency Powers provisions and Anti-Terrorist laws are presented by the IRA and their American apologists as anti-Irish legislation promoted by the British. These laws should be jointly enacted by the Dail and Westminster and jointly enforced. It would remove another propaganda tool from the IRA if such legislation was also incorporated into European law.

Reconciliation: A Message For All

One of the British groups which works for reconciliation, and has a special ministry in Northern Ireland, is Maranatha. It was founded jointly by Monsignor Michael Buckley and Denis Wrigley. Denis is a Methodist lay preacher and a lifelong Liberal. He attended the foundation meeting of the Epiphany Group and spoke at the Westminster Chapel Youth Day (see Chapter 4). I was very struck by a story which he told me arising out of that meeting. A young man who had harboured a longterm enmity for his brother had heard Denis talk about the need for reconciliation and healing in our broken lives. He left the meeting early to go and find his estranged brother, who lived in Croydon. His brother attacked him, violently assaulting him. The young man did not give up and when he returned the following day the second meeting culminated in his older brother bandaging up his wounds.

In the world of politics – and I suspect it is generally true – conflicting aims and ambitions frequently lead to conflict and confrontation. Here in the United Kingdom, especially, we have a very adversarial system of politics, which makes a virtue of rubbishing opponents and pitting one party against another. Britain generally pours scorn on the 'weak' systems of Europe where a party's strength is a true reflection of votes cast and where consequently parties have to learn to coexist and to co-operate. The notion that ours is the strong system and theirs the weak is laughable. More seriously, our parliamentary cockpit deters political consensus and etches deep divisions into our political life. Is it, therefore, any wonder that party politicians spend their time talking about eliminating their opponents rather than working with them; and about implementing their brand of dogma (never supported by or voted for by a majority of people), rather than working out a common programme for government? It is a system which lacks sophistication. It leads to instability and lack of continuity. By reinforcing division it also makes the job of healing the country's deep divisions that much harder.

Sinn Fein means 'We Ourselves Alone'. Many of our political leaders in Britain could take this as their own personal motto. We will all hold on to our strongly-held convictions. Standing up for your beliefs may well bring you to different conclusions from others. That is how it should be. A strong democracy can cope with diversity and should rejoice in it, not try to suppress it. But those who refuse to reach out and work with others from different political traditions will impede the work of reconciliation. They will also deserve to be ridiculed when they tell the Irish that the remedy is partnership and co-operation. Reconciliation is for everyone.

Chapter 8

Empowerment

In the last chapter we considered the importance of seeking reconciliation in divided societies and in divided lives. The achievement of this objective will often require a total change and softening of heart. Metanoia can only be achieved when old grievances have been set to one side and human fallibility and weakness admitted. Old allegiances must be critically re-examined and risks taken in opening ourselves to others. It is always easier to stay with the tribe, to play to the gallery, or to stay silent when speaking out requires a price. Such change or metanoia is the highest form of liberation and the truest form of empowerment. The Christian believes that such a change of heart is open to all.

Empowerment for the Christian cannot be about the pursuit of personal power. All authority derives from God and therefore the exercise of political power must be exercised in obedience and with responsibility. Self-seeking and personal ambition attempt to turn man himself into God. This distorts the use of power which instead of being used for the service of others becomes a weapon, ultimately leading to megalomania and totalitarianism. Concentrations of power are inimical to the true development of communities and the human personality. European Christian Democrats coined the term 'subsidiarity' to express their belief that all decisions should be taken at the lowest levels possible. In Britain, over the past decade, we have witnessed the peculiar phenomenon of a government providing a range of economic policies aimed at increasing individual choice, while simultaneously taking more and more power for itself. This emphasis on strong central control clashes directly with the Christian Democrat concepts of empowerment and dispersal of power; just as the cult of individualism clashes with Christian Democrat belief in the human personality.

How We See People

Gladstone said, 'Trust in the people'. He upheld the belief that democracy had its roots in Christian anthropology and therefore that each man and woman was a social and ethical person. Because they are made in the image of God they will always have it in them to transcend the earthly. Although, when justifying their Manchester School free market economics it suits the twentieth century free marketeers to lay claim to the Gladstonian mantle, they conveniently overlook Gladstone's belief that we are more than mere individuals.

The Christian Democrat thinkers, Jacques Maritain and Emmanuel Mounier, developed the ideas of personalism which in the 1930s began to link the disparate Christian Democratic movements of Europe. Maritain coined the phrase 'theocentric humanism' to underline basic respect for human dignity which permeates their political ideas. Personalism made possible an awareness of the anthropological and political limits of the contrasting historical models of individualism and socialism. More and more people are recognising that individualism alone is not enough, and that State domination is deeply corrosive of human dignity. An approach which emphasises the rediscovery of the meaning of the person and a new justification of what it means to be human provides a political language and praxis which goes beyond the old models.

This view of people emphasises the need for responsibility for critical self-analysis and examining institutions. Personal responsibility should lie at the heart of our claim to share in political power. This must hold true in democratic organisations, in professional associations and trades unions, and in faithful service to the vulnerable and needy. Hence, the whole concept of a Charter for Human Responsibility, being outlined in these pages.

Because of a basic antipathy towards regimentation, uniformity and oppression – which can happen when the State, the Church, a Party or an economic bloc accumulates too much power and becomes dominant – the human personality needs to be enabled to share in power and responsibility. These are the principles of subsidiarity and autonomy.

The Dutch Christian Democrat, Arie Oostlander, MEP, in *Politics Based on Christian Consciousness*[1] argues that 'the basic disposition of Christian-Democracy is anti-totalitarian and has developed two related and complementary societal structural principles, namely those of subsidiarity and autonomy'. What does this mean and how might it work out in practice?

Subsidiarity is a concept which comes from Catholic social teaching and philosophy. It points to the necessity of a division of power and competencies among various bodies at different levels. The responsibilities of the lower levels of government will always have priority. Only when justice, solidarity or effectiveness requires it should matters be determined at a higher level of decision making. This idea is being worked out in practice in Christian base communities.

The Protestant concept of autonomy refers to the necessity of acknowledging the qualitative difference between governmental power and social organisations. So, the State should not therefore subsume areas of society over which it does not need to have control. Similarly, the State guards against the domination of economic interests over social life, politics or culture and opposes the subjection of society to Church control. This pluralist approach recognises that each sphere of life has its own objective, its own character, its own autonomy and its own rights: each to be exercised with a sense of responsibility.

As we seek to empower the people of Britain it should be against this background of subsidiarity and autonomy.

While the human personality and the community in which it lives are the core of our approach, there must also be an emphasis on the interdependence of human beings and communities. This, surely, is the framework for a responsible society.

Freeing People

In 1989 Paul Mills of the Cambridge-based Jubilee Centre produced a paper entitled 'Interest in Interest: The Old Testament Ban on Interest and Its Implications For Today'.[2] There is probably no other measure more likely to empower and liberate communities and individuals than the abolition of interest. Equally, one of the most destructive pressures on human personalities and their families is the accumulation of massive debt.

During the House of Commons debate in the 1990 Budget,[3] I said that debt is insidious and destructive, and gave instances where crippling debts and unrepayable loans had led to disastrous consequences for family life and marriages. In 1989 2 million households found themselves falling behind with mortgage payments and taking together their other arrears their total debt amounted to £2.9 billion. Our nation of savers – who for hundreds of years had accepted the conventional wisdom of staying out of debt – have become a nation of debtors and borrowers. It is yet another example of Britain aping America: the trouble is, when America sneezes, Britain catches a cold.

The National Society for the Prevention of Cruelty to Children cites debt as a key stress factor in cases it had dealt with. Another survey showed that debt leads to emotional and physical problems, ranging from feelings of isolation to marital break-up and to suicidal tendencies. The Office of Fair Trading says that 3.6 million feel over-committed with credit, 4.5 million have had difficulty in the past five years with repayments, and 8.2 million have taken up commitments that they now regret. Meanwhile greedy moneylenders and loan sharks have been charging usurous rates of interest. One court case in Birmingham involved action against a borrower who had received money at an extortionate annual percentage rate of interest of 1,192 per cent.

As all of us who have a post box know, regular and inordinate rises in interest rates have not stopped enticing offers of new loans and easy credit facilities dropping daily through the letter box. Advertising simply stimulates further demand for more credit. Advertisers have obviously never heard the prayer 'lead us not into temptation'. Over £80 million was spent last year on promoting consumer credit on television.

A glance at the interest rates charged by some of the big High Street stores, with their own credit arrangements, during one typical week in 1990 illustrates the scale of the problem. Even allowing for their handling charges compare these rates of interest against High Street bank rates: John Lewis was charging 23.8 percent, Habitat 34.4 per cent, Marks and Spencer 34.5 per cent, and Next 39.9 per cent. Credit cards, during the same week, ranged from 22.4 per cent on Lloyds Gold Card (plus a £30 annual fee), to 31.3 per cent on the TSB Trustcard/Visa.

The institutions balance debt and investment and every bank and building society actively promotes credit. Their managers are given targets to see how many more people they can entice. In 1991 £49.6 billion is owed in Britain in consumer debt.

Lenders should ask themselves whether it is responsible to advertise and promote credit; whether it is right to encourage people to borrow, and to persuade a person to get into debt. Not only do I believe that woe will betide those who knowingly bring harm to others but also I feel we must to some extent actively be our brother's keepers – not the Nanny State but a responsible society.

Furthermore, lenders should also ask themselves whether it is right to set interest rates to maximise profits for their investors. Usury has become acceptable because the lender never meets the borrower. We are cushioned by the institutions. You never get to meet the man behind the Access Card. With consumer education, and responsible lending rather than aggressive lending, it will be possible to create a different relationship with money.

Freeing Money

In his fascinating paper on interest, already referred to, Paul Mills says that 'a ban on interest deserves more serious consideration . . . interest on consumption loans is inherently uncharitable whilst interest upon commercial loans is inherently presumptuous'. The alternative would be hire charges and profit-sharing relationships.

From a Christian point of view it is worth recalling that until about the year 1500 the Church had always opposed the use of interest. The early Church saw it as uncharitable and greedy and equated it with theft. The Church in the Middle Ages saw interest as inherently unjust but gradually outright opposition was replaced with qualifications, and Calvin rejected the view that interest was wrong *per se*. In modern society Mills points out that Christians rarely think twice about lending or borrowing money at interest. Of course, the truth is that for most of us there are few alternatives if we want to buy a house, own a car, or establish a business. A return to a clear biblical view might liberate the millions of people and communities now locked into a cycle of unremitting debt. It would also challenge the whole basis of Western capitalist economic thinking and create an economy which serves the human personality and communities instead of enslaving them.

Mills makes the point that modern society has drawn a distinction between usury and interest. However, usury initially referred to any charge made for the use of property, be it money, land or possessions. Therefore, rent on land or charges for objects could be described as usury as well as any charge made for a loan of money. Interest referred to payments made on a loan of money that acted as compensation to the lender for making the loan and interest payments were designed to ensure that the lender suffered no loss for engaging in the transaction. Under the euphemism 'interest' in contemporary society such compensatory payments amount to usury in its original sense.

The neo-classical view of interest sees the function of interest rate movements as being to bring saving and investment, and lending and borrowing into line with one another. Interest rates can ration funds but the social usefulness of borrowing is not the determining factor in deciding on priorities for loans. People who can invest most profitably and those who have the greatest time to see a return on their investment are the beneficiaries of this approach.

In his book *The General Theory of Employment, Interest and Money*,[4] Keynes argues that interest should not reward those who simply wait around and see their savings grow as a reward for non-consumption. Instead, interest was needed to stimulate wealth holders to part with their money rather than hoard it. Keynes believed interest rates which were set too high could be the cause of chronic unemployment and depression. He identified with the school of thought which advocated the abolition of financial return without effort, particularly from other people's debts.[5] Keynes held that it would take one or two generations to accumulate such capital to the extent that the rate of interest would fall to zero. In 1936 he said this would lead to 'euthanasia of the rentier'. Not since the 1940s has the institution of interest been questioned. The battle lines are now drawn around the issue of whether the government can and should attempt to set the rate of interest and the best means of doing so. Price inflation usually determines its chosen course of action.

Christian economists have, within the last few years, been returning to these neglected questions. Donald Hay[6] says that within the community of Israel: 'There are no returns on resources without a direct exercise of stewardship responsibilities in deciding the use to which they were to be put.'

Alan Storkey, in his visionary work, *Transforming Economics*,[7] sets out the case for relational economics and for a new view of economic structures:

> Relational questions are treated as 'externalities'. Yet clearly our day-to-day economic lives and decisions do

> have a profound effect on other people, and it is quite legitimate to take these effects into account when making decisions. We are our brother's and our sister's keeper.
>
> The fundamental biblical interpersonal commandment, 'You shall love your neighbour as yourself', creates the basis for another frame of reference. And it is not an abstract framework, but involves all kinds of detailed interpersonal norms which define how we are to treat one another justly in economic activity. Some of these, such as the prohibition of stealing, are widely accepted. Others, such as coveting, and the usury laws, are widely ignored. Yet they provide a coherent basis for looking at economic relationships.

Dr Michael Schluter[8] and C. J. H. Wright,[9] have both argued that the Old Testament law on interest should be seen as a model, or paradigm, for contemporary Christian social ethics. Mills develops these arguments, saying that the law is a model to be emulated, not slavishly applied, and to be set in the context of both the times and other laws. Schluter sees the Bible as prohibiting all interest because: a) it undermines kinship relationships; b) concentrates power through the concentration of finance capital; and c) leads to the growth of wide disparities in income and wealth.

Of course, it is one thing to point to the corrosive and damaging effects of interest on families, communities and developing countries, and quite another to provide a satisfactory alternative. A 'relationist' model would be based on the elimination of all returns on monetary loans and the legitimising of hire and rental charges and the financing of commercial investment through profit-share arrangements. At various points in their history, rabbinic, Christian and Islamic schools of thought have each embraced these concepts. N. M. Siddiqi in *Banking Without Interest*[10] sets out the Qu'ranic teaching and the basis for the Sharia, the Islamic concept of interest-free banking. Where interest-free banks have been established in the Islamic world they have performed as well, if not better, than their interest-based competitors. Often, though, interest rates have merely been concealed under the guise of arrangement fees and transaction costs.

We would need to start with an interest-free bank. If such a bank operated on the basis of moral law it could neither lend nor borrow with returns unrelated to the profitability of the use to which such funds were put or which did not constitute a hire charge for the use of property. The working principle of such a bank is partnership. When money capital is provided for commercial investment, any profit or loss is shared on a pre-specified proportionate basis. In addition, the bank can also engage in commodity and share trading, it can finance real estate purchases or engage in leasing equipment or property. When a depositor designates his deposit for investment purposes, it is added to the bank's overall portfolio and allocated a share of any profit or loss that the bank makes on its investments.

Essentially this is the unit trust principle, with the non-interest bank diversifying and distributing its investments so as to minimise the potential for loss.

The bank could use a proportion of its demand deposits for investment purposes and so be able to make current accounts available to its customers with few charges. If this practice became widespread the central bank would need to specify reserve requirements and provide a 'lender of last resort' facility to maintain public confidence – and to prevent any losses within the bank's portfolio from affecting its ability to honour current-account liabilities. The alternative model would involve the bank holding transaction deposits in cash and highly liquid assets, or using a proportion to provide interest-free short-term overdrafts to its profit-share borrowers.

The interest-free banking arrangements would be undergirded by parallel forms of finance. For instance, retailers' interest-free credit offers could be financed by banks who took a share of the retailers' extra profit arising from the additional custom generated. These forms of consumption finance would need to be complemented by interest-free loan funds provided for poverty relief and financed by local taxation or a proportion of bank current accounts.

The housing market would operate on the basis of the bank purchasing the property, letting it to residents who pay in excess of the market rent whenever they wish to or on a contractual basis. Gradually they then acquire an ownership share in the property, or they can finance intermediaries to do this on a profit-share basis. Millions of home owners caught up in crippling mortgage repayments, influenced more by the international money market than by the housing market, would find this alternative extremely attractive.

In the public sector finance would be available on a profit-share basis or the State could float marketable shares. Projects with no financial viability and those geared to current expenditure would have to be financed through taxation. The discipline of having to produce balanced budgets would be a downward pressure on inflation and ensure fiscal policies which do not irresponsibly encumber future generations with massive burdens of debt. By tying the money supply to the value of transactions the monetary system would have little intrinsic ability to create money.

One of the arguments used by those with a vested interest in manipulating money is that if interest were abolished it would massively reduce savings. Many people save, not for returns, but for future security or a future ability to spend. In any event profit-share arrangements do not eliminate returns: this might actually stimulate greater saving.

There is nothing to stop churches or voluntary organisations from establishing interest-free loans within congregations and for local communities – this has always been done by synagogues. If sufficient capital is not forthcoming, low-interest credit unions should be promoted. Bo Tsang of the Merseyside Credit Union Development Agency tells me that twenty-five credit unions are now established on Merseyside – with 40,000 people nationwide having joined almost 300 credit unions. In the USA more than 60 million people are in credit unions. In Britain, since 1990 they have been able to increase total loans from £4,000 to £10,000.

In the wider economic setting, for the commercial borrower the major benefit of the non-interest system is that it shares the risk of profit failure. The benefit is that when profits are unexpectedly low, the borrower is not saddled with fixed interest payments and when profits are unexpectedly high, they are shared by the bank. Clearly, an interest-free, profit-share bank would have to incur large information gathering costs in assessing the viability of ventures and in evaluating profits – and, like Japanese banks, would find advantage in developing long-term relationships with the firms it finances. West German banks are represented on the boards of companies where they have a profit-sharing stake. Whilst such a system would not solve every economic problem and would still carry risks, it would be more inherently robust and stable than the fragile interest-based system of finance which enslaves instead of enabling people today.

Freeing Property

In a system of politics which obsessively worships at the feet of the market or the State, human beings and their needs are of secondary importance. The objective is to impose one form or the other and, once achieved, to stop anyone threatening the equilibrium. In tracing out a third way – towards a community economy – money and property must be placed at the disposal of people and their communities; not the other way around.

Like money, property is predominantly private in ownership but social in purpose and function. Money and property, and all the goods of the earth, are meant by God to meet the needs of all the peoples of the earth. Private ownership is often the best way of securing this. But all must be given the opportunity of ownership, and owners must then remember their social obligations. Private ownership is not absolute. Speaking in Latin America, at Puebla, John Paul II said private property is like carrying a 'social mortgage'. In other words, having had the gift of access to money or property we must be unattached to our possessions and be willing to share these gifts with others. This is true empowerment.

Banks which profit-share should be mirrored by profit sharing companies and opportunities for share ownership schemes in housing. I have already described how a fairer system of house purchase might work but let me suggest some other models.

Although the majority of people will wish to have personal control over the ownership and management of their homes, it should not be assumed that this is the model for everyone. One of my chief complaints about the housing legislation of the 1980s is that it was largely irrelevant for those who are unable – for reasons of poverty or age – to take on mortgages. Yet, being the tenant of a large corporate landlord can be just as enslaving as the monthly worry about meeting an over-extended mortgage account.

It would be difficult to sit for nearly twenty years through weekly advice centres in a city such as Liverpool, and to have served as the city's Housing Chairman, without coming to some fairly radical conclusions about how to demunicipalise property.

Government should take a new look at housing finance. Most council housing is financed over a sixty-year borrowing period. The original building costs are paid back ten times and more. The absurd position has now been reached whereby local authorities are still repaying original construction costs and debt on properties now demolished. The demolition was financed through borrowing and those debts also have to be serviced.

More emphasis should be placed on what Dick Crossman called the 'third arm' of housing: the housing association movement. Non-profit-making organisations can often act as catalysts, providing expertise and know-how, helping tenants reclaim badly neglected and decaying properties. Their size means that they do not suffer from the appalling inefficiencies of the bureaucratic and impersonal council housing departments. They are closer to the people and better understand their needs. They have also undertaken some of the most important pioneering work in establishing housing co-operatives.

Merseyside Improved Houses is one of the biggest housing associations in Britain and is based in my constituency. Their no-nonsense Chief Executive, Barry Natton, has enabled thousands of tenants to have basic improvements undertaken to their homes, and in some cases to own and manage them themselves. Back in the 1970s we both rejected the corporatist 'we know best' approach. As the heart was ripped out of the city whole communities were torn asunder by bulldozers and redevelopment plans. In 1972 over half the homes in my Edge Hill constituency were without inside sanitation. Labour wanted to demolish them. I fought to save and improve them. By the end of the 1980s almost all had been improved and communities saved.

Natton sees other ways of enabling people to have greater power over their own destiny. He says that the demolition of inter-war-year tenements is costly and unimaginative, and proposes a system based on 'sweat equity', where the housing association gives the initial capital for improvements, and the tenant provides the sweat and physical commitment to improving the property. The rent and fulfilment of the improvements buys the tenant their ownership rights. While obviously not a housing solution for everyone, it could be very attractive to young couples trying to get into the housing market who cannot face huge debts and mortgages. It is a much more imaginative and better way of utilising property than simply demolishing it.

The principle could be extended further. Add together the total housing rent receipts of every local authority in the country. Examine the costs of subsidising tenants through housing benefits and local authorities through central government aid. Then take a look at the costs involved in running massive and inefficient centralised housing departments. In a city such as Liverpool it has led to perfectly good properties being badly maintained, not re-let quickly enough when vacated, subsequent vandalism and, in one year, the spectre of 8,000 council owned properties actually standing empty while people go in need of homes.

One solution, put forward by the Government, is to sell off council housing. This may be fine up to a point, but a) the worst property does not sell; b) it leads to a patchwork quilt approach; c) Councils are specifically prohibited from reinvesting receipts from sales into building new projects; and d) some people simply cannot afford to take up even the most generous discounts and are frightened that they will not be able to afford ongoing maintenance.

What is the answer?

It would be more efficient and would immediately empower millions of people if the estates were simply handed over to the tenants; if their housing benefits and subsidies were paid direct to a management and maintenance housing association or to a co-operative based on each estate; and, if those who could afford to pay, contributed an annual service charge. Each tenant would have the right of sale. Divested of this responsibility – and the ongoing debts – local authorities would have to compete along with private companies for the franchise to maintain the buildings and common areas. This would produce a direct system of accountability and local management.

There would still remain a need for sheltered accommodation and specialised housing for vulnerable groups and this would be best provided by housing associations and the private sector. Other groups who are locked out of the housing market, the homeless, for instance, will need an immediate and compassionate response. Although many of the able-bodied homeless might be very suitable candidates for the 'sweat equity' schemes outlined above, let's not pretend that this alone will be enough: more resources are needed too.

My family is fortunate enough to live in part of an early Victorian house near Liverpool's Sefton Park. When I moved in, in 1984, large parts of it were dilapidated and in urgent need of restoration. It has given me a great sense of satisfaction – as well as security – to invest time and labour. I was also fortunate enough to have sufficient capital to obtain the equipment, material and tools which I needed – and, from time to time, to buy in expertise. What I want for Britain is a property system which opens the same opportunities to all.

Augustine said this of possessions and the same is true of our homes: 'I do not say: "You are damned if you have possessions." You are damned if you take them for granted, if you are puffed up by them, if you think yourself important because of them, if because of them you forget the poor, if you forget your common human status because you have more of what are vanities.'

Christians believe in a God who took the form of a tiny embryo and who was born into a family that was temporarily homeless and then became refugees. Maybe that should give them a special appreciation of the security and importance of having a roof over their heads and a home of their own.

Freeing Families

Not everyone will marry or live in families but at some time in most people's lives it is the family which provides love, companionship and security. Where family life breaks down, the community should do all in its power to protect and care for the casualties. I am well aware from the bitter sequels to family breakdowns that the resentment and recriminations can have far-reaching and catastrophic effects on estranged partners and children alike. Rarely does a week go by without constituents consulting me about maintenance payments which have not been honoured, access arrangements which have broken down, and legal battles which sometimes continue for years on end.

During the week of writing this I met a woman who told me how her husband walked out on her when she was four months pregnant. He has never bothered to show the slightest interest in their now six-month-old daughter, although he does want access to their twelve-year-old son (who does not want to see his father). She contested his attempt to divorce her but was told by a court official at Liverpool Crown Court that her attempts to fight for her marriage represented attitudes from 'the dark ages'. She was subsequently rebuked in court by a judge who told her that her feelings 'didn't enter into it'.

Labour has increasingly argued that families are irrelevant in modern society, and that marriage should not be regarded as a permanent institution. A report from the Institute for Public Policy Research, the Labour Party's main source for new policy ideas, argues that two years is too long for couples to wait for a fault-free divorce. The authors of the 1990 report include Harriet Harman, MP, who is a Labour front-bencher, and Patricia Hewitt, a former advisor to Mr Kinnock. The Institute also argues for more publicly funded child care rather than tax relief to help parents who might prefer to stay at home. This is also the position of many members of the present Government.

In contrast, European Christian Democrats say quite specifically in their 1989 European Manifesto, 'On the People's Side', that their objective is

> to strengthen the importance of the family as the basic community. For us the family as a community for living and for teaching is the most important source of individual refuge and it is where values are transmitted, and where there should be solidarity and responsibility, with equality between parents and where each has autonomy and there is mutual respect for the aspirations of each.

How then might we hand more power to the family and strengthen its position?

First, all government departments should have to produce a 'relationist' assessment of whether policies which they are pursuing are helping or hindering family life.

Second, the divorce law should be reformed – not to make breaking up easier, but to make staying together easier. When a couple wed they should have to consider more seriously the nature of their contract. If they choose a Church wedding the marriage law should reflect the Christian belief in the lifelong nature of marriage, or the teaching of their faith if it is other than Christian. If a couple are unwilling to accept these vows then the secular route of the registry office – and divorce – would still be open to them. At least, at the very outset, both partners would have to consider what marriage actually meant to them.

Third, tax legislation should not penalise marriage; it should give financial recognition to the work of the spouse who undertakes the rearing of the children; if a parent does not return to work after the birth of a child, the family tax assessment should be weighted to make him no worse off than the parent who does choose to return to work; tax lesiglation should also take into account the real cost of family life, in particular the costs of caring for children. The European People's Party has advocated a European directive providing for a social insurance system in all European states guaranteeing parental leave and insurance against incapacity to work; full legal status; no loss of social security cover for the spouse who gives up paid work to care for children or dependent relatives; the number of children taken into account in calculating pension contributions; a mechanism to collect outstanding payments for the support of the spouse and children in the case of separated or divorced couples; and an assurance that when both spouses are engaged in paid work, marriage does not put in question the individual's social security rights.[11]

The State should empower and encourage family life, but never substitute for it. Family policy should, in part at least, make a contribution to changing demographic patterns. The 'extended family' that wants to provide a 'granny flat' in their home for an ageing relative should be given grants and incentives to do so.

The child, from the moment of conception, should be at the centre of a family-based policy. It must have its life and integrity protected. After birth it must also be provided for by both its parents, who both have rights, and obligations. When, for instance, a father walks out on his child direct attachments on earnings should automatically be made to enable the continuation of proper care and support for the child. Children deserve a world which can offer them all the best chances for development. Their good is the responsibility of parents, and the wider community.

An effective family policy must contribute to the self-fulfilment of each member of the family without favouring any one member at the expense of any other; each family member has the rights which derive from the family situation and in addition has individual rights.

Single-parent families must not be turned into a group apart. It is a truism that in an ideal world a child needs the love and security of both its parents. Many single parents courageously struggle to provide everything which two parents might ideally be expected to give. Many have eschewed the quick fix of abortion, knowing that their child's death is not the solution to the dilemma which faces them. They need strong support and practical help.

A family and community policy based on an approach which centres on the importance of the human being can hardly ignore the position of the single parent, those who choose not to marry, or those who live in community or in other relationships. A coherent family policy will recognise these different dimensions whilst never losing sight of the community's basic building block. The family is a kind of school of more abundant humanity. The Charter of the Rights of the Family (*Family Charter*), published by the Catholic Church, should perhaps be incorporated into European Community law.[12] In its preamble it states that

> The family constitutes much more than a mere juridical, social and economic unit, a community of love and solidarity, which is uniquely suited to teach and transmit cultural, ethical, social, spiritual and religious values, essential for the development and well-being of its own members and of society.

The Truth Will Set You Free

Freedom, then, is not simply about claimed rights. It is about responsibilities and duties. It is about using authority creatively to ensure a diffusion of power. Our progress should remain under man's control, not at the mercy of a few men or groups wielding too much economic power, nor at the mercy of the political community, or at that of some of the more powerful nations. On the contrary, at any level as many people as possible and, where international relations are concerned, all nations ought to have an active part in shaping our future direction.

Nothing is better for establishing a truly human political life than to stimulate a deep sense of justice, good will and public service, and to strengthen fundamental convictions about the true nature of a political community and about the purpose, the right exercise and the limits of public authority.

In our country too much power is concentrated in the hands of a few. Their legitimacy to govern is questionable. They are elected by minorities, but because of the perversity of the electoral system they command huge parliamentary majorities. They have taken an attitude towards local democracy not dissimilar to that adopted by Thomas Cromwell towards the monasteries: first list them, then bust them. They have vigorously opposed decentralisation and devolutionary measures and while adumbrating a belief in individual liberty, Janus-faced, they have strengthened their own hands by emasculating community control over everything from the administration of local government to the sale of council housing. Control of nationalised industries has passed from the hands of distant suzerains to privatised fiefdoms. It hasn't all been bad. I welcome the breaking of the power of industrial dictatorships and I welcome wider share ownership. But I look at the patterns of power in Britain and see only new dangers, new forms of servitude and new terrors. True freedom will only be achieved when man learns to harmonise his will with that of his Creator.

Freedom is not the liberty to do anything whatsoever. It is the freedom to do good, and in this alone will true happiness be found. People will become free and be empowered to the extent that they come to a knowledge of truth, and to the extent that this truth, and not other forces, guide that person's will. It is in a relationship with the Creator that human freedom obtains meaning and consistency; this truly guarantees dignity, liberating and empowering the human personality.

Chapter 9

Active Compassion

Western countries are at varying stages in the development of institutional provision of welfare. In this chapter I have taken four groups of people: the young, old, disabled and dying and have asked what an active and compassionate approach might mean for them.

In Britain the Liberal reformer, Lord Beveridge, was the pioneer of social welfare legislation. He concluded his booklet *Insurance For All and Everything*[1] with the question: 'Can we not join now to put one more fear beneath our feet for ever, to bring our country one stage nearer to the dream of the psalmist? "I have been young, and now am old; yet have I not seen the righteous forsaken, nor his seed begging bread?"'

It took Atlee's post-war Labour Government to implement Beveridge's proposals for social security and welfare. I would rank this in importance with the 1944 Education Act, promoted by the Conservative Minister, R.A. Butler. These two key pieces of post-war legislation ensured access to health, welfare and education, regardless of wealth.

Elsewhere in Europe, socialists, liberals and Christian Democrats made significant contributions in recognising the need for the State to be involved in anchoring social reforms by financing them and giving them legal status. European Christian Democrats had a distinctly Beveridgian view of life; and still do. Hence their support for the European Social Charter against the opposition of Mrs Thatcher.

Arie Oostlander, the Dutch Christian Democrat thinker and MEP, says:

> Neither the development of health and welfare services nor educational systems, nor decent living conditions for citizens can come about without the active involvement of the state . . . these are matters of the common good and have to be promoted by the state. The guarantee of a minimum standard of living is likewise one of the basic tasks which have to be accomplished by the state.[2]

This insistence on active involvement, active compassion for the vulnerable at institutionalised as well as personal level, contrasts sharply with the hands-off, opt-out approach of Britain's New Right. Instead of actively encouraging the citizen to opt out we should unashamedly be creating a responsible society where people opt in.

Oostlander says:

> Christian Democracy thinks principally in terms of various different forms of social organisation, each of which provides its own special service for society. It aspires towards a state that is aware of its responsibility in a responsible society. In this, the direct concern of one for another, the feeling of security in social groups, and the problem solving capacities of persons and associations, play a fundamental role.[3]

I strongly share this emphasis on social mediation through voluntary organisations and private initiative, undergirded where appropriate by the State. The narrow choices of individualism and collectivism offered by the continental liberals and socialists are far too restrictive. At a meeting of Liberal International in Stockholm I felt very ill at ease with the primacy placed on the individual and his or her freedom of choice. Many speakers called for the dismantlement of social welfare arrangements. This classical liberal, individualist view, has been championed in Britain by Mrs Thatcher and others.

Paddy Ashdown, in his leadership campaign against Alan Beith (who now sits for Beveridge's old constituency of Berwick-Upon-Tweed), clashed on the issue of choice, with Ashdown claiming that choice 'is the central political question'. In a speech in support of Alan Beith, made at Milton Keynes, I hotly contested this view. Those who believe in choice say that responsibility is simply a matter of regulating one's own affairs and one's own personal development. This explains the emphasis placed by Ashdown and others on the free, strong, and active citizen, and the inevitable and consequential survival of the fittest. The social liberalism of Beith, and before him of Beveridge, was a reaction against the extreme consequences of this individualism.

Socialism, and to a lesser extent European social democracy, have taken as their starting point not the individual person but the collective. The Socialists arrived at the opposite extreme. The State became the means of resolving all social problems. As time went by the State ceased to be Beveridge's safety net; it simply took decisions for the citizen and eroded personal responsibility. This also helps explain why in socialist-run cities such as Liverpool there has been such antagonism towards and victimisation of voluntary organisations and personal initiative groups, such as co-ops. The distortion in the extreme collectivist direction has created welfare structures which both shackle and discourage personal endeavour.

An alternative approach, based on personal and community responsibility, which encourages a variety of social organisations and associations – including the family – would lead to a less ideological approach. It would lead to a sharing of social burdens and place a premium on active compassion. It would also open possibilities to participate in the shaping of a responsible society in ways which are less anonymous, which stimulate a more imaginative response, which generate open-hearted generosity, and which create more solidarity between the giver and the receiver.

The Personalist Approach – Young People

Beveridge's quotation from the psalms spanned the generations: 'I have been young, and now am old.' Writing in the post First World War period, when so many young Europeans had been slaughtered in the trenches, he surveyed a country whose moral character and physical strength were then being sapped by poverty and want. He said, 'Their effects were felt in the break-up of families, in the waste of education on children too badly fed to learn, in the stifling of chances for the young through unaided struggles to maintain the old, above all in the sense of insecurity which breeds recklessness and bitterness'.[4]

Today, the challenges are different. Notwithstanding the grain of poverty which runs through our society (see Chapter 5) very few children are too badly fed to be unable to learn. According to a recent advertising agency report, the goals of the younger generation as they become adults will be to have more money and more luxury goods.

But, as in Beveridge's day, there is still insecurity and bitterness – especially among many young people. Perhaps it is the naked materialism, inversion of poverty, and the insatiable desire for consumerism, fuelled by advertising, which has created this new insecurity. What kind of Europe are we bequeathing to the coming generations? How can we address the issues that depersonalise and degrade our young people? Some of the statistics in Chapter 4 which relate to young people are very disturbing. Their position has worsened as the assault on the family has increased. They are entitled to a more vigorous and compassionate response.

Young People and Contemporary Values

In an address to the International Congress for the Family, in July 1990, Dr Michael Schluter said that 'consumerism undermines and destroys families . . . Consumerism, the pursuit of more luxury goods, attacks family relationships and family solidarity at three key points: Time, Stress, and Values'.[5]

Just being around as parents means providing time for the young of the family. Giving young people our exclusive attention is important for self-esteem and personal security. The treadmill of consumerism uses up spare time. To obtain more luxury goods people need more money – so they spend more time at work. Men end up doing more overtime (the working week now averages forty-four hours); more women have to go out to work and work longer hours; teenagers increasingly have to work weekends and vacations, and with student loans the pressures will be even greater. People trade off time for money, time for a bigger mortgage and a bigger house, time for a bigger car or foreign holiday.

One of the reasons given by the Government and the New Right in arguing for shops and stores to be open on Sundays is that because people are working extended hours they need Sundays to be able to shop. But this is just fuelling consumerism too. What will go if Sunday is spent in the hypermarket? Time with the family, time for relationships and friendships. Consumerism will have won again.

Young People and Home

Consumerism also creates stress at home. In Chapter 8, I looked at the corrosive effects and downward pressures of debt on families and young people. But it is our values which consumerism and pro-choice campaigners most seriously threaten.

If it is true that the next generation simply aspires to have more luxury goods and more money, then our country will become more selfish, and lack compassion and generosity. Consumerism and choice are always at somebody else's expense. The real choice, to use Schluter's phrase, is 'to be relationist or materialist', to decide what matters most, relationships or possessions.

In America it is now estimated that the average citizen spends eighteen months of his life watching advertisements on the television. In Britain we watch an average of five hours of TV daily, but as we have fewer adverts, about six minutes per day, we see only about eight days of ads a year.

The advertisements and the programmes which penetrate our homes have a radical impact on young people.

There is a nice story which Malcolm Muggeridge told about the world's greatest proponent of active compassion. Mother Teresa was on her first visit to an American television studio:

> She was quite unprepared for the constant interruptions for commercials. As it happened, surely as a result of divine intervention, all the commercials that particular morning were to do with different varieties of packaged food, recommended as being non-fattening and non-nourishing. Mother Teresa looked at them with a kind of wonder, her own constant preoccupation being, of course, to find the where-with-all to nourish the starving and put some flesh on human skeletons. It took some little time for the irony of the situation to strike her. When it did she remarked, in a perfectly audible voice: 'I see that Christ is needed in television studios.' A total silence descended on all present.[6]

The problem for parents concerned about the influence of television on their young people's attitudes stems from the nature of TV. For programme makers the medium is the message; violence and dishonesty are often portrayed as the means to achieve ambition and desire.

The media is often preoccupied with fantasy, not truth and reality. News is frequently manipulated and 'social realities' engineered. Just look at the disgraceful caricature of people and attitudes with which the programme makers and presenters are in disagreement. The appalling pro-choice bias on ethical questions such as embryo experimentation and abortion are classic examples. The TV reporting of the Human Fertilisation and Embryology Bill was distorted and unbalanced and usually told you more about the outlook of the presenter than about the issues before Parliament.

Muggeridge told another story, based on an experience in the Biafran War in Nigeria. It illustrates the nature of a medium so freely available in our homes and so influential in shaping many attitudes.

A news team was on hand just as an execution was imminent. As the command to fire was to be given the cameraman's battery went dead and needed to be replaced: 'He cried "cut!" . . . The execution waited until the battery was fitted. The cameraman shouted, "Action!"; then shots were fired and the prisoner fell down dead, his death duly recorded, to be shown in millions of sitting rooms throughout the so-called civilised world.'[7]

Coverage of the opening days of the war with Iraq was most notable for the continuous flow of pictures and instant analysis. The conflict, as seen through the TV, will inevitably have shaped many attitudes, especially of young people. Modern communications have a considerable influence on young people and their families. Home life for young people would be far more secure if the media had fewer portrayals of success measured in purely materialistic terms; progress equated with prosperity; and less exultation of brutal violence and degrading pornography as acceptable ways for people to treat one another. In a responsible society the media could play a constructive role in creating a climate which is supportive of the family and young people, and which created a climate in which both home life and school life might succeed. If they are not prepared to play that role parents might be well advised to limit the amount of television shown in their homes.

Young People and Education

Young people's values and attitudes are primarily shaped in the home and at school. The temptation for parents when things go wrong is to blame the school – and vice versa. An integrated personalist approach would consist of a partnership between the two.

School and family life are intimately linked and therefore schools must pay serious attention to the views of parents. The Christian Democrats, in their 1989 election manifesto, *On the People's Side*[8] put it well when they stated:

> School must, on the one hand, prepare children, by lessons for work and on the other hand, in their work of raising children, lead to a recognition of the values of family and citizenship. Lessons must offer boys and girls the same opportunities through education on the division of tasks within the family, profession, society and politics.

The first job is to ensure that families encourage educational progress and achievement. In Liverpool one of the worst insults you could hurl at a sixteen-year-old young woman is to call her a 'schoolie'. Outside of professional backgrounds many families still have a suspicion of education; and those who have left school with no qualifications and minimal literacy and numeracy often ridicule those who have stayed on.

The values transmitted at home and in the school are crucial to personal formation. Values are important because the world is meaningless and bewildering without a sense of right and wrong; and life is difficult without a sense of purpose and a confidence in oneself. Education is not just a means to a job; it is a preparation for life. Of course, if life is only about hedonism and material advancement then young people will see education as only being about obtaining qualifications to secure high-paying jobs.

Educational objectives and control of universities has become increasingly an arm of industrial policy. One member of staff at Liverpool University recently told me that provided a student brought private sponsorship and tuition fees for a project, space was available for that research. Yet, the majority of proposed Alpha-rated scientific research programmes are being denied public funding. Private money with near-market concerns will not necessarily nourish pure research; it is even less likely to nourish the arts. Should ICI, or discretionary ministerial powers rather than personal development and intellectual liberty, determine the shape of the educational opportunities available to our young people?

This dirigiste educational policy, which sees universities, colleges and schools as instruments of economic growth, has effectively nationalised education. Previously autonomous institutions are now under the thumb of Ministers who have arrogated huge powers to themselves.

Educationalists will find it increasingly difficult to encourage students to challenge preconceived ideas, to foster the ability to question and to recognise controversy, and to develop imagination. Ministerial directives and orientation towards market forces will be an impediment in the teaching of values.

Of course, Ministers would argue that theirs is a reaction against the emphasis placed by many educationalists on Marxist values. Certainly the reading lists and courses offered by some history, sociology and politics departments are ideologically slanted. Marx and Engels definitely would not have included in their view of education any emphasis on the value of the family and community. In *The Communist Manifesto* they bitterly criticised 'the bourgeois clap trap about the family and education, about the hallowed relation of parent and child'.[9] More recently, David Cooper put a more contemporary Marxist view: 'The bourgeois nuclear family (which in this context I shall henceforth refer to as "the family") is the principal mediating device that the capitalist ruling class uses to condition the individual, through primary socialization, to fit into some role complex that suits the system.'[10] The situation ethics and false liberation pedalled under the guise of Marxism and secularism has done as much damage to the family as consumerism.

So what is to be done?

Young People – Learning the Lessons

Parents must ensure that the quality and nature of our education system becomes a central political issue. Christians should particularly consider carefully the question of educational provision and the values which the system transmits. I strongly agree with Frank Field, who has argued that the Church of England has a unique opportunity to become a provider of Christian-based education.

I was disappointed that when, in the summer of 1990, I

wrote to Bishop David Sheppard on this subject he acknowledged that 'over the past few years there has been an increase in the demand for places in church schools, especially at the senior level' but he had reached the conclusion that 'it is unlikely we would see major expansion of schools as a high priority'. He said that the Church would be unable to raise the fifteen per cent of the costs required and was uncertain of the good will of the local education authority and the Government. This has been the Anglican position since the passing of the 1944 Education Act.

The author of the legislation, R.A. Butler, in *The Art of the Possible*,[11] recognised that Archbishop Temple's decision in 1944 for the Church of England to relinquish a major role in education would lead to the disappearance of Christian values in society: 'the perfunctory and uninspired nature of the religious instruction provided in all too many local authority and controlled schools had begun . . . to imperil the Christian basis of our society.'

Archbishop Temple did not accept the opportunity which the Butler Act gave the Church of England to develop its education service. Temple believed that the costs involved in maintaining church schools was not a priority. The Church of England opted out. Of the 9000 Church of England schools in existence in 1944 7000 closed. The secular consensus of 1960s middle England owed a great deal to the educational choices of the 1940s.

Christians from a Catholic tradition took a different view and began raising the massive sums needed to finance the building of parish schools and Catholic grammar schools all over the country. Bishop Sheppard himself admits that parental demand for church education (in Liverpool, and I suspect, elsewhere) has increased. The Church of England should meet this demand and make it a high priority. We should encourage parents and schools, which now have greater autonomy, to use it positively to re-create a Christian ethos. Given that motions were submitted to both the 1990 Labour and Liberal Democrat Conferences calling for the abolition of Church schools this battle promises to be a crucial one for the 1990s.

The second lesson to be learnt from 1944 concerns political consensus. When R.A. Butler became President of the Board of Education in 1941 he believed that there was a general consensus that a new deal in schooling was long overdue. Butler was a one-nation Conservative and an Anglican; his Parliamentary Private Secretary was Chuter Ede, a Labour MP and Free Churchman. This was still during war-time Coalition Government. Churchill advised against the Bill being laid before the Commons but Butler disregarded his advice and with still a year to go before the Japanese surrender, Parliament enacted a reform which was based on political and public agreement.

What a contrast with the ill-considered, meretricious, and often contradictory changes which central government and local authorities have implemented since. Education has become a political football and it is little wonder that young people and the teachers who work with them feel undervalued. It is a paradox that political parties who see the need to work together in times of war, cannot co-operate in peacetime.

Fifty per cent of qualified teachers now leave the profession within five years. They are over-burdened with bureaucracy, each teacher receiving 1438 sheets of paper to enable him to implement the National Curriculum. The system as a whole has generated half a billion sheets of paper. Perversely, the same teachers are given less to spend each week on books and equipment for the children in their care than the cost of four copies of *The Sun*. The buildings they work in are similarly neglected, with £3 billion of repairs outstanding in 1990. As our ambitions for young people seem to decline, consensus among policy makers has become a dirty word.

Higher education is not much better. Only thirty-five per cent of sixteen to eighteen-year-olds go on into full-time education or training, compared with seventy-nine per cent in the USA and sixty-six per cent in France. We also secure fewer graduates: 132 per 1000 twenty-one-year-olds, compared with 236 in Japan, 230 in America and 202 in France. From 1982 to 1987 graduations in the UK fell by 2.4 per cent. At a time when Britain was emerging from the early 1980s recession, higher education should have been the engine for pushing the country out of the mire, rather than a casualty of it.

I would like to see a clear objective of increasing the total number of students to 2 million by the year 2000. I would like closer co-operation between education and industry but not ownership of education by commerce. Parental means tests should be replaced by flat-rate grants repayable via taxation during the graduate's working life. Loans simply 'double tax' the student, add to indebtedness (see Chapter 8) and act as a disincentive to many who need to be attracted into education. In addition to secure funding for students and institutions, academics, researchers and teachers all need to be paid according to the high value which the rest of us recognise as their vital contribution. In the setting of Europe, Britain should give greater support to the ERASMUS programme, which enables young Europeans to continue their studies in one another's countries.

It used to be said that if education could not be cheap, let it be efficient; if it cannot be efficient let it be cheap. Perhaps we need now to provide a system which is both effective and provides value for money but, above all, recognises that education is a preparation of young people to become high-quality human beings.

The Personalist Approach – Elderly People

The pro-choice lobby in Parliament recently introduced its first attempt to legalise euthanasia (see Chapter 6). Although immoral, it would certainly be cheaper and more convenient than accepting responsibility for the care of the elderly. Perhaps that is why this approach finds such support amongst the New Right. Yet, the collectivist approach of dumping elderly people in badly maintained and inadequately staffed municipal or health authority institutions is hardly an attractive alternative. What is the compassionate alternative?

The demographic changes taking place all over Europe will mean that the number of elderly citizens will rapidly increase over the next few years. Instead of seeing this as a burden, society must see this opportunity as a blessing. The presence of so many people with a lifetime's experience is a major source of enrichment for our society. The elderly should be an integral part of the community for as long as possible. Our patterns of provision and care should reflect the diversity and needs of the users.

The Elderly and the Extended Family

Our present approach to provision and care for the elderly is a disgrace. Too easily we forget the sacrifices and the contribution which the elderly have already made. I heard recently of a Nigerian medic who had come to the UK to study geriatric care. After just three weeks she ended her studies and returned home, saying, 'There is nothing you can teach me about care and respect for the elderly.' We need to relearn from so-called under-developed countries a respect due to the aged.

I have already argued (Chapter 8) for grants and incentives where it is practical or desired for the 'extended family' to create granny flats and apartments within the familial home. In reaching planning decisions about house extensions a more relaxed approach should be taken, and perhaps help given with the applicant's costs, when the objective is to provide independent living within the family home for an aged relative.

In addition, more family homes could be provided if we accelerated our programmes for building sheltered warden-controlled units and small bungalows for the elderly. Every under-occupied house previously inhabited by an elderly person or couple so liberated provides accommodation for a family. This avoids the necessity of building new sprawling and impersonal municipal bantustans where people are dumped, miles from kith and kin, and which sever family mutual support systems. Grandparents often take particular delight in their grandchildren and a child's sense of belonging is greatly enhanced by frequent contact with grandparents and other members of the extended family.

The Elderly: Diversity of Needs and Provision

The provision of sheltered accommodation is best undertaken by neighbourhood-based housing associations and can often be accomplished on derelict in-fill sites within the same community where other family members live. Anchor Housing Association, and the Catholic Servite Housing Association have a particularly fine record in developing such projects. Here, too, is an example of actively and compassionately getting on with meeting needs without expecting it all to be done by the State.

Sheltered accommodation relieves its residents of many of the fears of living in increasingly insecure properties. I am a trustee of Liverpool's shelter for aged victims of violence, founded and administered by the redoubtable Joan Jonker.

Few things have upset me more than the sight of an elderly woman who has been beaten up and robbed of her few possessions, frightened stiff of returning to her family home. The security of sheltered accommodation, combined with the independent living it still allows, gives many elderly people a totally new lease of life.

I am also president of the Liverpool Old People's Hostels Association. This is the sort of residential nursing home accommodation which the elderly may require when even the sheltered blocks become too much for them. This particular association is a non-profit-making charity and operates on a relatively localised basis. In addition to voluntarism, the private sector also has a part to play.

Although there will always have to be proper scrutiny of the care provided, most of the operators of private homes offer good-quality care in buildings which are superior to many of the local authority homes which I have visited. It is ironic that the operators of the municipal institutions police the private and voluntary sectors and rightly insist on high standards. Sadly they rarely achieve the same standards in their own properties.

The policy of 'care in the community' will produce new demands on health authorities. In cases of dementia and psycho-geriatric illness there will always be a continuing need for closely supervised and well-staffed care in purpose-built premises. Instead of being a policy to respond compassionately to a person's needs, at present care in the community is seen by many authorities as simply an excuse for dumping seriously mentally ill elderly people into wholly unsuitable circumstances. Former institutions have been sold off and the profits from the land deals used towards the cost of implementing Kenneth Clarke's proposals to reorganise the National Health Service. Genuine 'care in the community' would itself be a more expensive policy than institutionalised care. Instead, it has been used as a way of saving money. By closing expensive facilities and leaving many to fend for themselves, vulnerable people have been placed at risk. One example I raised last year concerned an elderly lady with mental illness who had been dumped in a hard-to-let property on a council estate in Edge Hill, Liverpool. Her windows and door had been broken and simply nailed up with plywood. The decaying bodies of dead animals had been left to fester around her. Social services passed the buck to the health department and the police. No one wanted to accept responsibility for her and no one wanted to know. She was eventually carried out by ambulancemen after the flat caught fire.

The Elderly – Caring for the Carer

One form of care which is often wholly overlooked is the 'informal caring' which takes place in relatives' homes. People's serious needs are ten times more likely to be met by relatives than by friends or neighbours. This is particularly the case in old age or infirmity.

But caring is costly. Caring for another can involve house extensions, moving to a bigger house, extra heating, food and transport. Ofter a carer will forgo career and job prospects and incur considerable stress in taking on this responsibility. The trend has been away from caring for the elderly within the family setting. Many are simply left to live an isolated existence alone, often rarely seeing a neighbour or friend. In

1973 forty per cent of people over seventy-five lived alone. It is now nearer fifty per cent.

In their 1987 *Family Charter*[12] Dr Michael Schluter's Jubilee Centre say that the tax system at the moment provides little support for carers:

> There is a Dependent Relatives Allowance, offset against taxable income. But this is set at £100 per year, which actually amounts to a mere £29 per year for someone paying income tax at 29%. Indeed, tax allowances are now recognised to be a rather blunt instrument and of no help to non-earners or those on very low incomes. The defective Dependent Relatives Allowance is therefore being phased out.

What is needed is a general care allowance to be paid when someone cares for a sick or elderly person – not necessarily a relative – in his own home. This would encourage more active person-to-person compassion. The Invalidity Care Allowance is currently worth £28-£30 per week (1990 figure). This is only payable where a carer spends at least thirty-five hours a week looking after a severely disabled person, who in turn must receive Attendance Allowance. Only about five per cent of the elderly people receive Attendance Allowance; and thirty-five hours a week of direct caring is a fairly inflexible rule which acts as an impediment. Not surprisingly very few people (10,000 in 1987) get Invalidity Care Allowance. A spokesman for the Department of Social Security in the Edge Hill Office at Liverpool told me that 'After they fail to qualify for attendance allowance, there is little else we could do to help.'

Not only would a general care allowance ensure care in a permanent setting based on a sense of belonging and being loved, the costs would actually be far less. In 1990 the weekly cost of one place in a residential home ranged between £178 and £238 in London, and £155 and £215 outside London. Costs of nursing homes were even higher, ranging from £233 to £238 in London to £210 and £266 payable outside London. But it is not just costs – the limited number and changing nature of staff, restricted diets, and the general ethos of even the best institutions often contribute to an elderly person's decline.

The Elderly – Other Ways to Help

There are other ways in which a more humane approach could be adopted. The elderly are entitled to share independently and equally in the economic, social and cultural aspects of life. The right to a meaningful occupation should apply where appropriate. For instance, there should be legal protection of older workers and redistribution of work, giving older workers the chance to work part time, and flexible retirement should be organised on a voluntary basis. More and more companies are coming to recognise the importance of what Americans now describe as 'grey power'.

We could also introduce a national transport users scheme guaranteeing reduced fare access, and some free travel provision at off-peak times, for the elderly. Other non-material benefits, such as free use of local swimming pools and easier access to cultural and educational facilities, would also dramatically improve the quality – as well as the length – of life.

The Personalist Approach – Disabled People

If the opportunity to live a fulfilling and active life as part of the community and family is important to young and elderly people, how much more important it is to provide for the needs of disabled people. Here is an area of public policy crying out for a more compassionate approach.

I have already highlighted the prevailing attitude of eliminating disability by destroying the disabled child (see Chapter 6). But a positive pro-life ethic, which rejects quality controls and perfection tests, must also come up with practical proposals for improving the quality of life for disabled people. In creating a more human Europe we need to use several tools: legislation, resources and the challenging of attitudes. This approach was summed up well in 1866 by Samuel Howe, when he said: 'Good intentions and kind impulses do not necessarily lead to wise and truly humane measures. Meaning well is only half our duty; thinking right is the other and equally important half.'

Disabled People – Using Legislation

I was very pleased to see that the European Christian Democrats, in their 1989 document *On the People's Side*, recognise the need to legislate and to promote active and independent lives for disabled people. Amongst their proposals – which the New Right would adamantly oppose – is a Guarantee for the Right to Equal Opportunities in work, as outlined in the July 1986 EC document 'Recommendations on the Employment of the Disabled'; financial solidarity with the disabled in all fields of social security; and the Commission to draw up a draft directive, which will lay down the most important elements in the integration of the disabled.

Europe, on this occasion, could do a lot worse than to emulate the American Senate who, on July 13th, 1990, enacted the Americans with Disabilities Act. President Bush signed the document at a White House ceremony on July 26th, putting some flesh on the bones of his inaugural promise to help create 'a gentler America'. The Act prohibits discrimination on the basis of disability in employment, public services and public accommodation. It requires new buses and trains to be accessible to disabled people, and telecommunications companies to operate relay systems that will allow hearing and speech-impaired Americans to use telephone services.

This is quite a contrast with the feeble state of British law. A classic example is our attitude to training and employment of disabled people. During the week of writing this chapter I visited Twig Lane Workshops for disabled people in the Borough of Knowsley. On Merseyside alone there are over 7000 registered disabled people. Given that many disabled do not register, the workshop put the true number nearer 15,000 'with most being out of work'. The workshop is run on a shoestring with no clear source of funding. Education, social services and health departments simply play pass-the-parcel. Even worse, by tying the training scheme to Employment Training (ET), which is not designed for disabled people's needs or requirements, it means that after six months a trainee is a) unlikely to have acquired skills; b) unable to obtain a job; and c) unable to secure extra funding. Employment training is a wholly unsuitable instrument for people with special needs and denied proper political commitment and funding places such as Twig Lane Workshops face an uncertain future.

The Twig Lane syndrome extends to our legislative failure to provide proper safeguards for disabled people (despite attempts by MPs Tom Clarke and Bob Wareing, who both introduced Private Members Bills). Regrettably, it is difficult to imagine the present Government promoting legislation which sets out as its purpose the provision of

> a clear and comprehensive national mandate for the elimination of discrimination against individuals with disabilities; to provide clear, strong, consistent enforceable standards addressing discrimination . . . ; to ensure that the federal government plays a central role in enforcing the standards established under the act; and to invoke the sweep of congressional authority, including the power to invoke the 14th Amendment, and to regulate commerce, in order to address the major areas of discrimination faced day-to-day by people with disabilities.[13]

Legislation is important but by itself it is not enough. Attitudes towards disability and fear of disability have to be addressed as well.

Despite the work which my wife, Lizzie, did as a speech therapist with mentally handicapped adults – and with the Leonard Cheshire Foundation – and my own six years spent working with children with special needs, we are both acutely aware that disability is something every parent fears. It is only human to want your child to be healthy and able-bodied. I remember how shocked we both were on learning that our own little daughter, Marianne, would have to spend months in plaster when it was found that she had a congenital hip displacement. But there is little point bitterly asking 'Why?' Parents in this position need practical help and answers to the question 'What do we do now?'

Disabled People – Same Difference

I have already written about Ellen Wilkie who lived with muscular dystrophy for thirty-one years, until her death on August 7th, 1989 (see Chapter 6). Ellen, in *Pocketful of Dynamite*,[14] put it like this:

> I imagine various travel agents and travel companies that I have dealt with, saying behind my back. 'Oh, disabled people always complain. We can never get it right so let's not bother.' If we are, 'always complaining' it is because we have a lot to complain about! The problem stems from the images of disabled people as passive recipients who should be eternally grateful for every crumb that comes their way. This is not an image I wish to perpetuate.

In her poem *Same Difference*, Ellen summed up the desire of disabled people to be accepted as quality human beings on their own terms:

> I want you to know me
> without being nosey
> I want you to question
> without being inquisitive
> I want you to understand
> the delicate difference
> while treating me the same . . .
> I want you to get inside my skin
> without my explanation.[15]

Ellen also points out the inconsistency of claiming concern for disabled people but simultaneously espousing the extraordinary notion that their very right to exist is just a matter of individual choice:

> At the risk of sounding like a messenger of doom, only recently I read articles suggesting that any women refusing to have amniocentesis or similar tests for disability during pregnancy, or refusing to have abortions when they know

> their babies are disabled, should be denied the right to any state help in bringing up the child. Pro-life supporters may be accused of being right wing, but doesn't that sound rather fascist to you?[16]

People who argue that it is their right to choose to eliminate the disabled usually say something like 'the State does not provide sufficiently good help for the handicapped so they will not have a good quality of life. It will be even worse when they destroy the National Health Service. Therefore it is better that we abort them.' That is defeatism.

The answer is to stand up for both the right to live and for the right to a good quality of life. Nor do we have to simply wait for the Government – any government – to become more caring. Here Christians can point to a formidable record in caring for the powerless and vulnerable.

Disabled People – Doing Something

Kathryn Spink in *Jean Vanier and L'Arche – a Communion of Love*[17] records the development of L'Arche since its inception at Trosly-Breuil, just north of Paris, in 1964. The remarkable Jean Vanier invited three mentally handicapped people to leave the institution where they had been living and to make their home with him: 'Because Jesus wanted it'.[18] The revolutionary concept was not based on educating but on living together and sharing a life of communion. There are now eighty-five L'Arche communities scattered over several continents. Back in the 1970s I helped secure planning permission for the Liverpool house and subsequently opened their workshops. It would be hard not to be moved by the young people who give up time from their lives to share with disabled people. But they would be the first to admit that the disabled bring their gifts to this communion and flush out the disabilities which lurk inside every one of us. Most of us would rather not admit to our own disabilities but prefer to hide behind a parade of masks.

Whether it is L'Arche, the Leonard Cheshire Foundation, or the many religious organisations – like St Saviour's next door to where I live in Liverpool, where women have given their whole life to the service of other women, with disabilities – the spirit of active compassion shows that there are radical alternatives based on truly human values to the violence of eliminating disabled people. William Wilberforce summed up the need to speak and act in this way: 'Christianity calls her professors to a state of diligent watchfulness and active service'.

Endings: Dignity in Death

Increasingly, too, this active compassion will have to be extended to the dying among us. The AIDS pandemic is something which I have addressed in my contribution to *Aids: Meeting the Community Challenge*,[19] but suffice it to say here that just as each of us may have personally to face a disabling disease we will all have to face death. The dignity which we provide the dying is another test of how far we have come in creating a truly human society. In Britain, Dame Cicely Saunders is the latest of an illustrious band of Englishwomen – Florence Nightingale, Elizabeth Fry, and Emily Pankhurst are others – who have left a permanent impression on the history of their times. Dame Cicely's first foundation for the care of the dying, St Christopher's Hospice in Sydenham, London, was the first of many similar units in the UK and beyond. The founder of the modern hospice movement said in 1960: 'Suffering is only intolerable when nobody cares and one continually sees that faith in God and his care is made infinitely easier by faith in someone who has shown kindness and sympathy.[20] The Bishop of Stepney summed up the aim of the hospice movement as 'ministering to the whole personality that those whom we serve may be able to lose their fear of death'. In understanding what motivates a Cicely Saunders, a Jean Vanier, or a Mother Teresa, we can begin to understand why Christians in their private and public lives must place such a premium on active compassion.

Chapter 10

Good Stewardship

In the Westminster Declaration the founders of the movement for Christian Democracy are careful to accept both their fallibility and human weakness. The approach does not moralise but is based on the needs of the whole person, spiritual as well as physical. It is also unambiguous in setting out how we perceive the truth; nowhere more so than in our attitudes towards the heedless plunder of creation – the destruction of our own species; the animal kingdom; and the built environment. An approach to politics which measures political success in terms of the quality of our relationships with others and our relationship with the world around us could come to no other conclusion. When they come to assess how well we cared for the created world, future generations will judge successive governments to have been abject failures.

Political Will

In *What Kind of Country?*[1] I talked about the enquiries undertaken by the House of Commons Environment Select Committee into the disposal of nuclear waste and acid rain which took place during my membership of that Committee, between 1983 and 1986.

I warned then that we face an environmental catastrophe; that unless we urgently construct de-sulphurisation plants at our coal-burning power stations, fitted catalysers to our cars to cut carbon dioxide emissions, and recognised the dangers to human health from the nuclear industry, we would be poisoned by our own waste.

Despite a succession of speeches from the former Prime Minister and the publication of the 1990 Department of the Environment White Paper, it is clear that 'Green' sentiment does not match political reality.

Unless more resources are committed to public transport, and less to the private car; unless more resources are put into cleaning-up and conserving energy supplies; and unless every Department of State sees its prime responsibility as the promotion of environmentally sound policies, Britain's air, water, countryside, urban environment, and its call on scarce resources in the developing world, will remain unchanged.

By and large governments have done as little as possible to heed the many warnings. As long ago as 1977, when the then Energy Secretary, Tony Benn, gave the go-ahead to the £1 billion thermal oxide reprocessing plant at Sellafield, my late colleague, David Penhaligon, MP, was voicing disquiet and opposition. Since my own election to Parliament in 1979 I have consistently highlighted the dangers of the nuclear industry. In *What Kind of Country?*[2] I said: 'Unhesitatingly, I regard domestic nuclear energy as infinitely more dangerous and potentially more catastrophic than the nuclear weapons stashed away in our silos.' In addition to the environmental issues, during a time of conflict every major reactor becomes a lethal target.

In 1986 I was a member of the Environment Select Committee when it brought in its final report on nuclear waste.[3] I found myself in a minority of one on a number of issues but since Chernobyl and other nuclear accidents I am more convinced than ever about the rightness of the amendments which I moved.

Looking back to the drafting committee, held on Monday, January 27th, 1985, the Minutes record that my first amendment challenged the need to maintain a British civil nuclear programme:

> . . . in no sense does the civil nuclear programme have sufficient benefits to compensate for the serious problems

> produced by nuclear waste. We further believe that the ending of the civil nuclear programme will, in the medium term, significantly reduce the problems associated with nuclear waste disposal, as the size of the problem would be, for all intents and purposes, limited to its present level. We therefore recommend that the Government should set up an immediate independent enquiry into the continuation of the civil nuclear programme.

The amendment was defeated four votes to one. Five years later John Wakeham, the Energy Secretary, told Parliament that, for purely economic reasons, no further reactors would be constructed.

I then moved a further amendment that 'there may be long term environmental dangers associated with sea dumping and we should set ourselves against the resumption of this practice.' This was defeated by four votes to two.

Another amendment attempted to delete the phrase 'We are convinced that safe final disposal routes are available in the United Kingdom,' and was defeated by four votes to one.

I then attempted to delete the whole of Chapter 7 of the report and to incorporate a new chapter entitled, 'The Dangers of Radioactive Discharges'. This was based on the research of an American nun, a physicist, Rosalie Bertell, whose work has been published in her book, *No Immediate Danger*.[4]

This new chapter looked at the links between nuclear installations such as Sellafield and the high incidence of leukaemia, and stressed that given the great uncertainty surrounding the health effects of radioactive doses it was crass to assert that there were 'safe' levels of discharges. I quoted work undertaken by James Cutler of Yorkshire Television which suggested that Seascale, near Sellafield, had a leukaemia rate twenty-four times the regional average. Cutler challenged the findings of the earlier Black Report which failed to make any connections between outbreaks of cancer and radiation from nuclear installations. I also cited the excellent work of Stuart Boyle, of Friends of the

Earth[5] which suggested that it was implausible to dismiss the incidence of childhood leukaemia as a statistical freak.

My amendment stated that

> there is strong evidence to suggest that discharges emanating from nuclear sites at present bring with them a very serious health hazard. We therefore recommend that discharges from such sites are, as far as technically possible, ended unless irrefutable evidence is produced that they are safe . . . We also recommend that the Government establish an enquiry investigating the evidence of cancers around all nuclear establishments, examining the medical records of those working in, or living near to, nuclear establishments, and that such an enquiry does not repeat the logical and statistical errors of the Black Report.

Labour and Conservative Members on the Committee combined to defeat these proposals, five votes to one.

This is a small glimpse into the frustrations of political life and of society's failure to act early enough. It always seems to take another disaster before anything is done. Frustration pales into insignificance when measured alongside the grief of families – like that of little Gemma who died in the summer of 1990 from leukaemia, which the family believed was a direct result of discharges from Sellafield.

Frustration is also an inadequate word when placed in the context of the aftermath of Chernobyl. In Western Europe the political will to tackle the problems of nuclear waste, acid rain, the greenhouse effect and the pollution of our water and beaches, has been in short supply. But by comparison with Eastern Europe our leaders look positively virtuous.

I visited the Ukraine in the autumn of 1989. Then, in January 1990, while attending the Moscow Global Environmental Forum, I interviewed the Chairman of the Ecology Commission of Rukh (the Ukrainian Popular Movement) Nikolai Bidzilya who had been refused permission to attend the Forum.

Deeply disillusioned with the Soviet leadership, Bidzilya described the consequences of the Chernobyl disaster in the Ukraine. He told me that 300 villages in three regions, Nazodichesky, Ovzuchsky, and Polesski, had been evacuated because of the radiation and pollution. Wild animals such as boars and foxes had been discovered which had lost their fur, their baldness a direct result of contamination. I was shown a photograph of a mutant foal. That week Bidzilya told me fifty children had been sent to Israel for medical treatment.

In addition to the effects of radiation, Bidzilya described the condition of the environment in terms which could be applied to whole tracts of Eastern Europe: 10,000 small rivers have disappeared through bad land usage; there has been serious soil erosion and contamination of the air by harmful gases. At Rovenskaya, in the Roveno region, Bidzilya warned that an atomic power station was in danger of subsiding and that because there was simply no political will to tackle the problem, further environmental catastrophes were likely.

The Scale of the Problem

East or West, North or South, the degraded environment is an issue for everyone. In Britain alone, since the industrial revolution seventy-nine per cent of our wildflower meadows have been lost, 190,000 miles of hedgerow (enough to encircle the earth seven times), three-quarters of our internationally important heaths; and more than half of our peat bogs have disappeared.

How many today would be able to join Shakespeare in claiming: 'I know a bank where the wild thyme grows'? Native plants have been stripped from their habitat through development, pollution or neglect. No less than twenty-two differing flower species have already been lost and many more face imminent extinction. Names such as Wood Clamint and Lady's Slipper Orchid may soon just be memories. On a global scale, 60,000 plant species – one in four of the world's total – could become extinct within the lifetime of the next generation. One thousand species and subspecies of mammals, birds, amphibians, reptiles and fish also face extinction.

The deserts of the world are now expanding by 60,000 kilometers annually – almost the size of Ireland. Tropical rainforests are being decimated. An area the size of Belgium is disappearing every year. Since 1945, forty per cent of the world's rainforests have been destroyed. Fifty per cent of all the earth's species find their homes in the rainforests. Two hundred million tribal people, some four per cent of the earth's population, risk losing their livelihoods and their homes. Their habitat is being removed at a ruthless pace.

Once seventy to eighty per cent of a tropical rainforest is destroyed the remainder can no longer sustain the climate and the whole ecosystem collapses. This threat is even greater in scale than a major nuclear incident. In a major pastoral letter on ecology entitled 'What is Happening To Our Beautiful Land?'[6] the Catholic Bishops of the Philippines trenchantly set out the disaster looming in their country:

> How much of this richness and beauty is left a few thousand years after human beings arrived at these shores? Look around and see where our forests have gone. Out of the original 30 million hectares there is now only 1 million hectares of primary forest left. Where are some of the most beautiful creatures who used to dwell in our forests? These are God's masterpieces, through which he displays His power, ingenuity and love for His creation. Humans have forgotten to live peacefully with other creatures. They have destroyed their habitat and hunted them relentlessly.

Giving the Schumacher Lecture[7] at Clifton Cathedral, the scientist James Lovelock said, 'The two geocidal acts, forest clearance and suffocation by greenhouse gases . . . will usurp the political agenda . . . these predictions are not fictional doom scenarios, but uncomfortably close to certainty.'

Lovelock went on to argue that we must give 'substance to the Christian concept of stewardship and turn our hearts and minds towards what should be our prime environmental concern, the care and protection of the earth itself.' Sometimes the scale of what is happening seems quite beyond us.

Robert Louis Stevenson put into the mouth of a little boy the words, 'The world is so big and I am so small, I do not like it at all, at all.' Perhaps we can be forgiven for feeling like that child as we survey a planet booby-trapped with nuclear reactors, while bulldozers and chainsaws hack down forests; aircraft spray defoliants; factory ships ruthlessly deplete fish stocks; prospectors extract minerals; and industries and individuals pollute everything from the air, rivers and seas to the litter and refuse dumped on public open spaces. Our species resembles the Gadarene swine, about to make a final exit over the edge of the cliff.

A Global Response

It is now accepted as a truism that environmental degradation and pollution know no frontier posts. What happens in Eastern Europe or the Amazonian Forests has potentially disastrous consequences for the whole globe. During his address to the Moscow Global Environment Forum, President Gorbachev told us that 'the right to a healthy environment is a human right'. He said that the hour had struck and that unless we were predisposed to suicide, nations would have to act together. He suggested the establishment of an international Green Cross whose remit would be to assist with ecological disasters: a move which I subsequently welcomed in an all-party House of Commons Motion. Such a global initiative would be a start and I welcomed Mr Gorbachev's promise to put Soviet know-how and science at the disposal of the Green Cross. It might also be part of any 'peace dividend' – the release of resources and men who have previously been tied up with the arms race.

The World Commission on Environment and Development (the Bruntland Report, 1987) called for aid programmes to be geared 'to help restore, protect and improve the ecological basis for development'. Regrettably, commercial pressures have tended to put this on the back burner. The World

Bank has expanded the number of staff allocated to environmental management programmes and claims to have 'fully integrated environmental issues in the Bank's approach to development'. They have been so well integrated that you would now have difficulty in finding them. Commercial interests have taken priority.

If world priorities are to change there will be considerable social costs, especially for the poor. The World Bank has begun to recognise this and has now established a 'Social Dimensions of Adjustment' programme. Hopefully the International Monetary Fund will now work towards the Bruntland objective of marrying growth with social goals and environmental consideration. There is also much to commend the French Government's proposal in early 1990 for a special Global Environment Facility to finance programmes in developing countries to tackle specifically global environmental problems such as global warming, ozone depletion, and erosion of bio-diversity. To win the support of the developing nations it would clearly need to be additional to existing programmes. In summary, the proper environmental and ecological balance will not be found until we directly address the structural forms of poverty which exist throughout the world.

The European Response

In Chapter 5 I referred to the far-seeing Christian Democrat document, 'World Economy and Development'.[8] They say it is remarkable that so little attention is being given by European governments to the link between environmental problems and military conflict. Increasing pressure on natural resources have, in their different ways, contributed to conflicts as varied as those in the Gulf, Central America, the countries of Africa's Sahel region and Ethiopia. This is yet another reason for a European Development Programme (see Chapter 5) and for a more sensitive response.

European Community aid programmes have not always been environmentally sensitive. The EC has only three full-time staff working on environmental issues within the Development Directorate (one on loan from Britain's Overseas

Development Agency). This has led to inept decisions: for instance, a livestock programme in Botswana which culminated in overgrazing and deterioration of pastoral lands. The quality of our aid should be matched by improvements in the way we distribute it and by a sensitivity to the environmental impact of development.

The European People's Party, in their document *On the People's Side*[9] seem to understand the need to maximise European co-operation and they say they want 'to make Europe an environmental Community'. They add: 'Our commitment to protect the environment is part of our Christian understanding of man and his responsibility towards Creation.'

Some battles have been won. European Community countries now accept as binding the principle that the polluter should pay. The Community has also sought to establish common standards for the protection of the environment, particularly in connection with the handling of chemicals and waste, and for the protection of water and air. But, for instance, Britain's deplorable record in refusing to meet European Community targets over reducing acid rain emissions demonstrates that the Community is still only as good as its member States. The Single European Act will provide new legal and institutional opportunities to exert pressure on recalcitrant members. They should begin by insisting on common standards on emissions from cars, and by providing even more attractive incentives for the widest possible use of lead-free petrol. The ozone layer must be protected by forbidding the use of chlorofluorocarbons, except for medical purposes. Energy and transport policies which promote the better use of finite resources should be given greater priority.

Good stewardship demands that far greater efforts are made in dealing with the transportation and disposal of toxic and radioactive wastes. Chemical, nuclear and other dangerous waste should not be exported to Third World countries. Where waste can be recycled we should load the tax system to make this a desirable and viable proposition. If our common European home is not to resemble a slum we should also consider what will happen to waste products well in advance of their production. We should withdraw the deemed consent to pollute which allows many industries blithely to treat rivers such as the Danube, the Rhine and the Mersey as a huge toilet flush. The burning of chemical waste and the dumping of poisons in our rivers and at sea is a European scandal and should also be ended.

Eco-Fascism

Good stewardship is not simply a policy for governments. It is an issue for everyone and gets to the heart of how we perceive ourselves and our relationship with the created world.

For Christians and others the Green Movement poses challenges and dilemmas. In *Green Christianity*[10] Tim Cooper says that Christianity has failed sufficiently to address ecological issues and that consequently: 'In the recent past a more significant religious influence among Greens has been the New Age movement.' Dr Margaret Brearley, a Christian academic, speaking at Westminster to the Parliamentary Christian Fellowship, warned that the Green Movement had become dominated by New Age thinking: 'The jackboot of totalitarianism is hidden within the New Age agenda', she said.

Certainly I find the emphasis placed on draconian measures to reduce population and support for the abortion ethic inconsistent with a total respect for life. Good stewardship and responsibility must logically extend to our own species and in the use of our own fertility. Measures which either force or destroy can never be acceptable.

Ninety per cent of the expected global increase in population will occur in low-income countries, where food production cannot keep pace. Although the industrialised world has less than a quarter of the world's population, we consume seventy-five per cent of the world's energy resources, eighty-five per cent of the wood, and seventy-two per cent of all steel. We have depleted most of the world's energy and minerals; we have devastated the ecology of the planet; yet, we say the under-developed world is to blame in producing too many children. My mother came from a family of eight in impoverished rural West of Ireland. Families tended to have more children as an insurance against poverty. My mother emigrated to prosperous London. I was part of a family of two children. In other words, in addition to improving access to advice on family planning, we must address endemic poverty. Then families will naturally diminish in size. Nor, in assessing future population trends, should we ignore the devastating effects of AIDS, especially in Africa.

If some elements of the Green Movement, and New Age thinking, is totalitarian in outlook, it is also pantheistic. Brearley's article on Matthew Fox, an American Dominican whose writings have been condemned by mainstream theologians, 'Matthew Fox: Creation Spirituality for the Aquarian Age'[11] suggests that

> modern New Age occultism has caused a massive increase in astrology, occult spiritual mediumship, tuning in to natural forces in creation such as ley lines and witchcraft, including Satanism. New Age teaches, as does Fox, that Man is evolving into a Godhead, that transcendent deities are now superfluous and that all morality is relative.

The Greening of the Church,[12] written by the Irish Columban missionary, Sean McDonagh, has some sympathy with Fox's views, describing them as a creation-centred theology. Fox, he says, argues that the fall/redemption theology had superseded and restricted creation theology. While there is truth in this, Fox goes to an extreme which is hard to equate with Christianity. Eliminating the Fall and subsequent redemption eliminates the central claim of Christ.

New Age claims there is no Creator God; that the spirit deifies everything. Thus man will become God in the age of Aquarius; that we are now living on the cusp between the Piscean Age and the Aquarian Age; and that in the New Age Christians must cease to be Christians and Jews to be Jews; they must become pagan as part of one world religion. This belief in eco-spiritualism manifests itself in slogans about world peace, unity and harmony. New Age followers seek to balance and align 'energies' and use psychotherapeutic programmes and mind-expanding drugs. Their occult meditation is based on the principle 'Build an altar to oneself' – an appropriate epitaph to the relentless selfishness of a post Judaeo-Christian civilisation.

Of course, Hitler too, claimed that he believed in 'God in nature, God in our people, God in one's own fate, and in one's own blood'. Eco fascism – foreseeing a 'violent planetary cleansing', insisting on enforced population programmes, and support for the destruction of our own species is totalitarian and anti-democratic. This mixture of paganism and Eastern mysticism presents a major threat to Christianity. It can also be a challenge.

Communion with Creation

In 1972 the Lifestyle Movement was founded by Canon Dammers, Dean of Coventry Cathedral. Its slogan has been to 'live more simply that all of us may simply live'. To make ourselves smaller and thus more acceptable to God has been a recurrent Christian theme. The Beatitudes exalt us to be meek and gentle. Indeed, it is the gentle who shall have the earth as their heritage. We are urged to hunger for what is right, to show mercy, to be peacemakers and to accept persecution if it is the price of pursuing what is right. And we are taught that the poor in spirit will inherit the kingdom of God. It is the poverty of spirit which must impel us to reject personal consumerism and to choose a simpler lifestyle through which we become better custodians and stewards of that which we have been given.

Ian Bradley in a BBC Radio Four 'Seeds of Faith' talk,[13] said that Psalm 8, which emphasises Man's dominion over the earth, is too often interpreted as a warrant from God ruthlessly to exploit and ravage the natural resources. Bradley argues that it is rather a command to exercise that loving concern that God Himself shows over all His Creation: 'If we are, indeed, fashioned in the image of God, then that surely means that we are intended to love, nurture and cherish the rest of Creation.'

Bradley defines Christian stewardship as a good steward acting as a faithful deputy of God, sustaining His Creation and preserving it for future generations: 'Stewardship also suggests an active and creative role with regard to the Earth we have been given responsibility for. We are to be gardeners as well as gardens.'

Stewardship alone, he goes on to say, may not be enough. Jesus clearly related to the world around Him in a way which implies far more than stewardship. He showed an intimacy and familiarity with God's creatures and the processes of nature. Born in a stable, surrounded by animals and greeted by shepherds who had left their flocks, Jesus often used the seasons, the crops, the flowers and the animals to illustrate his teachings and parables. He stilled storms, walked on water, coexisted safely in deserted and wild places with the beasts of the wilderness.

The Bible tells us that God created a beautiful and fruitful world for all his creatures and that He has given us the task of being stewards of His creation.[14] The relationship which links God to us and the rest of His Creation is emphasised in the covenant which was made by God with Noah after the flood. The rainbow remains as a reminder of the special bond and challenge.

This communion with nature can be seen in the lives of many of the saints. The Celtic saint, Columba, is reputed to have saved the trees at Calgach, near Derry, to have secured an early ripening of harvest after prayer, and to have had an encounter with the great boar on Skye.

Six hundred years ago the English contemplative, Mother Julian of Norwich, reflected on the tiny hazelnut which she held in her hand and wrote: 'I looked at it thoughtfully and wondered, "what is this?" And the answer came, "it is all that is made" . . . In this little thing I saw three truths. The first is that God made the earth; the second is that God loves it; and the third is that God sustains it.'[15]

Ignatius Loyola, in his *Spiritual Exercises* suggests that we may acquire a love of God through contemplation and consideration of his creatures: 'Consider how God dwells in creatures, in the elements giving them being, in the plants giving them growth, in animals giving them feeling, and in men giving them understanding . . . Consider how God works and labours for me in all created things.'[16]

The English Jesuit nineteenth-century poet, Gerard Manley Hopkins, perhaps found his inspiration from Loyola when he wrote in 'Pied Beauty':

> Glory be to God for dappled things -
> For skies of couple-colour as a brinded cow;
> For roses-moles all in stipple upon trout that swim;
> Fresh-firecoal chestnut-falls; finchs' wings.

While, for G.K. Chesterton, Christ was Lord of all and God's hand could be detected in everything: 'All the flowers looked up at Him, and all the stars looked down.'[17]

Perhaps the most famous Christian assertion of the beauty of God's handiwork comes from the author of the 'Canticle of Brother Sun'. St Francis rejoices in the flora and fauna and praises his Lord for the nourishment of the precious, humble and chaste Mother Earth. John Paul II[18] says that Francis

> offers Christians an example of genuine and deep respect for the integrity of creation. As a friend of the poor who was loved by God's creatures, St Francis invited all of creation – animals, plants, natural forces, even Brother Sun and Sister Moon – to give honour and praise to the Lord. The poor man of Assisi gives us striking witness that when we are at peace with God we are better able to devote ourselves to building up that peace with all creation which is inseparable from peace among all peoples.

John Paul says that the seriousness of the ecological issue lays bare the depths of man's moral crisis.

Totality of Respect for Life

Christianity has always refuted the pagan idea that we should worship nature. It does not see pantheistic divinities in the trees, rivers and hills, but it has a long tradition of worshipping God through nature and from the Book of Genesis onwards the Judaeo-Christian tradition has rejoiced in contemplation of God's exquisite craftsmanship. Christianity must also stand in solidarity against the heedless misuse and plunder of creation.

Respect for all life will require us to show concern for the animal kingdom and for our own species. It will surely require opposition to abortion and destructive experiments on human embryos as well as cruelty to animals. As Tim Cooper rightly concedes:[19] 'The unborn child is not merely an extension of the mother; it thus has a right to exist whether or not it is wanted. Greens, of all people, would be wrong to suggest that rights only begin at birth.'

C.S. Lewis in a little post-war pamphlet for the National Anti-Vivisection Society[20] saw the link between our respect for human life and our commitment to other created life:

> No argument for experiments on animals can be found which is not also an argument for experiments on inferior men. If we cut up beasts simply because they cannot prevent us and because we are backing our own side in the struggle for existence, it is only logical to cut up imbeciles, criminals, enemies or capitalists for the same reason. Indeed, experiments on men have already begun. We all hear that Nazi scientists have done them. We all suspect that our own scientists may begin to do so, in secret, at any moment.

Lewis argued that the victory of the vivisectionists marked 'a great advance in the triumph of ruthless, non-moral utilitarianism over the old world of ethical law'. He would not have been surprised to learn that by 1990 the British Parliament had voted to legalise experiments on the human embryo. It is perfectly logical for them to have done so.

Many Christians believe that humanity has a role as mediator between the realm of the spirit and the realm of the flesh; and certainly that there is a spiritual continuity between humans and other living creatures. Joel and the Psalmist compare the cry of the animals to a spirit yearning for God.[21] Genesis describes a covenant made between God and animals made of 'flesh'[22] and describes how the Creator breathes life into the animals and birds.[23] In the First Book of Kings animals emerge as helpmates: during a long drought the prophet Elijah was fed by ravens 'and the ravens brought him bread and meat in the morning, and bread and meat in the evening'.[24] It is because the animal world belongs to God that man is required to treat it with love and respect, to cherish it and not to ill-treat those entrusted to his care. This is not to equate the animal kingdom with humanity but to recognise its place in God's plan for all creation. For this reason alone, society should reconsider its attitude towards vivisection, the genetic manipulation of animals, appalling, unnatural and often cruel factory farming of animals, and towards blood sports.

This linkage between the world of animals, plants and human beings demonstrates that the pro-life argument needs to be seen within the widest context of the fragility of the living world. Just as it is anti-life to allow an avoidable increase in infant mortality or abatable hunger which leads to the death of millions of children, it is anti-life to allow the extinction of hundreds of thousands of living species. I might also add that if a passion for the welfare of animals leads to a hatred of the human species – or, at any rate a criminal disregard for the lives and safety of members of it – that is anti-life too. Concern for the welfare of Brother Beagle by recourse to Brother Bomb is a corrupt and warped view of the world.

A total respect for life – and above all for the dignity of the human person – is crucial for sound economic, scientific and industrial progress. No society which wishes to survive can afford either to neglect to have a profound respect for life or to be negligent stewards of creation. If it does, the future will be bleak indeed.

As Gerard Manley Hopkins wrote in 1879,[25] those who come after us will never guess what beauty there has been:

> O, if we but knew what we do
> When we delve or hew -

Hack and rack the growing green!
Since the country is so tender
To touch, her being so slender
Take, like this sleek and seeing ball
But a prick will make no eye at all,
Where we, even where we mean
To mend her we end her,
When we hew or delve:
Aftercomers cannot guess the beauty seen.

The Good Steward

To sum up, the concept of good stewardship requires us to have a sense of responsibility and duty towards all of God's creation. It requires us to empower, enable and to enrich the human personality and the communities in which we live through subsidiarity and decentralisation of power and wealth. Good stewardship requires us to reconcile our needs with the needs of all; to wisely share the fruits of creation with others; to seek co-existence and justice; to exalt the gentler and less aggressive side of human nature; to wonder at the beauty of our endowment. The issue of good stewardship should be addressed at global and continental level, by nations, communities, families and individual people.

The good steward will recognise that relentless consumerism and obsessive materialism is generated by greed and is incompatible with sustaining life; that 'my choice' is always made at someone else's expense; that we are trustees for future generations, and not sole heirs and owners. The good steward knows that each person is made in the image of his Maker and is both precious and accountable to Him. The good steward will exist in fraternity, solidarity and communion with his Creator, alongside the good and beautiful things which the Creator has given us.

Conclusion

These preceding six chapters have looked at how we might work out in practice a commitment to the six foundation principles of the Movement for Christian Democracy. These six themes – social justice, a respect for life, reconciliation, empowerment, active compassion and good stewardship – are a good framework for getting right our relationships with Creation and with each other. Together they form a Charter for Human Responsibility. The active ingredients in each have been the ideas of 'personalism' and 'communitarianism', with political success measured in terms of the effect of policies on the human personality, the family, the community, and on our relationships. It is a third way between the popular exaltation of the individual and the slavery of the State.

I have freely owned that the Christian contribution to public and political life has not always been benign; but I have also pointed to examples of great and enriching achievement.

The temptation is to stay neutral and to take no risks.

Neutrality was not the spirit which motivated Wilberforce and Shaftesbury, Gladstone and Hardie, Tawney, Schuman, Adenauer and de Gasperi. Nor has it been the spirit of Eastern Europe: of men like Alexander Ogorodnikov and Ivan Hel. Wilberforce rejected neutrality and populism with these words: 'We never ought to deviate from the paths of duty in order to procure the applause or to avoid the reproaches of men.' What is true for each of us as individuals is true for our country. We must not be neutral bystanders in the battle for Europe.

Britain's future lies in a federated Europe. Our politics must come to terms with the political realities of Europe, especially the contribution of Europe's Christian Democrats. Their record is no doubt as open to criticism as any other political party. But it is intellectually unacceptable to dismiss them or to categorise them without even attempting to understand their motivation, their history or outlook. Christian Democracy is influential in most European governments. 35 million Western Europeans support them with their votes – and they are emerging as the non-socialist alternative in Eastern Europe.

There are also still many in Britain who care for their faith and wish to see Judaeo-Christian values central to policy making and to the shaping of political priorities. In the centenary year of the publication of *Rerum Novarum* and at a time when evangelicals are re-emerging as a significant force in Britain, it is the right time to be reconsidering these questions.

Christian Democracy's was the visionary spirit which founded the European Community. They are clearly going to be leading players in Europe's future development. Britain will need to address this challenge. We need not do so with suspicion or fear, but with a sense of faith in Britain. We need a willingness both to receive and to learn. Through a deep faith in our own country and its people we should also have confidence in what we might offer others. Each of us should consider and apply to ourselves the graffiti slogan which appeared all over Eastern Europe in 1989:

> If not now, when?
> If not us, who?

Notes

Chapter 1: The Christian Democratic Tradition in Britain

1 Spring Harvest Seminar, 'Where Truth and Justice Meet', 1989.
2 *The Extraordinary Black Book*, London, 1831, pp 20–21.
3 Donald Reeves (ed), *The Church and the State*, Hodder and Stoughton, 1984.
4 *The Universe* (*The Christian Supplement*, No 4, 1990).
5 Garth Lean, *God's Politician*, Helmers and Howard, 1987.
6 Thomas Gisborne, MP for Stafford, 1830–1, Derbyshire, 1832–7, and Nottingham, 1843–7.
7 *Presbyterian Herald*, March, 1989.
8 One-nationism has its genesis in Disraeli's novel, *Sybil or The Two Nations*, and contrasts the rich and poor. It has since been used as a popular description of those Conservatives who believe in public spending as a way of maintaining social cohesion and bridging the gap between the affluent and least well off.
9 An extract from Anthony Trollope's *Framley Parsonage*, published in 1861, vividly illustrates this type of Conservatism. This is how Trollope describes Lady Lufton, a High Church Tory: 'She liked cheerful, quiet, well-to-do people, who loved their Church, their country, and their Queen, and who were not too anxious to make a noise in the world. She desired that all farmers round her should be able to pay their rents without trouble, that all the old women should have warm flannel petticoats, that the working men should be saved from rheumatism by healthy food and dry houses, that they should all be obedient to their pastors and

masters – temporal as well as spiritual. That was her idea of loving her country.

10 F. B. Czarnomsky, *The Wisdom of Winston Churchill*, Allen and Unwin, 1956.

11 Lord Hailsham, *A Sparrow's Flight*, Collins, 1990.

12 *Marxism Today*, February, 1991.

13 John Locke (1632–1704), philosopher. Locke argued that knowledge is the result of experience and that sovereignty depends on contract.

John Stuart Mill (1806–73), economist and philosopher. Initially an exponent of Utilitarianism, he later altered his views on more altruistic lines, advocated universal franchise and did much for the poor.

Utilitarianism: doctrine which finds the basis of morals in utility. Its advocates ask whether or not a certain course of action tends to make mankind happier or better, and by this test they approve or condemn. Exponents of this theory were Jeremy Bentham and John Stuart Mill and it had great influence on the political movements of the nineteenth century.

Jeremy Bentham (1748–1832), author. Bentham advocated that the aim of politics was the greatest good of the greatest number. His ideas influenced the great nineteenth-century reforms.

An example of the increasing materialism of the age can be found in the works of Samuel Smiles (1812–1904), Scottish author, best known for a series of books on character building, the first of which, *Self Help*, had an enormous circulation. The books advocate the virtues of honesty and industry, connecting the practice of such virtues with the reward of material prosperity. Other titles include *Thrift*, *Character* and *Duty*.

14 Lord Harris, 'The Morality of the Market', *The New Right and Christian Values*, CTPI, 1987.

15 Ben Patterson, Lord Bethell, Amadee Turner, QC, *An Introduction to Modern Conservatism*, European Democratic Group, Strasbourg, 1990.

16 Ibid.

17 Peter Broadbent, 'The Soul of the Parties', *New Way*, March, 1989.

18 Donald Reeves (ed), op cit.

19 Robert Owen (1771–1858), social reformer, started working aged ten, by twenty-eight he was the part owner of the

New Lanark cotton mills. He encouraged his workpeople in thrift and cleanliness, helped to establish infant education and tried unsuccessfully to run experimental communities on co-operative lines.

Otto von Bismarck (1815–98), German statesman. With King William I of Prussia he helped to forge the German Empire of which he was the first Chancellor. He was a determined reformer and German industries benefited from his protectionist policies.

F. D. Maurice (1805–72), theologian, founder and first principal of the Working Men's College. A friend of Charles Kingsley, his forceful personality and sympathy with the oppressed made him an influential figure in religious life, and the Christian Socialist movement was an outcome of his teaching.

Fabian Society: political society founded in 1884 to forward socialism by steady and deliberate methods. Its members have included Beatrice and Sidney Webb and G. B. Shaw, and it has exercised great influence on the socialist movement.

20 Brooke Fosse Westcott, *Lessons from Work*, London, 1901.
21 Edward Norman, *The Victorian Christian Socialists*, Cambridge University Press, 1987.
22 Until the publication of *Rerum Novarum*, an encyclical letter on capital and labour published by Pope Leo XIII in 1891, the Catholic Church had little to say about social justice. This letter was a watershed in the thinking of a Church which gradually began to emerge from the sacristy and to address the injustices of the world.
23 John Ludlow (1821–1911), social reformer and one of the founders of the Christian Socialist Movement.
24 Frank Field, *Politics of Paradise*, Fount, 1987.
25 William Temple (1881–1944), Archbishop of Canterbury, 1942–4.
26 *The Times*, March 23rd, 1966.
27 William Temple, *Christianity and the Social Order*, Penguin, 1942.
28 Pilgrim Trust, *Men Without Work*, 1938.
29 Church of England Board for Social Responsibility Report, *Faith in the City*, 1985.
30 House of Commons Library biographical note on Keir Hardie.

31 For twelve years, as Eric Heffer's MP, I have found myself both in conflict and co-operation with a man whom I have come to respect as a sincere exponent of traditional socialism. A curious mixture of High Church Anglican and Liverpool dock worker, he enlivened many parliamentary debates by his pugnacious attacks on both the Conservatives and Neil Kinnock alike. Field has a similar churchmanship but his politics owe more to R. H. Tawney, the inter-war years' proponent of social democracy, than to Marx.

32 R. H. Tawney, *Commonplace Book*, Cambridge University Press, 1972.

33 R. H. Tawney, *The Acquisitive Society*, George Bell and Sons Ltd, 1921.

34 G. D. H. Cole (1889–1959), left-wing journalist.

35 *Guild Socialism Twenty Years Ago and Now*, New English Weekly, September 1934.

36 David Owen, *Face the Future*, Oxford University Press, 1981.

37 Donald Reeves (ed), op cit.

38 David Owen, op cit.

39 Wilberforce's Diaries, 25 July 1853.

40 Wilberforce, op cit.

41 Palmerston's Divorce Bill, 1857. Previously divorce could only be obtained by a special Act of Parliament. The 1857 Act allowed the husband to apply for a divorce if his wife had committed adultery. A wife had to prove adultery coupled with desertion or cruelty in order to apply.

42 Oxford Movement: movement to reform the Church of England, aimed at bringing more reverence and order into its worship.

Cardinal Newman (1801–90), a leader of the Oxford Movement, converted to Catholicism. He became a Cardinal in 1879.

Cardinal Manning (1808–92), vicar of Lavington, attracted by the Oxford Movement. He was ordained following his conversion to Catholicism and made a Cardinal in 1875.

43 J. J. Parry, *Democracy and Religion*, Cambridge University Press, 1986.

44 E. S. Purcell, *Life and Letters of Ambrose Phillips de Lisle*, London, 1900.

45 Arthur Henderson, leading trade unionist and MP, Home

Secretary and later Foreign Secretary in the first Labour administration. In 1932 he chaired the disarmament conference in Geneva.

46 George Lansbury, Labour MP for Bow and Leader of the Opposition from 1931 to 1935.

47 J. J. Parry, op cit.

48 Henry Campbell-Bannerman's Liberal Government was formed on December 5th, 1905, but the General Election was not held until January 12th, 1906 (and was a Liberal landslide). Campbell-Bannerman brought Asquith, Lloyd George and Churchill into his celebrated Cabinet and allowed them to develop the radical legislative programme which came to fruition under Asquith after Campbell-Bannerman's death.

Lloyd George's Budget of 1909 proposed taxation on land and was rejected by the House of Lords, precipitating a constitutional crisis which resulted in two General Elections in 1910 and the passing of the Parliament Act of 1911, making the Lords subordinate to the House of Commons.

49 G. Tupini, *I Democratici Christiani*, Ganzanti, 1954.

50 Ramsay Muir, *The New Liberalism*, The New Way Series, Liberal Publications, 1929.

51 Alan Beith, John Gummer, Eric Heffer, *Faith in Politics – Which Way Should Christians Vote?*, SPCK, 1987.

Chapter 2: The Christian Democratic Tradition in Western Europe

1 Edmund Burke (1729–97), writer and political philosopher. His rich and stately prose championed the cause of the American colonists and denounced the French Revolution.

2 Prof. Michael Fogarty, *Christian Democracy in Western Europe, 1820–1953*, Routledge and Kegan Paul, 1957.

3 Robert Papini, *Tradition und Aktualitat christlich-demokratischen Denkens*, Vol. I, Geistige und Historische Grundlagen Christlich-Demokratischer Politik, Verlag Ernst Knoth, Melle, West Germany, 1988.

4 Prof. Michael Fogarty, op cit.

5 Christian Democratic Union, *Freiheit, Solidaritat, Gerechtigkeit: Grundsatzprogram der Christlich-Demokratischen Union Deutschlands*, Bonn CDU Bundesgeschaftstelle, Ludwigshafen, October, 1978.

6 Georges Bernanos, *Journal d'un Curé de Campagne*, 1936.
7 Civardi, *Manuale di Azione Cattolica*, 12th ed, 1952.
8 Prof. Michael Fogarty, op cit, p 179.
9 Konrad Adenauer resumed office as Lord Mayor of Cologne after the Second World War. In 1948 he became chairman of the Christian Democratic Union and was elected Chancellor of the West German Federal Republic in 1949.
10 Clay Clemens, 'Christian Democracy: The Different Dimensions of a Modern Movement', Brussels, 1989.
11 Robert Schuman, *Heart of Europe*, EPP Publications.
12 The Second Vatican Council (1963) continued the process of change inside the Catholic Church and a series of encyclicals addressed issues of justice and peace.

Chapter 3: The Christian Democratic Tradition in Eastern Europe

1 William Wilberforce, *A Practical View of the System of Professed Christians Contrasted with Real Christians* (1797).
2 Mikhail Gorbachev, *Perestroika*, Collins, 1987.
3 Father Men was one of the new generation of Orthodox leaders openly preaching spiritual renewal and opposition to State corruption and Communist domination.
4 Michael Bourdeaux, *Risen Indeed, Lessons in Faith from the USSR*, Darton, Longman and Todd, 1983.
5 The Siberian Seven were seven Siberian Christians who took refuge in the basement of the American Embassy in Moscow and who were ultimately allowed to leave the USSR after a vigorous campaign in the West during the 1980s.

Valeri Barinov was a well-known Russian Christian rock musician who was jailed by the Soviet authorities. In 1986 I led a small human rights delegation to Leningrad to meet his family and then visited the head of the Religious Affairs Bureau in Moscow on Barinov's behalf. Barinov was allowed to leave the USSR the following year and now lives with his family in Great Britain.

Raoul Wallenberg was a Swedish diplomat serving in Budapest during the Second World War. He rescued many Hungarian Jews by issuing them with Swedish passports. He was captured by the Russians at the end of the war and disappeared into the Russian labour camps.

6 Michael Bourdeaux, op cit.

7 Jane Ellis, *Religion in Communist Lands*, Vol 8, No. 2, Keston College, Summer 1980.

8 Dr Andrei Sakharov was a prominent physicist and worked on nuclear fusion. A tireless campaigner for peace, married to fellow dissident Elena Bonner, he spent some time in internal exile in the Soviet Union before being reinstated by Mikhail Gorbachev. He won the Nobel Peace Prize in 1975.

9 Irina Ratushinskaya, *No, I'm Not Afraid*, Bloodaxe, 1986.

10 Ibid.

11 *The Independent on Sunday*, September 23rd, 1990.

12 Quoted by Michael Bourdeaux, op cit.

13 Ibid.

14 Jan Huss (*c.* 1370–1415), reformer and champion of the Czechs against the Germans, he was burnt as a heretic for preaching Wycliffe's doctrines.

Jan Masaryk (1886–1948), son of Thomas Masaryk, who founded the modern state of Czechoslovakia. Jan was a member of the Czech Government-in-exile during the Second World War, and held the post of Foreign Minister when the Government was restored. He found himself unable to co-operate with the Communists and committed suicide a month after they came to power.

15 John Amos Comenius (1592–1670), theologian and educational reformer.

16 The population of Czechoslovakia is made up of Czechs and Slovaks, the Czechs populating the western regions, their language kept alive through the efforts of Jan Huss and the Moravian Brethren, the Slovaks on the east having been under Hungarian rule till 1919.

17 David Alton, *What Kind of Country?*, Marshall Pickering, 1988.

18 Primarily an attempt by central government to force agricultural reforms through centralisation, the wholesale bulldozing of villages also had the effect of destroying the way of life of many rural minority communities.

19 Tinothy Garton Ash, *We The People*, Granta Books, 1990.

Chapter 4: The Movement for Christian Democracy

1 RU486 is the 'abortion pill' manufactured by Roussel-Uclaf. It is given to a pregnant woman in tablet form, followed

two days later by either an injection or a pessary containing prostaglandin. Contractions are induced which dislodge and expel the human embryo from the womb.

2 William Temple, *Christianity and Social Order*, SPCK, 1942.
3 William Wilberforce, op cit.
4 Ibid.
5 Tom Cullinan, OSB, *The Passion of Political Love*, Sheed and Ward, 1987.
6 Peter Hebblethwaite, 'Missing the European Bus or How to be Communitaires', Epiphany Group Papers, April 22nd, 1989.
7 *Christian Democracy*, June 1990.
8 Ibid, July 1990.

Chapter 5: Social Justice

1 Luke 16:26.
2 *New Day Magazine*, August 1990.
3 Alan Storkey, *Transforming Economies*, Third Way Books, SPCK, 1989.
4 Ibid, pp 200, 202.
5 Frank Field, *Inequality in Britain*, Fontana, 1981.
6 Archbishop Temple, 'An Appeal to the Christian Conscience on the Subject of Unemployment', *The Times*, March 5th, 1934.
7 David Alton, op cit.
8 Hansard, February 28th, 1989.
9 C. M. Klare, 'Le rôle de l'Union Sovietique dans les rentes d'equipements militaires au tiers monde', *Le Monde Diplomatique*, Vol 31/361, April 1984, pp 8–10.
10 European People's Party, 'World Economy and Development – A Christian Democratic Contribution', Occasional Paper 3, Brussels, 1990.
11 Ibid.
12 Ibid.
13 Ibid.
14 *Populorum Progressio*, 1967.
15 European People's Party, 'World Economy and Development. . . ', op cit.
16 John Stott, *Issues Facing Christians Today*, Marshall Pickering, 1984.

17 *Populorum Progressio*, op cit.
18 Synod, 1971, quoted by Owen Hardwicke, *The Gospel and Social Justice*, CTS, 1989.
19 Matthew 16:26.

Chapter 6: Respect for Life

1 John Stott, op cit.
2 Desmond Doig, *Mother Teresa: Her People and Her Work*, Collins, 1976.
3 David Alton and Alison Holmes, *Whose Choice Anyway? The Right to Life*, Marshall Pickering, 1988.
4 *Family Charter* (The Charter of the Rights of the Family), CTS, 1983.
5 Lords Hansard, February 8th, 1990.
6 Francis Schaeffer and Everett Koop, *Whatever Happened to the Human Race?*, Marshall, Morgan and Scott, 1980.
7 European People's Party, *On the People's Side*, 'Action Programme 1989–94', EPP, Brussels, 1988.
8 *Warnock Committee Report on Human Fertilisation and Embryology*, HMSO, 1985.
9 *The Times*, December 11th, 1989.
10 *The Tablet*, February 3rd, 1990.
Professor Edwards together with Patrick Steptoe pioneered research into in vitro fertilisation.
11 *Le Quotidien du Medicine*, April 30th, 1990.
12 *Nursing Mirror*, November 22nd, 1989.
13 *The Pharmaceutical Journal*, November 4th, 1989.
14 Ellen Wilkie, *A Pocketful of Dynamite*, Hodder and Stoughton, 1990.
15 Ibid.

Chapter 7: Reconciliation

1 George Berkeley (1685–1753), Irish philosopher, Bishop of Cloyne, he wrote *The Treatise on the Principles of Human Knowledge*.
2 Cecil Kerr, *Just a Moment*, Christian Journals Ltd., Belfast, 1982.
3 Inter-Church Group on Faith and Politics, *Choose Life*, Corrymeela, 1986.

4 David Armstrong was a Presbyterian Minister who became friendly with the local Catholic priest in their town of Limavady. He was driven out of the town by bigots who made his family's life unbearable, and they came to live in the UK. I visited Limavady subsequently and asked to meet some of the local Christian leaders who confirmed that this early attempt at reconciliation between Protestants and Catholics had led to an outpouring of hatred.

5 The integrated schools have a genuine mix of Catholic and Protestant children but to date the institutional Catholic Church has not felt able to give them public support. Schools such as Laggan College offer a full range of subjects and a Christian ethos, with topics such as religion and history being approached in a very balanced manner.

6 Ephesians 2:14-15, Jerusalem Bible, Darton, Longman and Todd, 1966.

7 David Alton, *What Kind of Country?*, op cit.

8 The Northern Consensus Group is made up of mainly lawyers, many of them active Christians, and constitutes one of the most positive and constructive influences in Northern Ireland.

9 Fenians: a patriotic secret society founded *c.* 1860 to make Ireland an independent republic and restore the land to the Irish peasants.

Michael Davitt (1846–1906), born in Mayo, he was brought up in Lancashire where he lost an arm in an industrial accident. He became a Fenian and was imprisoned for arms trafficking. He founded the Land League and the United Irish League and sat as MP for South Mayo.

10 James Connolly, Irish labour leader, was born in County Monaghan but brought up in Edinburgh. He was wounded in the Easter Rising of 1916 and executed after it. Jim Larkin was the leader of the Irish Transport and General Workers' Union, founded in 1908.

11 Liberal Unionists opposed to Home Rule for Ireland joined the Conservative Party, which then became known as the Conservative and Unionist Party. Lord Randolph Churchill rallied the Protestant North with the cry, 'Ulster will fight and Ulster will be right'.

12 Garret Fitzgerald, *Towards a New Ireland*, Torc Books, Dublin, 1972.

13 Ibid.

14 Cahal Daly, *Dialogue for Peace*, Irish Messenger Publications, Dublin, 1985.

Chapter 8: Empowerment

1 Arie Oostlander, 'Politics Based on Christian Consciousness', *Efforts to Define a Christian Democratic Doctrine*, European People's Party, Brussels, 1989.
2 Paul Mills, 'Interest in Interest: The Old Testament Ban on Interest and its Implications for Today', Jubilee Centre, 1989.
3 Hansard, March 20th, 1990.
4 John Maynard Keynes, *The General Theory of Employment, Interest and Money*, Macmillan, 1939.
John Maynard Keynes (1883–1946), economist, Governor of the Bank of England, he helped to negotiate the Anglo-American loan agreement of 1945. His theories on inflation were highly influential.
5 John Maynard Keynes, 'Saving and Usury', *Economic Journal*, 1932, pp 135–7.
6 Donald Hay, *Economics Today*, Inter-Varsity Press, Leicester, 1989.
7 Alan Storkey, op cit.
8 Dr Michael Schluter, *The Old Testament Ban on Interest: Its Relevance for the Reform of Britain's Industrial Structure in the 1980s*, Jubilee Centre, 1986.
9 C. J. H. Wright, *Living as the People of God*, Inter-Varsity Press, Leicester, 1983.
10 N.M. Siddiqi, *Banking Without Interest*, Islamic Foundation, Leicester, 1983.
11 European People's Party, *On the People's Side*, op cit.
12 *Family Charter*, op cit.

Chapter 9: Active Compassion

1 Lord Beveridge, *Insurance for All and Everything*, New Way Series, Liberal Publications, The Daily News Ltd, 1924.
2 Arie Oostlander, op cit.
3 Ibid.
4 Lord Beveridge, op cit.
5 Dr Michael Schluter, *Consumerism and the Family*, Jubilee Centre, 1990.

6 Malcolm Muggeridge, *Christ and the Media*, Hodder and Stoughton, 1977.
7 Ibid.
8 European People's Party, *On the People's Side*, op cit.
9 Karl Marx and Friedrich Engels, *The Communist Manifesto*, Penguin, 1967.
10 David Cooper, *The Grammar of Living*, Penguin, 1974.
11 R. A. Butler, *The Art of the Possible*, Hodder and Stoughton, 1971.
12 Dr Michael Schluter, *Family Charter*, Family Base, Jubilee Centre, 1987.
13 Americans with Disabilities Act, 1990.
14 Ellen Wilkie, op cit.
15 Ibid.
16 Ibid.
17 Kathryn Spink, *Jean Vanier and L'Arche – a Communion of Love*, Darton, Longman and Todd, 1990.
18 Ibid.
19 David Alton, *Aids: Meeting the Community Challenge*, St Paul's Publications, 1987.
20 Shirley du Boulay, *Cicely Saunders*, Hodder and Stoughton, 1984.

Chapter 10: Good Stewardship

1 David Alton, *What Kind of Country?*, op cit.
2 Ibid.
3 *Sessions 1985–86, Radioactive Waste*, HMSO.
4 Rosalie Bertell, *No Immediate Danger*, Women's Press, 1985.
5 Stuart Boyle, *What Price Windscale?*, Friends of the Earth, 1985.
6 Bishops of the Philippines, 'What is Happening to our Beautiful Land?', Manila, January 29th, 1988.
7 The Schumacher Lecture, November 5th, 1989.
8 European People's Party, 'World Economy and Development . . . ', op cit.
9 European People's Party, *On the People's Side*, op cit.
10 Tim Cooper, *Green Christianity*, Hodder and Stoughton, 1990.
11 Dr Margaret Brearley, 'Matthew Fox: Creation Spirituality for the Aquarian Age', *Christian Jewish Relations*, Vol 22, No 2, 1989.

12 Sean McDonagh, *The Greening of the Church*, Geoffrey Chapman, Cassell Ltd, 1990.
13 Ian Bradley, 'Seeds of Faith', abridged in *Christian Democracy Bulletin* No 3, September 1990.
Ian Bradley is now a Church of Scotland clergyman who was previously a journalist, writer and Liberal historian.
14 Genesis 2:19–20.
15 Mother Julian of Norwich, *Revelations of Divine Love*, Hodder and Stoughton, 1987.
16 Ignatius Loyola, *Spiritual Exercises*, Westminster, 1949.
17 Both quotations are cited by Edward P. Echlin in *The Greening of the Church*, op cit.
18 John Paul II, 'Peace with God and the Creator; Peace with All of Creation', January 28th, 1990.
19 Tim Cooper, op cit.
20 C. S. Lewis, National Anti-Vivisection Society Pamphlet, Vivisection NAVS Ltd, London.
21 Joel 1:20; Psalms 42:1.
22 Genesis 9:9–10.
23 Genesis 2:7, cf Genesis 1:30; Psalms 104:30.
24 I Kings 17:1–6.
25 Gerard Manley Hopkins, *Poems and Prose*, ed W.H. Gardner, Penguin, 1952.

Bibliography

Alton, David, *Aids: Meeting the Community Challenge*, St Paul's Publications, 1987.

Alton, David, *What Kind of Country?*, Marshall Pickering, 1988.

Alton, David and Holmes, Alison, *Whose Choice Anyway? The Right to Life*, Marshall Pickering, 1988.

Ash, Timothy Garton, *We The People*, Granta Books, 1990.

Beith, Alan, Gummer, John and Heffer, Eric, *Faith in Politics – Which Way Should Christians Vote?*, SPCK, 1987.

Bernanos, Georges, *Journal d'un Curé de Campagne*, 1936.

Bertell, Rosalie, *No Immediate Danger*, Women's Press, 1985.

Beveridge, Lord, *Insurance for All and Everything*, New Way Series, Liberal Publications, The Daily News Ltd, 1924.

Bourdeaux, Michael, *Risen Indeed, Lessons in Faith from the USSR*, Darton, Longman and Todd, 1983.

Boyle, Stuart, *What Price Windscale?*, Friends of the Earth, 1985.

Bradley, Ian, 'Seeds of Faith', abridged in *Christian Democracy Bulletin* No 3, September 1990.

Brearley, Dr Margaret, 'Matthew Fox: Creation Spirituality for the Aquarian Age', *Christian Jewish Relations*, Vol 22, No 2, 1989.

Broadbent, Peter, 'The Soul of the Parties', *New Way*, March 1989.

Bruntland Report, The World Commission on Environment and Development, August 4th, 1987.

Butler, R.A., *The Art of the Possible*, Hodder and Stoughton, 1971.

Butt, Ronald, *History of Parliament*, Constable, 1989.

Christian Democratic Union, *Freiheit, Solidaritat, Gerechtigkeit: Grundsatzprogram der Christlich-Demokratischen Union Deutschlands*, Bonn CDU Bundesgeschaftstelle, Ludwigshafen, October 1978.

Church of England Board for Social Responsibility report, *Faith in the City*, 1985.
Civardi, *Manuale di Azione Cattolica*, 12th ed, 1952.
Clemens, Clay, 'Christian Democracy: The Different Dimensions of a Modern Movement', Brussels, 1989.
Cooper, David, *The Grammar of Living*, Penguin, 1974.
Cooper, Tim, *Green Christianity*, Hodder and Stoughton, 1990.
Cullinan, Tom, OSB, *The Passion of Political Love*, Sheed and Ward, 1987.
Czarnomsky, F.B. *The Wisdom of Winston Churchill*, Allen and Unwin, 1956.
Daly, Cahal, *Dialogue for Peace*, Irish Messenger Publications, Dublin, 1985.
Doig, Desmond, *Mother Teresa: Her People and Her Work*, Collins, 1976.
du Boulay, Shirley, *Cicely Saunders*, Hodder and Stoughton, 1984.
Ellis, Jane, *Religion in Communist Lands*, Vol 8, No 2, Keston College, Summer 1980.
European People's Party, *On the People's Side*, 'Action Programme 1989-94', EPP, Brussels, 1988.
European People's Party, 'World Economy and Development – A Christian Democratic Contribution', Occasional Paper 3, Brussels, 1990.
Extraordinary Black Book, The, London, 1831.
Family Charter (The Charter of the Rights of the Family), CTS, 1983.
Family Policy Studies Centre, 'Family Change and Future Policy', 1990.
Field, Frank, *Inequality in Britain*, Fontana, 1981.
Field, Frank, *Politics of Paradise*, Fount, 1987.
Fitzgerald, Garret, *Towards a New Ireland*, Torc Books, Dublin, 1972.
Fogarty, Prof. Michael, *Christian Democracy in Western Europe, 1820-1953*, Routledge and Kegan Paul, 1957.
Gorbachev, Mikhail, *Perestroika*, Collins, 1987.
Goricheva, Tatiana, *Cry of the Spirit – Christian Testimonies from the Soviet Union*, Collins, 1989.
Hailsham, Lord, *A Sparrow's Flight*, Collins, 1990.
Hardwicke, Owen, *The Gospel and Social Justice*, CTS, 1989.
Harris, Lord, 'The Morality of the Market', *The New Right and Christian Values*, CTPI, 1987.
Hay, Donald, *Economics Today*, Inter-Varsity Press, Leicester, 1989.

Health Education Council, 'Young People's Health and Lifestyles' (Mori Poll), March–May 1990.
Hebblethwaite, Peter, 'Missing the European Bus, or How To Be Communitaires', Epiphany Group Papers, April 22nd, 1989.
Hopkins, Gerard Manley, *Poems and Prose*, ed W.H. Gardner, Penguin, 1952.
Inter-Church Group on Faith and Politics, *Choose Life*, Corrymeela, 1986.
John Paul II, 'Peace with God the Creator; Peace with All of Creation', January 28th, 1990.
Julian of Norwich, Mother, *Revelations of Divine Love*, Hodder and Stoughton, 1987.
Kerr, Cecil, *Just a Moment*, Christian Journals Ltd, Belfast, 1982.
Keynes, John Maynard, *The General Theory of Employment, Interest and Money*, Macmillan, 1936.
Keynes, John Maynard, 'Saving and Usury', *Economic Journal*, 1932.
Klare, C.M., 'Le rôle de l'Union Sovietique dans les rentes d'equipements militaires au tiers monde', *Le Monde Diplomatique*, Vol 31/361, April 1984.
Lean, Garth, *God's Politician*, Helmers and Howard, 1987.
Lewis, C.S., National Anti-Vivisection Society Pamphlet, Vivisection NAVS Ltd, London.
Loyola, Ignatius, *Spiritual Exercises*, Westminster, 1949.
Marx, K., and Engels, F., *The Communist Manifesto*, Penguin, 1967.
McDonagh, Sean, *The Greening of the Church*, Geoffrey Chapman, Cassell Ltd, 1990.
Mills, Paul, 'Interest on Interest: The Old Testament Ban on Interest and Its Implications for Today', Jubilee Centre Publications Ltd, 1989.
Muggeridge, Malcolm, *Christ and the Media*, Hodder and Stoughton, 1977.
Muir, Ramsay, *The Challenge to Liberalism*, The New Way Series, Liberal Publications, London, 1928.
Muir, Ramsay, *The New Liberalism*, The New Way Series, Liberal Publications, London, 1929.
National Association of Housing Associations, 'Taking Stock', 1989.
Norman, Edward, *The Victorian Christian Socialists*, Cambridge University Press, 1987.
Northern Consensus Group, 'Untying the Knot', February 1990.

Oostlander, Arie, 'Politics Based on Christian Consciousness', *Efforts to Define a Christian Democratic Doctrine*, European People's Party, Brussels, 1989.

Owen, David, *Face the Future*, Oxford University Press, 1981.

Papini, Robert, *Tradition und Aktualitat Christlich-Demokratischen Denkens*, Vol I, Geistige und Historische Grundlagen Christlich-Demokratischer Politik, Verlag Ernst Knoth, Melle, West Germany, 1988.

Parry, J.J., *Democracy and Religion*, Cambridge University Press, 1986.

Patterson, Ben, Bethell, Lord, and Turner, Amadee, QC, *An Introduction to Modern Conservatism*, European Democratic Group, Strasbourg, 1990.

Philippines, Bishops of, 'What is Happening to our Beautiful Land?', Manila, January 29th, 1988.

Pilgrim Trust, *Men Without Work*, 1938.

Purcell, E.S., *Life and Letters of Ambrose Phillips de Lisle*, London, 1900.

Ratushinskaya, Irina, *No, I'm Not Afraid*, Bloodaxe, 1986.

Reeves, Donald (ed), *The Church and the State*, Hodder and Stoughton, 1984.

Schaeffer, Francis and Koop, Everett, *Whatever Happened to the Human Race?*, Marshall, Morgan and Scott, 1980.

Schluter, Dr Michael, *Consumerism and the Family*, Jubilee Centre, Cambridge, 1990.

Schluter, Dr Michael, *Family Charter*, Family Base, Jubilee Centre, Cambridge, 1987.

Schluter, Dr Michael, *The Old Testament Ban on Interest: Its Relevance for the Reform of Britain's Industrial Structure in the 1980s*, Jubilee Centre, Cambridge, 1986.

Schumacher Lecture, The, November 5th, 1989.

Schuman, Robert, *Heart of Europe*, EPP Publications.

Sessions 1985-86, Radioactive Waste, HMSO, 1986.

Siddiqi, N.M., *Banking Without Interest*, Islamic Foundation, Leicester, 1983.

Spink, Kathryn, *Jean Vanier and L'Arche – a Communion of Love*, Darton, Longman and Todd, 1990.

Spring Harvest Seminar, 'Where Truth and Justice Meet', 1989.

Storkey, Alan, *Transforming Economies*, Third Way Books, SPCK, 1989.

Stott, John, *Issues Facing Christians Today*, Marshall Pickering, 1984.

Tawney, R.H. *Commonplace Book*, Cambridge University Press, 1972.

Tawney, R.H. *The Acquisitive Society*, George Bell and Sons Ltd, 1921.
Temple, Archbishop, 'An Appeal to the Christian Conscience on the Subject of Unemployment', *The Times*, March 5th, 1934.
Temple, William, *Christianity and the Social Order*, SPCK, 1942.
Tupini, G., *I Democratici Christiani*, Ganzanti, 1954.
Warnock Committee Report on Human Fertilisation and Embryology, HMSO, 1985.
Westcott, Brooke Fosse, *Lessons from Work*, London, 1901.
Wheatley, John, *The Catholic Working Man*, 1909.
Wilberforce, William *A Practical View of the System of Professed Christians Contrasted with Real Christians*, 1797.
Wilkie, Ellen, *A Pocketful of Dynamite*, Hodder and Stoughton, 1990.
Wright, C.J.H., *Living as the People of God*, Inter-Varsity Press, Leicester 1983.

Hansard, February 28th, 1989; March 20th, 1990.
Lords Hansard, February 8th, 1990.

British Journal of General Practice, March 1990.
Christian Democracy Bulletin, June 1990; July 1990; September 1990.
Independent on Sunday, *The*, September 23rd, 1990.
Marxism Today, February 1991.
New Day Magazine, August 1990.
Nursing Mirror, November 22nd, 1989.
Pharmaceutical Journal, *The*, November 4th, 1989.
Presbyterian Herald, March 1989.
Quotidien du Medicine, *Le*, April 30th, 1990.
Tablet, *The*, February 3rd, 1990.
Times, *The*, March 23rd, 1966; December 11th, 1989.
Universe, *The*, (*The Christian Supplement*, No 4, 1990).